John Kelsey

Rich Texts:
Selected Writing for Art

Institut für Kunstkritik
Frankfurt am Main
Daniel Birnbaum
Isabelle Graw

John Kelsey

Rich Texts:
Selected Writing
for Art

Sternberg Press

Preface
John Kelsey

For a brief moment, this book was going to be titled *Texte zur Kunts* [*sic*]. But the bad joke didn't seem to work in Germany, not really in New York either, and was quickly replaced by *Rich Texts*. Somewhere near the bottom of a growing, indecisive list of proposed titles I'd sent the editors, *Rich Texts* sounded "new wave" to their Berlin and Frankfurt ears, and also echoed the title of Isabelle Graw's recent book, *High Price*. The reason a title was giving us so much trouble here was that none of these texts were written with the slightest idea of ending up in a book. Each of these reviews, short articles, and catalogue essays was produced for a particular context and in response to a particular moment or task, and so they remain blind and somehow indifferent to the package that contains them now. I am still not sure if the texts finally *agree* with their own elevation (exhumation?) here. They do and they don't, just as they agreed and at the same time disagreed to be written in the first place. Sequenced in alphabetical order, rather than according to theme or chronology, they can in this way assume at least a degree of belonging within the logic of the present selection.

Rich Text Format (RTF) is a document file format developed by Microsoft Corporation in 1987. It is a means of making writing travel efficiently between digital platforms while maintaining its "human readability." Many of the texts included here attempt to engage (and perform) the problem of their own participation within (and extension of) the networked, communicational space they share with art. They are produced on the same screen that's used to visualize, organize, and mobilize contemporary art, and so no matter what they say, or however inaccurate their perceptions and judgments may be, they know they are close

to art, in fact simultaneous with it. "Rich texts" also refers somewhat ironically to the medieval "book of hours" (*Les Très Riches
Heures du Duc de Berry*), but in this case, the hours are relatively
poor ones: the writer is among the least remunerated of workers in the art industry, however much the market depends on
his service to make the world we call art continue to function as
it does. What is a "rich hour"? Like most art writing, these texts
are very deadline-driven, written quickly and according to the
schedules of others. They sometimes even find a certain pleasure in matching the anonymous and displacing speed of art
today. Another possible title for this book was *The Tray Table*.

Written in the midst of my involvement with the founding and
operation of Reena Spaulings Fine Art in New York; and with the
production of collectively authored texts such as the novel
Reena Spaulings, 2004, and the epic poem *A Billion and Change*,
2009 (both by Bernadette Corporation); and in between various
other activities, jobs, and exhibitions, these "rich texts" are also
immediately involved with the question of how to elaborate
(habitable) rhythms of production today. The reason for avoiding
the professional identity of either a writer or an artist, a critic
or a dealer, is to bring ourselves closer (and in a more fascinated
way) to the problem of *how* art works under its present conditions. To get closer to a possible and paradoxical definition of art
through assuming art's increasing loss of distinction from other
communicative activities. Doing several things at once has been
a way of remaining unemployed even in the midst of constant,
inescapable employment. Writing, too, can be a form of unem-
ployment within employment, and so is closer than ever to art.

Many thanks to Matthew Evans, Miriam Rech, and Caroline
Schneider at Sternberg Press; to Daniel Birnbaum and Isabelle
Graw at the Institut für Kunstkritik; and to Carly Busta, Tim

Griffin, Don McMahon, Scott Rothkopf, and everyone else at *Artforum*. Also thanks and love to Emily, Julien, Carissa, Antek, Bernadette, Jim, Jutta, Fulvia, etc., who are all very much present in these pages; and to all the artists who've invited this writing.

New York, July 2010

Introduction
Daniel Birnbaum and Isabelle Graw

"When the critic chooses to become a smuggler, a hack, a cook, or an artist, it's maybe because criticism as such remains tied to an outmoded social relation."[1] This is what John Kelsey told us a few years ago during a conference at the Städelschule in Frankfurt am Main. Could there be a more challenging and provocative assertion for a newly founded Institut für Kunstkritik? The critic, Kelsey furthermore explained, might be a character who belongs to the past, and her disappearance is not necessarily something to mourn, especially if she's not up to the task of reinventing herself in order to meet the conditions she's working under today. "If the old critical distance is lost, then we need to invent new distances, or learn to deal with the loss of distance." This task of inventing new distances indeed seems to be the central operation that criticism has to perform nowadays. Once the critic has renegotiated distance, it is nevertheless very probable—as Kelsey foresees—that she will return without being recognizable as such.

Who knows? Perhaps things are changing again in times of the often-invoked "crisis," but during the last decade, we've indeed witnessed the marginalization of all the functions in the art world that at least *suggested* the possibility of something truly significant taking place outside of the commercial sphere. And the critic, it seems, was first to go. She was marginalized by the international curator, who in turn was pushed aside by the art advisor, the event manager, and—most importantly—the dealer and the collector (who sometimes happen to be the same

1   John Kelsey, "The Hack," in *Canvases and Careers Today: Art Criticism and Its Markets*, eds. Daniel Birnbaum and Isabelle Graw (Berlin and New York: Sternberg Press, 2007), 73.

person). What could the critic's task possibly be in this new environment, other than discussing her own obsolescence on panels financed by more powerful actors in an art world transformed into a money-drenched segment of the entertainment industry?

In a conversation with Kelsey and Claire Fontaine member Fulvia Carnevale, French philosopher Jacques Rancière commented on the inconsistencies accompanying the persistent desire among artists and critics to escape the logic of the art market:

> The critique of the market today has become a morose reassessment that, contrary to its stated aims, serves to forestall the emancipation of minds and practices. And it ends up sounding not dissimilar to reactionary discourse. These critics of the market call for subversion only to declare it impossible and to abandon all hope for emancipation. For me, the fundamental question is to explore the possibility of maintaining spaces of play. To discover how to produce forms for the presentation of objects, forms for the organization of spaces, that thwart expectations. The main enemy of artistic creativity as well as of political creativity is consensus—that is, inscription within given roles, possibilities, and competences.[2]

While it is certainly true that consensus is a problem, and that dissensus has become rare, one would nevertheless have to point to the fact that it is precisely this expansion of "given roles" advocated by Rancière that suits the market so well. By now, Kelsey certainly has occupied most roles that the art world provides, but without simply fulfilling the expectations built in to them, and without giving up his other professional identities, even when the conflicts of interest were glaring. Taking plenty of liberties, he has managed to maintain his own spaces of play—and also invent new ones. He is not,

---

2   Fulvia Carnevale and John Kelsey, "Art of the Possible: An Interview with Jacques Rancière," *Artforum* (March 2007): 258.

however, an inventor of the multitasking so typical of today's art world, but he does embody this type in a rather unusual fashion—as a writer, critic, teacher, editor, translator, artist, and art dealer, who often works under pseudonyms ("Reena Spaulings," "Bernadette Corporation"). While, on the one hand, his work thwarts the expectations of and confuses, if not irritates, the more purist minds, it has also been very popular in the art world. Because amidst this impurity, he has produced a body of mostly commissioned "critical" texts—what else could we call them?—that seem to us to be among the most pertinent written today. With a keen sense of the way objects and subjects appear in the spaces we share, and how we inhabit our bodies, he writes texts at once playful and true to the situations under observation. He does not write from an imaginary critical distance, but as someone fully aware of being immersed in the commercial world, commodified and for hire—i.e., as a "hack"—yet constantly searching for new forms of experimentation: "To play is not to calculate profits, it's to explore multiple forms of distance from oneself. If the critic is always right, the hack is always there—always in play."

These texts, it seems to us, were written in a state of spectacular distraction that their author shares with one of his inspirations, Stéphane Mallarmé, the poet and anonymous editor of the fashion magazine *La dernière mode*. We would like to thank John for letting us present his extremely articulate and elegant essays.

Frankfurt and Berlin, June 2010

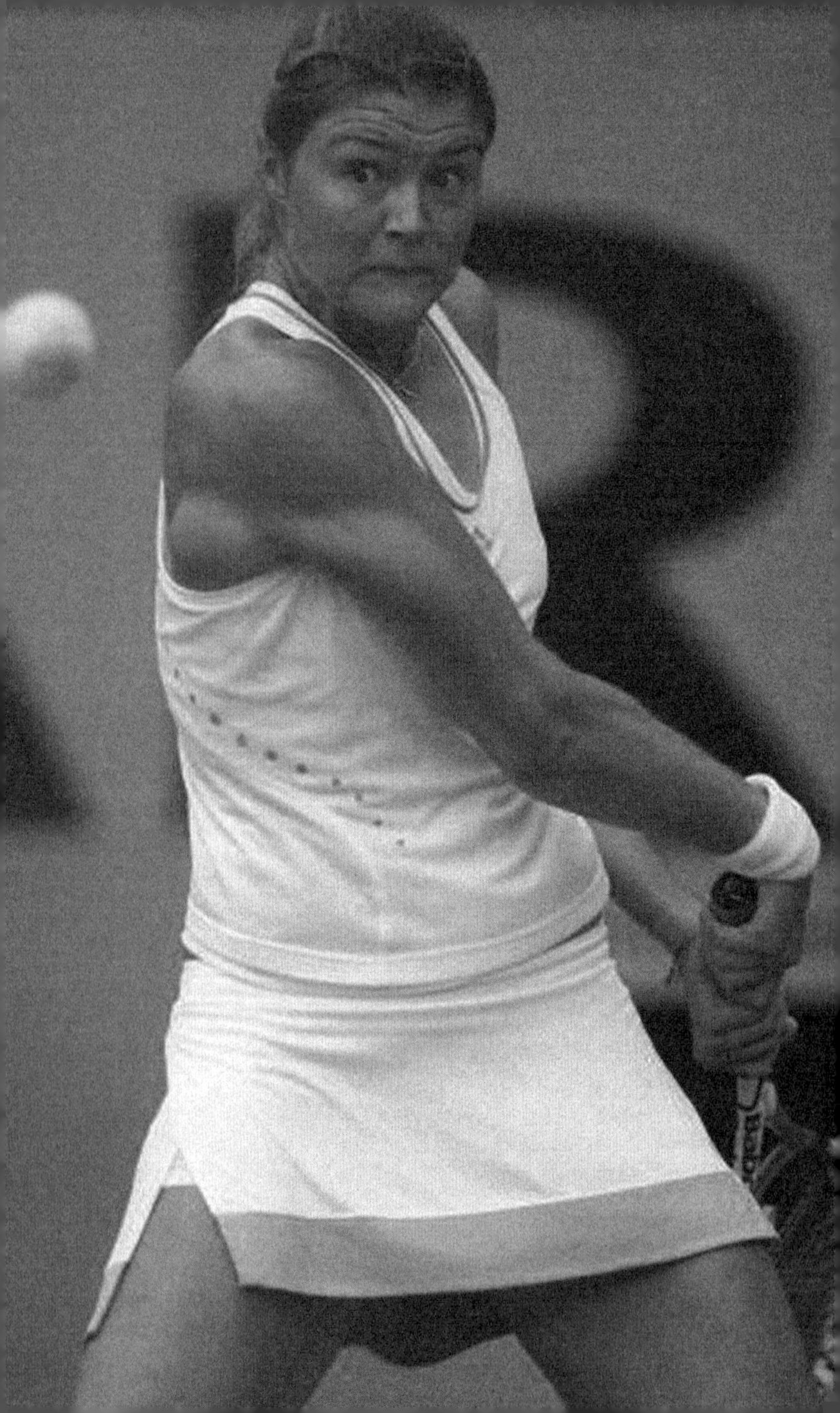

100%*

How much of the painting is already in the TIFF? And in the end, after the file has been selected and commanded to print, how much actually comes out of the Epson? Where does painting go when it's sent and received like this—as a *code*? The work of art seems to go outside of itself when it decides to picture the weightless, groundless, dimensionless, and genderless qualities of information, in the cybernetic sense; or when the image itself assumes such qualities in order to experience how abstraction happens today. The first thing the work abandons is the *act* of painting, and with it, manual space. Replacing the "diagram" with the program or code, painting suddenly leaves the ground and approaches something like a post-Fordist condition of abstraction. Now the space of the work is no longer either optical or manual, but communicational, extending itself along a network that links one apparatus to another. The object in the gallery is now like a hard copy or alias of the source file on the drive, and what we are looking at is perhaps less a painting than a "rendering." What this work displays is the difference between sending information and receiving aesthetic objects in the gallery, or what happens when "black" moves from desktop to printer to museum, and whatever is lost along the way. The monochrome is a record of a circulation. As it is copied and communicated, discrepancies are produced. And these are what now stand in for painting.

We are no longer experiencing painting as a relation between a manual diagram and an optical catastrophe, which was how Deleuze theorized the practices of Jackson Pollock and others.[1]

---

*   Originally published in *Wade Guyton: Black Paintings*, JRP Ringier, Zurich, 2010.

1   Gilles Deleuze, "The Diagram," in *The Deleuze Reader* (New York: Columbia University Press, 1993), 193–200.

If diagrammatic abstraction was linked to the work of the hand and to the introduction of a sort of blindness within the visual order, programmatic abstraction is more about the displacement or neutralization of the painterly act itself. And where the diagram produced blindness and visual violence, the program only functions, displaying the hands-off violence of design, perhaps, or something like designer violence. Instead of blindness, there is now only the possibility of interrupting communication. Painting is either on or off.

Printing out mailing-address labels might be something like degree-zero painting in a world still coming to terms with the increasing loss of distinction between the production of art objects and the daily labor of communication. "Print" is an action selected from a menu; nobody actually performs it. The rest—the printing, the painting—is mostly automatic: a connection between the design program and the printing apparatus has been okayed as the artist manages and monitors his production from the side. This could even be a definition of contemporary art: an encounter with our own absence in the midst of the very activities we manage and monitor. Such encounters also involve a reckoning with the ways in which we ourselves are inhabited and even predicted by the readymade programs whose users we say we are.[2] Most of the time, we don't realize how *activated* we've become as artists and users. The monochrome is a means of displaying this. At the same time, it can be a way of reducing to a minimum the degree of our activation in the midst of communication. In this case, the monochrome signals

2   Vilém Flusser, *Towards a Philosophy of Photography* (London: Reaktion Books, 2000). In theorizing an emergent postindustrial era in terms of a shift from a text-based to an image-based culture, Flusser proposes that the photographer is, first of all, already a function of the camera's program.

the creative subject's possible deactivation, or even disconnection, from the program of painting. If the "blank" TIFF (Who would still call this rectangle a "field"?) is still related to the painterly blank, the former no longer pretends to be anything less than 100% information. It is this 100% that also now stands in for the act of painting.

For the eye that still inhabits the modern spaces of literature and painting, and that scans pages and walls for sense and sensation, the monochrome is the image of a radical minimum. It is a spiritual or ascetic void, a pictorial purification. But in the discursive or "connexionist" space, where work and life now lose their difference, 100% black is the *most* a machine or an artist can say, do, or send, a total saturation and total activation of the space of communication. Here, black may still stand for a minimum, but from the angle of function or performance, it is a maximum. If Mallarmé were still here, he might say that black is the full dress of sense (and its shadow too), the formal attire of every possible transmission.

On the contemporary screen, where writing, too, finds its image, black is the color of "automatic." It is what 100% looks like. Here, in the visual space that writing now shares with design and communication, black is both a kind of information and a means of informing. When it is not selected, it is the default color of anything we do or send, including literature. Here, writing and painting are no longer so much about spilling ink, but about managing shades, sizes, styles, and quantities of information. And writers and painters have never been so neighborly: they share the same screens and same postures. Already the canvas—like a Rorschach—starts to resemble the sequenced pages of a book, with a seam or margin (some say "zip") down its middle. It is a picture of information without a message, a post-literary document. It is also a sort of shadow painting of the TIFF it was composed with.

Do graphics exist? The "painting" commands the wall and the room, but its source file is only a few compressed kilobytes of code. And just as the designer fills in a rectangular box with what is referred to as "#000000" (or black) in the invisible source code of a digital "page," Wade Guyton has filled or blackened exhibition spaces in New York, Paris, and Frankfurt. These three shows are like one show repeated in or communicated between the three cities. The filling in of digital windows is followed by the distribution of ink across canvases, and then by the ritual installing and staging of black in the galleries. In order to show itself here, communication becomes décor.

But the TIFF is nothing in itself. It only really exists or becomes visible through use, or when one device communicates it to another. It is much less than an idea, and much more efficient. A means of circulating information between two or more machines or galleries in a network, the TIFF, we could say, is potential communication, the pure possibility of transit, which in Guyton's case is used to send "black" from hard drive to printer to canvas to wall. Black is circulated and also at a strange standstill in the paintings and in the gallery. Here, the installation produces an optical rhythm that departs from the painterly dance of the diagram in order to approach the on/off, on/off of the program. This binary pattern will sometimes produce effects reminiscent of Bridget Riley's Op art.

In the gallery, a false floor of black plywood introduces a material hollow beneath the viewers' feet. It's a strange feeling to real-ize that one is standing in the same space as information, as if formatted along with it, a body dragged and dropped in a room full of ink. It's the same in the city, where we transmit ourselves through the urban program of Manhattan. We say we are like tourists here, but we are also like files on the move, opening and closing, constantly updating and duplicating ourselves. Under our feet, the hollow, flimsy feeling of a stage renders the body strangely present in the act of scanning the show. And this feeling is accompanied by a perception of how completely absent the body has become in the paintings.

The gallery is no longer a theater of human activity or even passivity, but an activated space where information, bodies, and money are rapidly circulated, and where this power of circulation is momentarily frozen in images and objects. In other words, the canvases on view are not so much finished, final things as they are a series of interrupted movements. These are abstractions torn from and at the same time irretrievably lodged in a condition of productive mobilization. And in its interruption, "painting," too, is put at a strange, fresh distance. The blankness that surrounds us here is both "on" and "off," and is perhaps working on a third possibility in the relation between the two.

Because their surfaces expose information dropouts and discrepancies between source image and printout, we could say these paintings are failed attempts at picturing TIFFs, a serial repetition of this. Often, a canvas is over-printed multiple times so that several copies occupy a single surface, overloading it. But no matter how awash in ink they are, these images will never achieve the thickness of painting. And we wonder if the Epson is even capable of failing the way a painting can.

Connoisseurs will insist on the many subtle and unpredicted differences produced by the Epson's struggling printer heads, mechanical glitches, and even the rough traces of the studio floor on the canvas's sensitive surface. As if whatever escapes the program is now painting. As if painting occurred finally as information dropout (or overload), as mechanical malfunction. These minor traffic accidents are what produce images of transit and transmission: They make us see the TIFF in the room precisely because it never finally arrived here. And 100% black is a way of displaying the fact that the artist and his gestures have already exited the space and the moment of the picture's production. We are in a sort of shadow land of painting.

In a way, Guyton is dragging and dropping these shows into New York, Paris, and Frankfurt. We get the feeling that the spaces he fills have in the meantime abandoned the possibility of experience, that they are more like magazine pages than rooms. At an opening, bodies circulate against walls of TIFFs, and we remember that Warhol's shadow paintings were used as a backdrop for fashion shoots, and that his wallpapers, films, and publishing ventures were also means of displaying the being-in-mediation of postindustrial, post-Expressionist bodies. Against such backdrops, Warhol elaborated a real style of disappearance, or disappearance as a style of use. Guyton's updated décor, on the other hand, stages the productive relation between communication and appearance: Work is not what we do, but how we show up, like on a screen. Making the Epson struggle, the artist causes a sort of material stammering within the program, putting communication in closer proximity to interruption. It is a stammering of the Epson and also of painting.

The monochrome is a document that tells us of nothing but its own circulation, presenting the pure possibility of communication by a possible artist. And if the artist no longer locates himself in manual space, if the picture is automatic, then the painter is somewhere out here on the floor with us, another dislocation. Here is where black is momentarily extracted from its program, casting a shadow that's as good-looking as Kasimir Malevich and Calvin Klein.

The contemporary artist's productive displacement is constantly encountering its own image—also like a shadow—on the screen, on the wall, and on the page. So if the artist, as he works, is already producing images of communication, he must find ways of intervening exactly there, in this space and moment where displacement becomes appearance. In this way—by working on both the distribution and display of information—he can perhaps begin to recover what Giorgio Agamben has called the "gestural sphere."[3] How can we picture and interrupt our own endless transmission within the networked spaces we inhabit and extend today? The monochrome can be taken up as a means of re-appropriating everything that already disappears us in the midst of our productive activities. On the one hand, the Epson is exploited to produce the feeling of an easy, convincing, institutional décor. On the other hand, this décor is a direct occupation of discursive space, returning the possibility of use. And if the painter prefers not to show up here, the user—his double—is already working overtime.

Not long ago, Guyton was printing over other artists' images, using pages torn from catalogues and the back issues of art magazines. Sending these pages through a desktop printer, interrupting them with his programmed marks, Guyton intervened directly within the mediation of artistic practice, discourse, and value. Taken up as a pure means, employed as a

---

3   Giorgio Agamben, "Notes on Gesture," in *Infancy and History: On the Destruction of Experience* (London: Verso, 2007), 150.

discursive and material support, the magazine or catalogue became a display system for new and possible gestures. And as the painter or printer elaborates ways of using that somehow remain out of reach or blind to the author, he also learns to displace himself with a strange ease between discourse and design, communication and image. This ease is accompanied by a certain indifference to the ownership of messages and signatures. It also involves simply letting the program function. The artist intervenes where the production of communication by means of communication happens, in the black of the font and in the sending of the image, outputting paintings like pages and putting transmission on display.

One could imagine a rule (≠ law) of the Neutral: it would consist in finding a way to disseminate intelligent stuff, as though between the lines (cf. the monochrome) of a flat, dumb (verbal) fabric.
—Roland Barthes, *The Neutral*

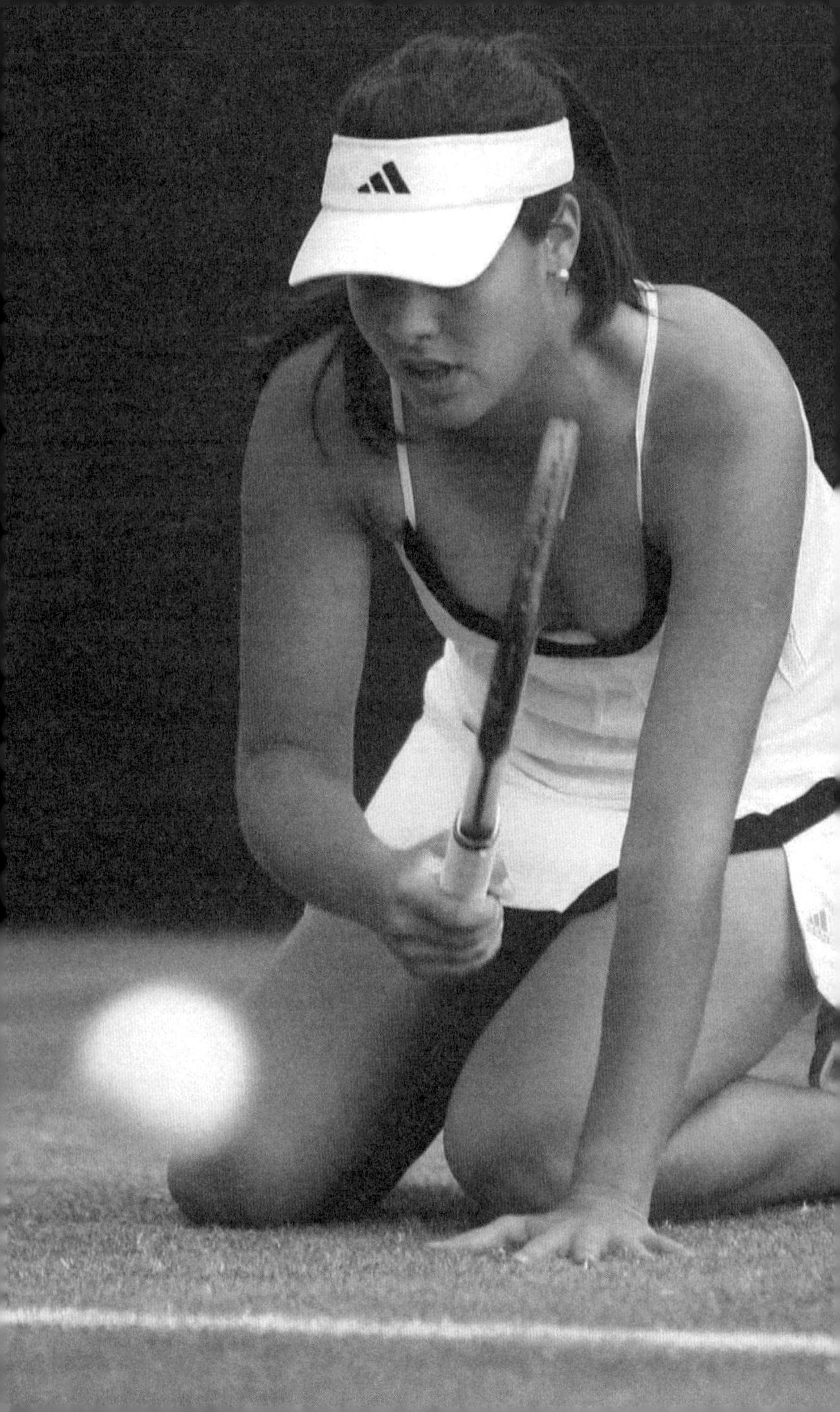

Alice in 3D*

When the Cheshire Cat's disembodied head comes unmoored from the picture plane and, like a ball in oil, begins to roll in our RealD glasses, it asks through its floating grin whether Alice is really *the* Alice. We are actually watching two movies when we watch 3D, thanks to a circularly polarizing technology that involves splitting the projected light into two series of rapidly alternating images—a right-eye image that circles clockwise, like the cat's head, and a left-eye image that circles counterclockwise; 3D glasses with oppositely and circularly polarized lenses ensure that each eye can see only one image. Plunked onto the picture's CGI ground is Mia Wasikowska, the live-action actress playing an Alice who's once again losing track of both her direction and her identity, this time in the visual woods of Tim Burton's *Alice in Wonderland*, which has been loosely adapted from Lewis Carroll's books *Alice's Adventures in Wonderland* (1865) and *Through the Looking-Glass* (1871). No longer a child, in this version Alice returns to the site of her original adventures as a nineteen-year-old who has fallen back down the rabbit hole on the very day of her wedding engagement. And Wonderland, it turns out, is actually called Underland—on her first visit, as a seven-year-old, she had misheard the word. Meanwhile, Underland has been festering in a sort of depression and is now ruled by the tyrannical Red Queen (Helena Bonham Carter). Burton's *Alice* is a gothic, young-adult revisitation of Carroll's books via a complex amalgam of the latest digital filmmaking technologies. And Alice's job now is to keep her head and unseat this terrorist queen.

---

* Originally published in *Artforum*, May 2010.

Given *Alice in Wonderland*'s conceit of a teen's return to a lost and buried childhood, a soundtrack featuring Avril Lavigne's song "Alice (Underground)" makes total sense, helping to rescript the children's storybook as an angsty, emo-inflected self-help message: "I, I'll get by / I, I'll survive..." (In the end, Alice will regain control of her destiny, emerging from Underland to refuse a marriage proposal and launch herself as an independent businesswoman instead.) Carroll's popular Alice books were the products of an age that was hugely invested in the idea of childhood, inventing complex, perverse topologies to navigate the enforced cultural split between childhood and adulthood on which Victorian England was based. Burton's Underland (like the fictive universes of his other films), on the contrary, reflects a contemporary world of never-ending adolescence, where adults and animals are teens, too. His Alice could easily be a character in *Harry Potter*, and *Alice* screenwriter Linda Woolverton seems to take many devices from the latter (and from the fantasy-adventure genre in general), basing her narrative on a good-versus-evil conflict, chases and battles with villains and mean monsters, etc., while tying Alice's progress to the mastery of visual problems (and of sword fighting) so that she can finally return victorious to her proper garden-party reality. So whereas Carroll's seven-year-old encounters the enchanting nonsense of adult institutional codes (discourse, lessons, logic, rules, etiquette) distorted in a looking glass and on the page, Burton's protagonist confronts something more like a fully saturated and operative media-space (which the film itself extends and inhabits) as a site of self-discovery and self-mastery. The new Alice is neither child nor adult; she is a *jeune fille* who struggles to integrate herself within a highly engineered image program (in order to be free!).

"Off with her head!" screams the Red Queen, whose own head has been filmed separately with an ultrahigh-resolution camera so that, when magnified to three times its original size and pasted back onto her now slightly reduced body, it looks seamless, its pixels no larger than the others. So the queen's head is both off and on. Carroll's books include jokes about heads, too: Alice is told that she can travel Wonderland by mail, since she has a head and so do postage stamps. In the film, digitally enhanced heads are frequently "stitched" onto live-action bodies and vice versa: Crispin Glover's live-action head is glued to a body stretched to over seven feet tall, and the Mad Hatter (Johnny Depp) sports a head rigged with inhumanly large green eyes. These hybrid visuals are one of the ways that Burton translates Alice's disorienting movements through the twisted topologies of Carroll's books. They are also the latest instance of the director's ongoing pursuit of a designer image in which humans and cartoons trade places or finally lose their distinction. With 3D (Burton shot the film in 2D and later transferred it to 3D), heads are allowed to float and roll not only free of bodies, but (as if) freed from the screen. Yet if the movie screen has become a sort of looking glass through which Burton's characters can pass in occasional sequences, drifting in the space between our polarized eyeballs and our brains, why do we remain so disenchanted throughout the experience? One reason is that the stretched-out space of IMAX 3D is not at all infinite: It feels as though the screen space has extra depth now, but we only seem to gain about twenty or thirty immersive feet on either side of the usual rectangle. It's like an oversize, animated pop-up book. Also, the depth of field in most shots seems somehow squashed, and all the CGI-generated and baroquely ornamented forests and waterfalls seem a little dim and soft in focus behind the characters that bulge from the frame's center. 3D works best with heads and logos (the IMAX logo itself), or when sharply focused heads are floated like logos against a receded, softened background. The most effective 3D moment in *Alice* is the final credits sequence, where giant mushrooms begin to sprout around the scrolling text. Here, the film functions like an illuminated manuscript and the audience remains captivated until the lights come on, finally tripping out to the credits for Grip and Best Boy. We almost think the best 3D treatment of Carroll's text would have been this—to simply float his flat pages in front of us.

The Wonderland that Carroll's Alice wanders though is composed of language, and each of her displacements is somehow linked to a pun, a rhyme, a misinterpretation, or some other play on words. Even the bizarre creatures she encounters are generated by wordplay (the Jabberwock, the bread-and-butterfly, the Mock Turtle, etc.). Once she plummets underground, her movements quickly become horizontal, sometimes echoing moves across a chessboard, other times sliding across surfaces such as tabletops and mirrors, behind which she meets characters as flat as playing cards. In other words, the adventure plays out both on the page and *as a page*, which, through nonsense, becomes a highly non-orientable and complex surface. But when Burton chooses to transpose this tale back into depth, or the illusion of depth, going so far as to psychologize Alice's adventure as some kind of repressed trauma that needs to be "treated" by high-tech cinema, the magic of misinterpretation is exchanged for a lavish exercise in programming and illustration, right down to the dripping 3D fangs of the Bandersnatch, which Alice is eventually able to tame. On the page, Alice is not a deep girl, or if she experiences depth, it is like that of a Möbius strip, which by definition cannot be polarized without losing its power of disorientation.

A recent formula in cinema has been the casting of relatively inexpensive, non-marquee actors whose performances become the bases for multimillion-dollar "digital puppets": Andy Serkis played Gollum in the *Lord of the Rings* trilogy (2001–2003), Zoe Saldana was the female lead in *Avatar* (2009), and so on. At this point, human extras can be almost entirely done away with, especially in blurry battle scenes where detail isn't so noticeable. Virtual actors are being painstakingly concocted on computer screens, and technology now allows both the reanimation of dead talent (whose images can be licensed through a company called GreenLight) and the cloning of younger versions of "agèd, agèd" actors (a spry Jeff Bridges will return in the upcoming *Tron: Legacy*) through the scanning of earlier films' frames, which are then reprocessed using digital-animation programs. In other words, the boundary between animation and live performance is quickly dissolving, and we are already hearing terms like "virtual performance" and "virtual camera," already watching seamless hybrids at work in films like *The Curious Case of Benjamin Button* (2008). With the plotting of live-action facial performances onto head-shaped digital grids, the insertion of motion-captured gestures into virtual camera movements and CGI environments (*Avatar*), or the building of these from the raw, dead material of digital scans, the "shoot" is no longer what (or when) it used to be. Most of what normally happens on set is in these cases generated later by programmers and animators on banks of hard drives that cost more than the actors. The industry term "uncanny valley" describes the disturbing effect of an animation that looks all too human but nevertheless lacks life—like a mobilized corpse. It is said that once we master lighting effects and the subtlety of skin movement, however, the valley can be successfully crossed.

But none of this wizardry can translate the systematic distortions of sense or the flat-out joys of Lewis Carroll's books (which are already so screen-like). Depp's performance, it should be noted, remains somehow faithful to Carroll's inventiveness: It is all on the surface and is generative of surfaces. Interpreting the hatter's madness as the spread of mercury poisoning, he plays mental deterioration out on the skin, communicating sudden mood shifts as a rapid shuffling of masks, via makeup, costume, and abrupt changes of accent in his speech. Mostly working against green screens, Depp manages to tap Carrollian speed: His solution is to become a screen himself. But the surface speeds on which the literary adventure depends are otherwise lost in the film.

While "revolutionary" film technology allows the hyper management and control of every square millimeter of screen space, we may miss the holes and gaps (in space and in meaning) movies once had. Cutting is not so easy in 3D: The images have to be melded and synthesized, and rapid or hard edits (as with sudden shifts in depth of field) disturb the viewer's experience of immersion. So we are losing the differences and intervals between images, too, and movies forget to breathe or think as they once did. It's now a matter of compositing multiple layers (live and animated), performances, and shoots to produce a single, seamless sequence, and this requires many slow months of work by roomfuls of technicians. So now there is no end to shooting: Once the performances have been "captured," they can be endlessly re-shot after the fact, with virtual cameras. Virtual cameras have no lenses; they are programs used to re-angle and recompose raw performances on the computer, and these can also be layered onto CGI bodies or backgrounds and inserted into pans, zooms, or tracking shots that are all digitally constructed in what was once called postproduction. But there is no more postproduction, because there is no longer a defined time and place of production. And if there is no established set (*Avatar* was captured in a "volume"), then neither is there an off-set (and therefore no exit from work, or "performance"). As movies attempt to move off-screen, too, seeming to colonize and fill this "other," unrepresentable space that films once produced in an erotic and dynamic relation to the on-screen image (the space of performance), we wonder what happens to seduction. It seems impossible to imagine an erotics of full immersion and full-time programming.

Carroll was a "logician with a taste for children," an upstanding representative of the institutional order (as a lecturer in mathematics at Oxford) in relation to which his experimental nonsense was elaborated. His perversion involved luring proper little girls into the comedy of meaning, enchanting them with double and contradictory interpretations of both words and social codes, with anarchic games of cultural decoding and recoding. Burton submits his Alice to the pure power of the code, and every displacement has been programmed. When Alice grows and shrinks, he shows her slipping into and out of her variously scaled dresses, a sort of programmed, 3D (PG) strip-tease. How much stranger and more perverse were the light-sensitive photographic plates that Carroll himself produced, posing his child subjects stock-still (as if dreaming) against the backgrounds of their Victorian homes and gardens. Burton moves his teen Alice through the film like a JPEG within a design program, submitting her to various manipulations and mobilizations. What we get on-screen is a young woman successfully coming to grips with the function of her own self-image, learning from the program how to finally (endlessly) put herself to work.

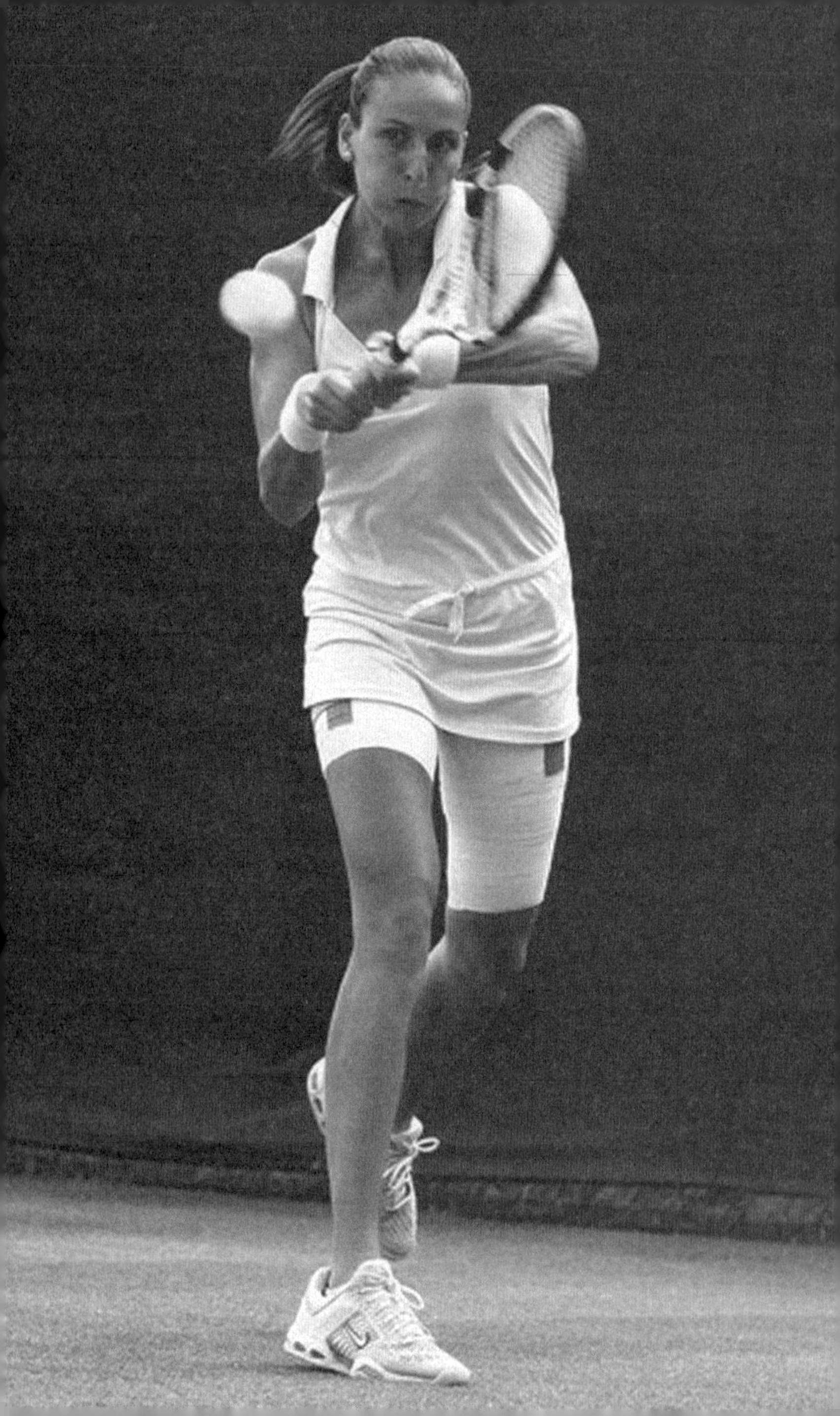

Big Joy Time*

> Here's my advice: take some pills and purge your head; fuck a lot or
> work out until your arms are twenty inches thick. Finally you will be
> a brute, if not a visionary.
> —Arthur Cravan

> Let the person who wants a vision hang himself by his neck. When
> his face turns purple, take him down and have him describe what he's
> seen.
> —Eskimo

Some painters start with a vision and then go to work. Charline
von Heyl works her way toward a vision that never would have
been possible before the work and the painting materialize.
The burning question here is not what to paint, or even why to
paint now, but *how to*: not a problem (problems are for the
experts, the historians) but a constantly renewed, lived question
of tactics and techniques. How to paint now, in a world ordered
by visual communication and, consequently, drained of what the
Eskimos called visions? Or how to free the practice and processes
of painting from the imperative of merely communicating the
world's visual order back to itself, and restore their potential to
make it see again?

In so many ways, von Heyl's work inhabits the question of
how an image resulting directly from the real work of painting
also radically departs from the real—inspired or uninspired—
time of that work; the image she is going for interrupts and
extends seeing in time. And the work is about finding ways of
splitting or unfolding its own "now," of complexifying the
relationship between its gestures and the present of their own
enactment. The question of time is key, contaminating both
the "hows" elaborated in the working hours of the studio and

---

* Originally published in the exhibition catalogue *Charline von Heyl*, Secession, Vienna, 2004.

perception as it encounters the painted object. As we shall see, the specific virtuosity of the painter and the painterly marks and erasures she performs are all contaminated by this attention to time. Because time is at the root of what we might call abstract attention. And what we call an image is both something to see and something that infects and alters seeing with rhythms.

By shifting the question in this way (to the how), the painter derails the problem of painting into actions and attitudes. Here, painting has no choice but to revise itself in its brutal exposure to decisions, events, and the contingencies of doing and seeing as they *take place* in the living-dead material of paint. But "when" is the act of painting? Von Heyl makes it oscillate between a before and an after. In a world where the work of seeing is ever more efficiently compressed into the production of a recognized now (which works by remaining somehow blind to its own work and to how we are implicated in it), von Heyl insists on never letting the painting's present sit still or become naturalized and neutralized in its presentation.

These paintings are seeing-machines, in which visions are artificially and materially fabricated. This work never quits, and there is no right way to go about it because they are images that don't yet know what they want to see. What follows are notes toward a possible definition of abstract attention (or a sort of manual for the painter without a vision), encountering some of the tendencies particular to von Heyl's production of perceptions, which could have never been predicted.

Portrayed Abstraction
Histories of modern art are dramatized by painting's many suicide attempts (the first abstractions resonated this way, and then for a while, abstraction seemed to be the only possible life

for modern painting). Some were considered more successful or sincere than others, but all of them were stage-deaths that painting has lived to tell about. Always these psychodramas, and always these expressions of surprise at painting's new, acted-out recoveries. Von Heyl seems drawn to another kind of drama, as catastrophic as suicide, but not so black. Her colors and gestures, her lines and speeds, pile up and fade out before our eyes, and seem to stage everything *but* death. Which is not to say they present us with a mere imitation of life. They are alive precisely to the extent that they activate the false and its powers, sometimes going so far as to produce and multiply haunting or humorous "portraits" of possible paintings within themselves. In her works, we may recognize a manly, postwar move here, a 1950s color scheme put back to work there, a baroque idea of space crashing up against an Abstract Expressionist handling of material, etc. There seems to be an urge to work through what abstraction looks like (all the painting that comes before the painting), so that the painting can finally get around to what it needs to do. And these partial portraits or portrait-moments, which may sometimes seem to blatantly represent and advertise painted abstraction, are worked and un-worked until a new, unexpected image starts to happen in their midst. These are intensely *suggestive* moments, and the new image occurs as the rhythm at which such suggestions are played. They make up a kind of sensational and gestural vocabulary that von Heyl is teaching to speak again; but differently now, making them sing and stammer like standards ("My Favorite Things") do in jazz. Sometimes, they contradict or trip over themselves as they get caught in her off-speeds. What is particular about von Heyl's abstraction is that it produces an image in which abstraction never stops *doing* itself, knocking itself off or out, and sometimes even lip synching its own greatest hits for a second here or there; and it has no shame. A von Heyl picture is melodramatic and shameless. A title like *Big Joy* brazenly declares itself in 2004. The painting knows it is a stage and that performance is its highest power. It is even what is most real in painting, which exists for real because it wants to and has already moved beyond the question "what for?". These paintings are brutally and comically up front about their own precursors, and address them without the least bit of cynicism. Joys, depressions, enthusiasms, and idiotic hilarity are real *and* performed feelings, stammered and kicked out in colors and lines we may have seen somewhere before, but never experienced in this particular arrangement, tempo, or key.

False Moves and Forged Gestures
Painting and seeing are and always will be physical experiences, involving the eye and the body together (sometimes pulling them apart), and the eye's precarious relation to lived time and space. If postwar abstraction pursued a method-actorly wedding of the unconscious and the performed gesture, emotion, and action, then von Heyl communicates all of this expression via another kind of virtuosity. Her approach is more Nouvelle Vague: like, say, Anna Karina in Godard's *Pierrot le fou* (1965), there is no way here of distinguishing the actor from the role, the per-formance from its image, the Léaud before from the Léaud after "action!" Here, there is always painting before and after, and the image happens *as* their indiscernability. In a von Heyl, the spontaneous, thrown, sudden, physical gesture is often the most labored part of the painting. Drips, smears, and other "painterly" moves are not always what they seem: They can be highly conscious additions, executed with slow care and a virtuosic attention to effect, to the look of emotion or to the painterly qualities that make something like spontaneity feel the way it does. Conversely, the parts of the painting that look slow and composed are sometimes the result of fast, unthinking,

near-blind activity or accident. A portion of the canvas attacked at top speed with acrylic (sometimes using a squeegee) is washed off moments later, producing the effect of a planned scaffolding or skeleton, upon which subsequent layers of oil are built up. Here, too, the body is put to work, thrown into action, but in a way that its habitual gestures (the spiral, or vortex, that always seems to happen as a result of the arm's length, the way the shoulder swivels in its socket, the body's natural distance from the canvas, etc.) are later undone, backtracked from, and worked against. A gesture isn't the truth of the painting; it is one of its many tools. Some gestures are forged and pictured. Others can be buried or extrapolated. But most interestingly, they are systematically and experimentally disengaged from their supposed "now." In almost any von Heyl painting, a before is always put into contact with an after, and the time of painting, of its action or activity, is opened up, shifted, and remixed in an intensely undecideable way.

Reverse and Other Speeds
In a demolition derby, the skillful driver knows when to suddenly slam it in reverse to avoid, or cause, a crash. We could also talk about dancing or boxing. In a painting like *Boogey* (2004), for example, initial, under-painted layers are suddenly brought forward again at the end, and made to seem as if pressing back up to the picture's foreground. There are different ways of painting in reverse: refilling in a background or negative space with an aggressive color, such as cadmium yellow, so that negative space reverses into positive, and vice versa; washing out of acrylic layers so that only the outlines of the initial brushstrokes remain (becoming complex networks of lines surrounding excavated pools of freshly cleared space); un-earthing buried lines and making them crawl or fly again on the surface; etc. These tactics are some of the many ways of

putting the painting in reverse, of making the image oscillate between its own before and after so that it always inhabits the frontier between its own past and future, coming and going as does our eye when we encounter it. Speed is everything in works such as *Defenester 2*, where sections of the brown storm's vortex are strangely slowed, making gusty areas suddenly hang awkwardly in space like dumb, frozen planks, everything flying about them gone back over again, but with patience this time, their blurs nailed down, arcing arm motions weighted down again by hand. Von Heyl uses speed against the grain, against itself, confusing the body's and eye's natural reflexes in order to open the image into unforeseen rhythms. And, once again, the time of seeing unfolds and dilates in the oscillating, constantly shifted time of painting. Forth and back, flying and freezing … the turning point of the image happens precisely where gesture and material are squatted with off speeds. In this way, the act of painting is decentered from its own clumsy present, and put back in touch with both a forgotten past and a future poised elegantly on the tip of the tongue.

Collapsed and Phantom Lines
Lines usually want to trace a form, and the eye can't help wanting to see them work that way. One of von Heyl's tactics is to dismantle the line's habitual operation by adding lines to lines until a floating or heavy line-mass is produced (*Boogey, Schluckspecht*). The line's tendency to trace a contour is hijacked, shifted over, and made free (as is color) to do everything else but represent: it becomes intensely rhythmic, unearthing new times and spaces. Here, at the point where illustration collapses, the illustrational line remains somehow charged as outline, but doesn't outline. In paintings like *Blue Noir*, we get phantom lines. Lines are interrupted in mid-flight, whited out here, but picked up again there, in the calm mapping of lavender fields.

The line's power is slowed and stilled in such passages, but the eye is continually drawn back off the map by the line's irrepressible, phantom movement. The line stops and the eye keeps going, and neither ever arrive at the destination of a recognizable form. Here, the line's potential to suggest and unleash many, sometimes contradictory speeds is played to the hilt. And the image is happening at all of these speeds at once, which is a pleasure the brain still doesn't want to admit.

Dirt and Attitude

The "dirt" in some of these paintings is made by hand-grinding dry charcoal or un-thinned, black or brown pigments straight from the tube into the grain of the clean or under-painted canvas. Dirt often dances with bright and pretty colors, as if not only the flowers, but also the soil in which they grew, were uprooted all at once and thrown into a compositional blender. A painting can start with dirt, gradually cutting it in with colored planes until it pops back out as 3D clouds (*Black Pink*). Dirt can also be applied later, as a nasty, smoggy atmosphere that chokes off the girlish or kitschy impulses in a certain color scheme. Or used to defocus the crisp, clean flatness of a surface such as that of *Red and Yeller*. Dirt is an attitude as well as a part of the image. Some parts of the image seem to have their own personal attitudes—rebellious or humorous—that carry on loud, sometimes deaf conversations with the uptight or lame attitudes of other parts. This is painting that refuses to commit to any one attitude, that's always ready to throw dirt in its own eye makeup. And the different attitudes happen in different speeds, generating rhythm and variation. One hand running circles around the other. A fistful of dirt versus a steady-handed, glossy lipstick. The eye drawn along by both at once.

Happy Catastrophe

There is a perverse joy in killing a picture at the very moment it might be finished, and in the challenge of making this dead body get up and try to dance again. Von Heyl likes to renew this challenge in many of her canvases. It is how the painting is made to plunge back into a catastrophic or clumsy present that doggedly returns between its own heroic before and after. She also wonders if "uncreative," cowardly, or lame moods aren't in fact just as interesting and productive as their supposed opposites, and will put these to work at the moment a painting starts to seem too sure of itself. The completed, final image is always kept in suspense, never presented but intensely and constantly suggested: this is the image she wants, but also doesn't want. What she really wants is the next image, the unshowable one beyond (before and after) the one she's working on, or even between the different paintings in a show. Maybe catastrophe is another word for the hysteria of painting, for how a suppressed sensation keeps erupting on a given surface, or at a given speed—one more way of explaining how and why the painting is always both before and after itself. Forgetting itself is one of the painting's best powers: Abstract attention is about knowing how to lose an image in order to find an image. The painter always provokes a new catastrophe because here and nowhere else is where the possibility of the next image is opened.

Aesthetic discussions always return to definitions of beauty, pleasure, and taste in painting. It would be interesting to turn our attention instead to painting's health, and ask after the happiness of the image. Because it seems the image is happiest when it learns to transform its own collapsings into a new way of dancing or seeing. To speak of painting without a vision is another way of announcing painting's potential to fabricate images and ways of seeing that undermine a culture's demand to not only have any art finally locate its end in that culture's transmission, but to also tie its processes down in a product. The question of happiness is a question of dislocating painting's means from its ends, its gestures from any efficient or programmatic result. It is a question of how to continue to invent ways of exposing the image to its own unworkings, and of elaborating, in the words of Giorgio Agamben, means without ends.[1] More than anything, abstract attention might be an attention to happiness.

1   "Once again Walter Benjamin, in the 'Theologico-Political Fragment,' leaves no doubts regarding the fact that 'the order of the profane should be erected on the idea of happiness.' The definition of the concept of 'happy life' remains one of the essential tasks of the coming thought ..." Giorgio Agamben, "Notes on Politics," in *Means without End* (Minneapolis, MN: University of Minnesota Press, 2000).

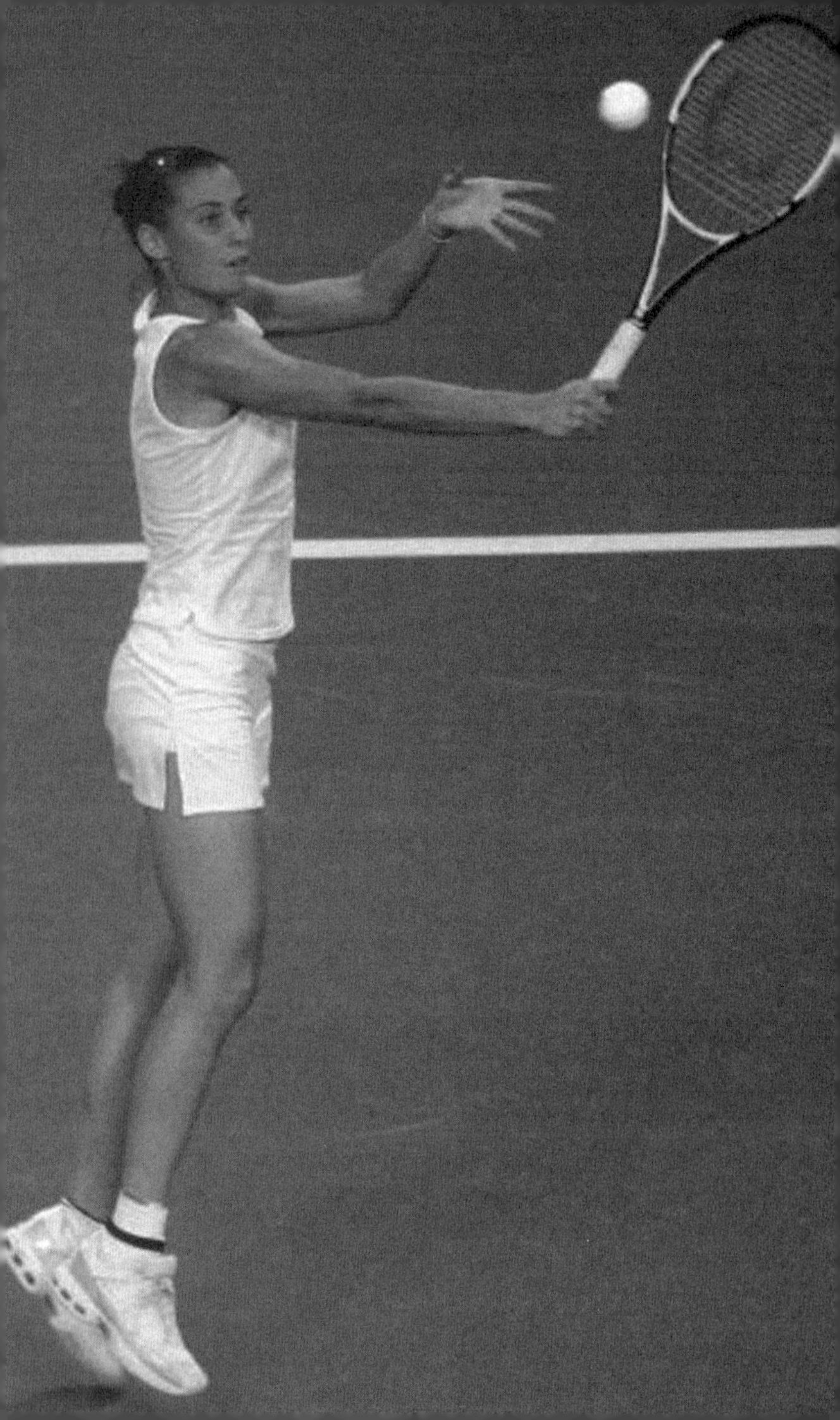

Bohemian Monsters*

Playing with dolls is a pastime for sissies and shut-ins, and as artists from Hans Bellmer to Todd Haynes have shown, it is also a hands-on means of objectifying the terrors and traumas of one's time, whether in psychotherapy or in the gallery. Indeed, as the credit crunch hits the headlines and now the city, the moment seems right for this series of hilariously downsized allegories of subjective and economic crisis. And what genre could be more fitting than schlock horror? For his first solo exhibition in New York, "Bohemian Monsters," at Broadway 1602, Daniel McDonald peopled miniature yet epic tableaux with mummies, zombies, and other mass-produced "action figures" bought on eBay. Surgically restyled by the artist, these figurines depict the lower depths of the art-world food chain—a downtown pressure—cooked by gentrification and the crackdown on "quality of life" crimes and terror, first under Giuliani and then Bloomberg.

McDonald, who also makes jewelry under the name Mended Veil, is brilliant in small scale. Obsessive, DIY craftsmanship and an arch, conceptual approach to found objects inform the artist's move from gothic costume jewelry to these new, intricate sculptures, which condense two decades of Lower Manhattan's mutant history into tightly arranged scenes that play out at comic-book speed. *Goodbye (The Wolfman and Frankenstein)*, 2008, presents a hipster werewolf clutching a bouquet of roses, in the act of kicking down the door of a cramped apartment where a little Jack Pierson-style text-work spells out "GOODB . . ." on the wall, and a mini Y props open the window. A second figure, holding an E, is already up on the roof, about to jump. In *An*

---

*   Originally published in *Artforum*, December 2008.

Experiment in Self-Medication (Doctor Jekyll as Mr. Hyde), 2008, a solitary figure wearing a paint-smeared lab coat guzzles alcohol in a studio strewn with bottles. The scene is itself bottled—an allegory of addiction trapped under a bell jar. There is a perversity in McDonald's reduced scales and self-enclosed forms that calls to mind certain works by Duchamp, such as *Belle Haleine, Eau de Voilette* (1921), a small sculpture based on a readymade perfume bottle, and *Boîte-en-valise* (1935–41), whereby the artist carefully reproduced his own works as a miniature, foldout career retrospective inside a small suitcase. Playing on a confusion between artistic subjectivity and the readymade commodity, McDonald's project underlines the living-dead status of products and selves that outlast their expiration dates, while foregrounding a hobbyist's approach to making objects— self-sufficient, self-sustaining, never in a hurry. You can imagine McDonald producing this show at home, in front of the TV, in an apartment not unlike the ones he fabricates in miniature. In his case, the joke is in how the hobbyist's detached and retiring attitude collides with the end-of-the-rope urgencies that dramatize his sculptures.

McDonald experienced the previous economic recession as co-director of American Fine Arts gallery in New York, where he and other Cooper Union grads joined forces with dealer Colin de Land to form Art Club 2000, a collective whose mid-1990s work portrayed urban youths striking ironic and critical poses against the backdrop of SoHo's collapse and the rise of the megastore. Soon, all the good nightclubs would be closed down. In that context, DIY was both a mode of humble resistance and a real necessity for those interested in keeping some version of bohemian self-invention alive in the city. It was the era of club kids, Wu-Tang Clan, Tommy Hilfiger, Alleged Gallery, cable access, Narcotics Anonymous, and other mutant formations.

This time around, however, McDonald shows us the impotence and absurdity of stereotypical underground lifestyles in the face of unstoppable urban development. In *Demolition of Affordable Housing (The Phantom of the Opera)*, 2007, a dandyish ghoul stands paralyzed next to a tiny typewriter and a bin full of even tinier crumpled pages, while a toy crane stands ready to raze his crumbling, claustrophobic world. These are not only images of the artist destroyed by madness, starving hysterical, etc. These are metaphors for bohemia in the process of being disappeared by the far darker forces of global finance. In *Forced to Sell Artwork from a Personal Collection in Order to Offset Living Expenses (The Wicked Witch of the West)*, 2008, a green-faced collector-hag creeps into a gallery with the obvious intention of selling back an artwork that also happens to be her own Warhol celebrity portrait. "Bohemian Monsters" presents the new downtown: a creaking ruin, now fractured into a series of isolated freak-outs and cooped-up crisis couples, trapped in airless art studios and overpriced apartments that resemble B-horror sets.

During the Great Depression, films such as *Frankenstein* (1931) and *Freaks* (1932) resonated with common fears of disaster and misfortune, and for Western consumers living through the Cold War, Hollywood B movies in the sci-fi and horror genres tapped popular anxieties about the bomb and Soviet invasion. Referencing these histories in "Bohemian Monsters," McDonald reflects a contemporary dread particular to New York: a feeling that what we once imagined as the "artist's life" is no longer possible here, or only possible as a sort of "bad," no-budget movie. He also orchestrates a couple of crowd scenes: *Available Space (Various Figures)*, 2008, depicts a horde of mutant/monster creative types lined up in the street outside a padlocked door bearing the words "alternative space"; *Artists Under Consideration* (2008), appropriately installed in the gallery's office, is a gruesome filing cabinet overflowing with corpses and CVs—a bohemian graveyard. Strung like rotten pearls on a very thin thread, the figures in these scenes populate the dark side of what we call the creative network, spooked by the possibility that they could soon find themselves as uselessly adrift in this world as yesterday's hedge-fund managers and other, less-privileged sectors of the global multitude.

We've carried the notion of the freedom-seeking outsider into these times, but find no proper space in which to live it. Given the spiraling of the global financial crisis, artists may find it necessary to elaborate other, more cunning (and therapeutic) relations to their own crisis, and to the real estate they haunt. If the credit-driven economy is a fiction that no longer functions, art, too, will have to put dysfunction back into play. It will get smaller, weirder, and more monstrous.

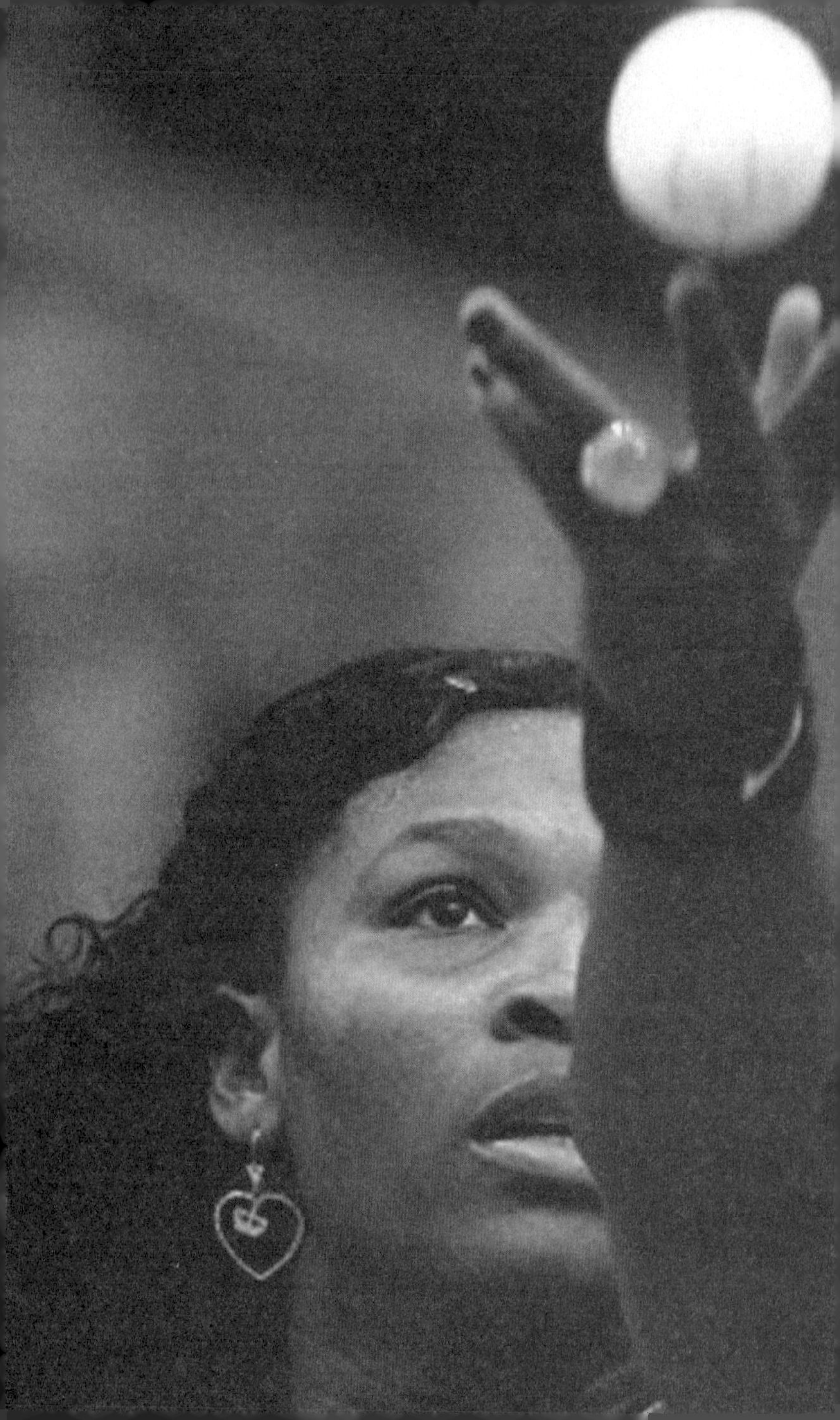

Cars, Women*

The frequent flyer and the traffic jam are just two examples of the fact that, in our days, production and circulation are one and the same process. If we are moving, we are probably working. If something produces value, it is probably moving too, not just a thing, but a transportation. "AM I MY CAR?" is one of the many big or small questions posed in Peter Fischli's and David Weiss's book *Will Happiness Find Me?* (2002). Big and small, these are the questions that works like *Autos* (*Cars*) and *Frauen* (*Women*, formerly titled *Stewardesses*) were already asking in the late 1980s, even if they were hidden behind other, more immediate ones like, "Is it too easy?" and "Is it good?"

Cars and *Women* are works that have often appeared together, and one of the basic qualities they share is a ghostly, dry whiteness. Being made of plaster, this is a quality they both also happen to share with galleries and museums. Cast in the same stuff, both sets of objects and the gallery walls that echo and contain them have a way of undermining the old figure/ground structure—being not exactly one or the other—and at the same time announcing a sort of zone of indistinction between idea and surface, content and packaging, information and format. Haunting the gallery and catalogue with their chalky blankness, these objects have a disconcertingly easy way of showing us what's so strange about the ordinariness of our world. This is an effect we know from other Fischli/Weiss works too, and one way they do it (when they're not busy animating static objects) is by stopping and freezing a thing or an image that normally moves. Many works do it by robbing an ordinary thing of its utility, and these do it with cast plaster.

*   Originally published in the Peter Fischli and David Weiss exhibition catalogue *Flowers & Questions: A Retrospective*, Tate Publishing, London, 2006.

A material so cheap and common seems perfectly and strangely adequate to forms as ordinary as cars and working women. Reduced and then immobilized in plaster, the perfectly normal desires these objects speak to—desires for mobility, independence, belonging, completeness, etc.—are made to stumble over themselves, over their own strangeness. Because *Cars* and *Stewardesses* are libidinal stumbling blocks. Some part of us is moving toward them only to be met by this dry, airy frozenness, and also this awkwardly reduced scale. This is how a material as cheap and common as plaster shows us how strange we are in our wanting and recognizing these things. They've also done it with clay, acrylic, and black rubber, but with plaster, they do it cheaper and faster.

If I were Rosalind Krauss, I might explain how the blank, white *Cars* and *Women* are also mothers and breasts, and that if they figure anything, it is their own absence.[1] Because what we encounter in them is in fact a repeating missed encounter with the real. Fischli/Weiss make sure we recognize these objects, and at the same time that we recognize our misrecognition of them, since they are nothing but substitutes for the images in our world. The plaster, causing a confusion between the blankness of the page and what appears on the page, reminds us that what we see is like an automatic ghost rising up, and even producing the gap, in our seeing. So we see that seeing is also not seeing.

The *Women* come in three sizes: small, medium, and large (one meter tall). They come individually and in sets of four (cast in formation, along with the square of floor that supports them). The *Cars* are roughly one-third the actual size of a car. These

1   Rosalind E. Krauss, *The Optical Unconscious* (Cambridge, MA: MIT Press, 1994).

off-scales give them the "look" of art: Greek or Neoclassical statuettes or Minimalist blocks presented on plinths, they occupy the place of art in a casual way, simply parked or posing here. They might be aesthetic stand-ins or sculptural surrogates. Even in heels, the *Women* manage to mimic the relaxed beauty of classical *contrapposto* poses, one leg supporting the body's weight, the other slightly bent. The alternating scales of these working women, when distributed in a gallery's expanse, produce optical illusions of depth perspective or odd fore-shortenings of rational, functional space. Standing next to a photograph, she is like a prop, a signifier of "art" in a bourgeois salon. They are stewardesses and cars in the form of décor and vice versa. Returning us to the safety and comfort of a world whose values are always in order, they also haunt this place with their ordinariness and ease. They remind us that this space of inventory is always already filled, like a parking lot.

These women aren't particular people. The cars, too—parked in all their showroom obviousness—are approximations of the most average automobiles, as brandless as the women are anonymous. Examples of the normal, stripped of almost every identifying feature but that of being normal, they really are strange. We could say that anonymous or whatever-art is art that doesn't identify with itself, and that isn't non-art either, but has a devious way of exemplifying and absorbing the art/non-art paradox, which has haunted the aesthetic regime at least since Duchamp stripped a urinal of its use value in order to suddenly charge it with a disorienting exhibition value (in order to present exhibition value as such). *Cars* and *Women* are "examples" of readymades, and are, in fact, made that way by the artists, nonchalantly cast, and cast into our midst as examples of automatic or mass-produced things. Have you ever seen a model kitchen, for example, displayed in a shop window? It is an abbreviation, life-like but smaller than life, and the faucets don't work. This could be something to cast in plaster too, an example of an installation.

The word "automobile" is close enough to "automaton" that a question like, "Am I my car?" and the robotic look of the working women can be posed together, in the gallery, in order to also ask the question of happiness in an automatic world. Ever more subtly calibrated to the production and circulation, to the making-moving, of our post-Fordist economy and its value-producing transportations, are the processes by which we are simultaneously subjectivized as individuals, travelers, workers, and consumers—not only of an automatic world, but of our own automation. Ever since the first readymade, modern art has attempted to match the automatic force of non-artistic, industrial processes, and not always in order to critique or sabotage them. Because there is still the promise of the joyride and the desiring machine. Automatic, familiar images such as *Cars* and *Women* are like molded blocs of late twentieth-century subjectivity laid out in plain view. They are our own whateverness. And in plaster as white as a gallery wall, they show how this whateverness links production and desire. Cast, dried, and frozen, but not in the glamorous permanence of marble or bronze, these static productions seem caught in the beams of oncoming traffic, of our own automobilized gaze.

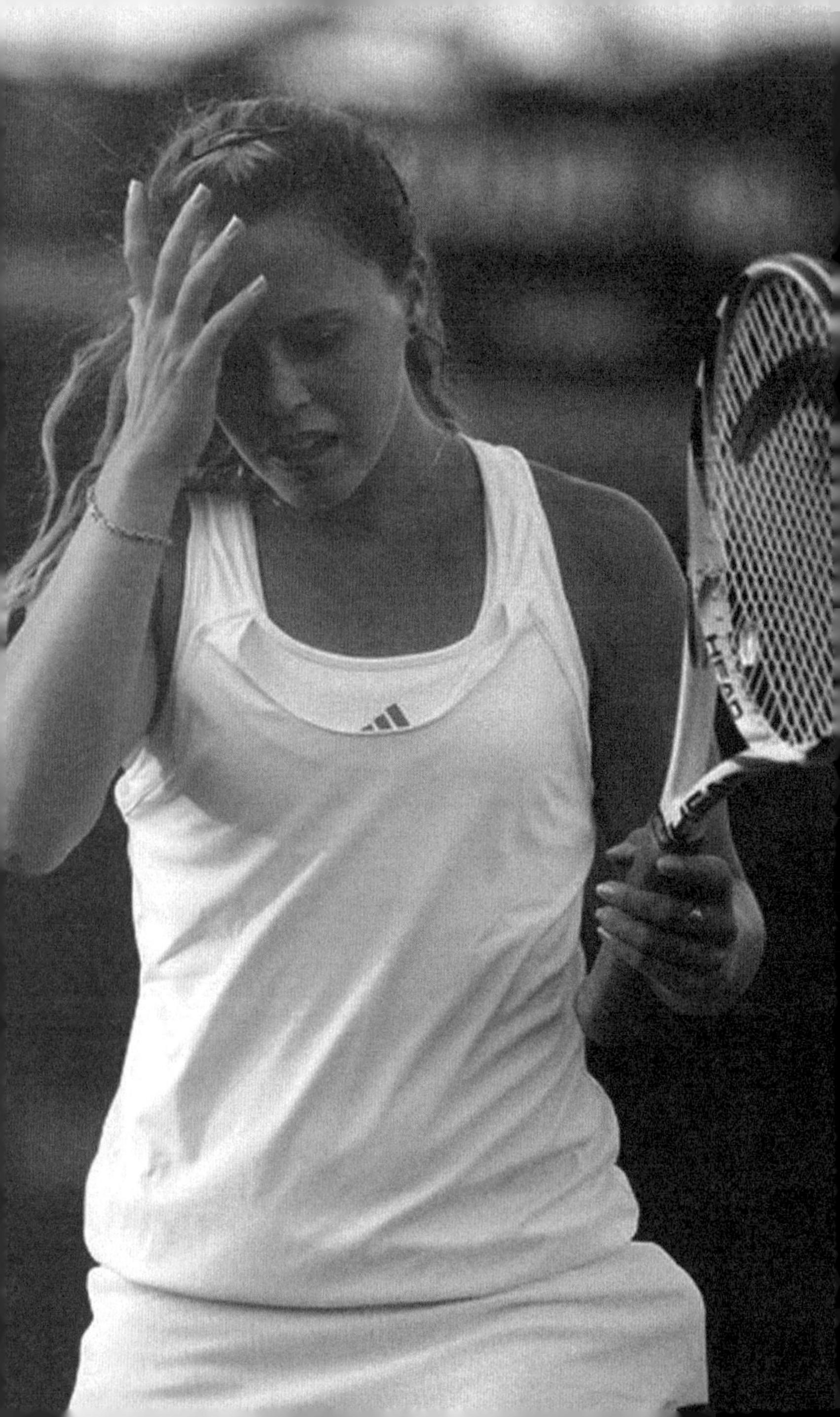

Collage and Program (Rise of the Readymetal Maidens)*

The miracle is produced with the same exactitude that is
required of banking and commercial operations.[1]
—Salvador Dalí

As his dealers push Albert Oehlen the master painter in a market
now ready to receive him as such, we wouldn't want to forget
the Oehlen who, before and after picking up his brush, is always
busy with other, less grandiose, less noble activities, such as
tearing up magazines, cycling, or passing hours in front of the
computer. It has already been said that collage plays a primary
role in the artist's process—as the starting point or foundation
of almost every one of his paintings. But what kind of foundation
is it? Is it a structural base giving rise to towers of paint, or a
false bottom, ensuring that the painting will always already be
confused with and undermined by something else, and never
totally itself? While collage serves the painting's compositional
process—if only by providing information to paint against,
to graffiti over—it also seems to persist in and infect the canvas
with a certain indifference to the rising and the proper time
of painting. The wasteful, constant activity of cutting and pasting,
appropriating, and recombining readymade images produces
moments both against and within the time of painting, unbalancing it by always getting between the legs of the finished
product.

If almost every major Oehlen is to some degree slung over the
bones of a collage, it's also true that the painting itself is a
collage of different moments and gestures, and that, in many cases,
the moments we would call painterly are often followed and

* Originally published in *Parkett*, no. 79, 2007.
1 Salvador Dalí, "Photography: Pure Creation of the Mind," in *Oui: The Paranoid-Critical Revolution: Writings 1927-1933* (Boston: Exact Change, 2004), 12.

extended by further layers of actual collage. For example, a painted table might be set with appropriated, ink-jetted reproductions of fruit. Or a photographic headshot might be hung on the wall of a painted field of color, decorating and making a canvas room-like. All of this to say that the paintings never seem to depart or finally distinguish themselves from collage, or from the persistence of the readymade image, which might come back as décor or content within an otherwise abstract picture. Meanwhile, in small collages on paper, painting returns again and again as readymade-painting, art history snipped and sampled from catalogues and magazines, now joining rank with reproductions of nude cyclists, Scandinavian heavy metalists, computer graphics, antique furniture, tattoos, etc.

We could visualize this constant exchange between collage and painting as a motor that never stops turning over, with the readymade as a kind of drive shaft at its center:

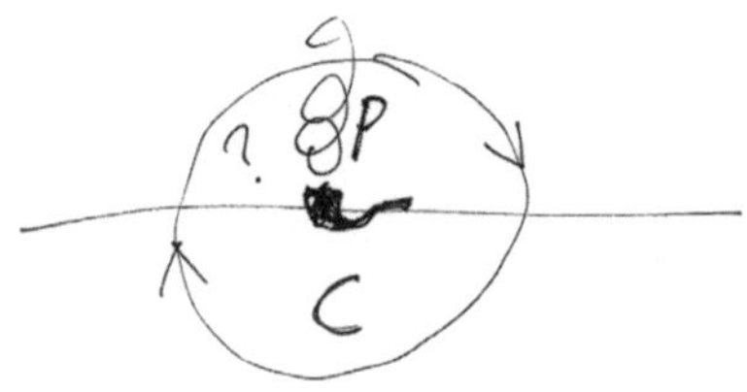

Collage (bottom) both founds and undermines painting (top), but both procedures lose their specificity as they orbit around the readymade, which already contaminates even the most spontaneous-looking painterly gesture. Collage could be defined as the guerilla occupation of a prescribed and ready-made field, where it sets itself up as a machine for reprocessing the idea of painting in terms of so much other programmed in-formation. Our diagram depicts a cycle whereby collage appropriates readymade images that might serve as the foundation for a coming painting, while painting returns as readymade material in another collage. What remains unknowable about painting, sometimes calling itself abstract as it arises like a zombie from collage, but entirely unsure of its own status now, is indicated by a question mark. But this simplistic schema, while maybe helpful in its grasp of a dynamic relation linking two activities, will not bring us very close to either the specific character of Oehlen's collages or to the influence of digital programs in his recent work.

Glancing at Oehlen's small-format, cut-and-paste collages on paper, we immediately discern two basic types: grids and rooms. The grids are often composed of appropriated newspaper or catalogue pages, taken whole in order to exploit their orderly stacking and sequencing of blocks or columns of information, while the page's squareness is sometimes disturbed by the odd, round eyeball or the snaking curve of a flamingo's neck. These grids also recall the didactic charts and layouts of art-history or biology textbooks, and so are asking to be vandalized. The rooms, on the other hand, appropriate the order and contents of designer homes, taking reproductions of these from lifestyle magazines and furniture advertisements, and are usually visited by pasted-in figures and other intruding objects. Oehlen begins with readymade systems of display—the real estate of the page and the real estate of real estate—and then pirates their logic. Pages and rooms are structuring devices that permeate daily life and are essential to the distribution of value, property, and meaning within a policed, orderly world. Sometimes the most joyful way of attacking bourgeois order and the systems that maintain it is simply to redistribute its properties, put fine-art bronzes next to Spandex thongs, Spanish Fascism next to gym equipment, lip gloss next to corpses, etc. The structures of the grid and the domestic interior remain intact, but they no longer inform or comfort us; they terrorize us both with their sudden uselessness and by faking miracles in the face of everyday life's impoverishment.

In one collage, Oehlen simply pastes a picture of an armchair into an image of a tasteful, designer kitchen. The chair is slightly misaligned with the perspective of the room and floats a little off the floor. It's more of a living room chair than a kitchen chair, but it's not exactly an umbrella on an operating table. In this collage, nothing collides with nothing. Oehlen prefers to add things to a world of things: collage as inventory, or as a simple stocking of images in the place where they already belong. We are a long way from the Surrealist chance encounter here. Or rather, we are in a world where chance is already included in every communications package; bizarre juxtapositions never stop coming anyway. This is collage with an eye on the redundancy of the present.[2]

2 "To the reservoir or inventory of this series of stand-ins Lacan gives the name automaton to indicate the quality of uncanniness that surrounds the finding of each of these objects, the sense not only of anxiety the encounter produces but also its aura of happenstance, an encounter one was not prepared for, a meeting that always, one insists, takes place by chance. But the term automaton also underscores the inexorability and order that rule this series ..." Rosalind E. Krauss, *The Optical Unconscious* (Cambridge, MA: MIT Press, 1993), 72.

Elsewhere, a sort of "automaton" rises up within the pictorial field, haunting the inventoried spaces of metropolitan life. It rises up as a figure, or as figured information. It might come as a heavy-metal ghoul or a clay figurine lifted from some lame arts and crafts manual, but it always returns. Painting, too, returns when a drunken Bruegel peasant crashes out on a yuppie bedspread, or when someone else we know from art history, maybe one of de Kooning's Ab-Ex monsters, stalks and squats a picture-perfect interior. As figure and information, painting visits the collage like any other customer in the supermarket, dragging its reproduced, drippy, living-dead paint-flesh into our lifestyle, something obscene and nude hogging the photo-genic bathroom and raiding our refrigerator. Hanging out with face-painted guitarists, airbrushed "booty" girls, and peppy aerobics instructors, these art historical figures are as naked and strange here as the bald cyber-mannequins that populate so many Oehlens. Painting returns as automaton to occupy this void, rising up in the collage like the Commandante's ghost at the end of *Don Giovanni*. A psychoanalyst might have something to say about castration at this point, seeing so many figures detached from their paintings and set adrift among all these other sad and ridiculous objects of desire: claw-footed bathtubs, lamps, asses, cannons, gilded frames, palm trees, naked teenagers from the 1930s, etc. But it is not for us to explain the relation be-tween collage and the phallus, or what paint has to do with shit and punishment. We only see creeps and monsters, the eternal return of these invading, severed bodies.

And then, from the gleaming depths of cyberspace, a third type of image comes to join the grids and rooms: the poster or flyer-like pictures that are designed with computer programs and printed onto large sheets of paper. These, too, exploit and occupy readymade systems of display. In the posters, where collage is assisted by graphic design software, or already (like chance, like Surrealism) absorbed into the smooth operation of a cybernetic program, Oehlen exploits all the chaos and flashy juxtapositions of rave flyers, porn sites, and cheap travel brochures. These are organizing devices already infected with psychedelic culture and "bad Surrealism," which, for all their mind-bending ambitions, are no less banal than the rooms and grids. Here, we are not only dealing with readymade images, but with a readymade program and its built-in palette of effects. The first impulse is to use too much at once, too many colors and too many tools, and to push the program to a creative and functional limit that never seems to come. The artist makes it work and work, forcing it to simulate inspiration. What better way to announce one's upcoming art exhibition, or nothing in particular, than to present announcement as such? From now on, the event *is* the announcement—its own poster.

When Oehlen uses a program like Illustrator or Paintbox, with its virtual "brushes" and "spray paint" option, he elaborates another kind of relation between the readymade, painting, and collage. As collage merges with the readymade program, painting is suddenly put into a threatening relationship with the mid-1990s cyborg, a digi-graphic automaton at least as terrifying as its old grandmother, the Surrealist mannequin. And this might be a good time to show how the introduction of ready-made digital-collage effects and painting effects complicate the matrix of Oehlen's practice:

When the new mannequins begin to march across the twilit field of painting, they not only lay waste to what was once called gesture (ever more integrated into the program, where it is neutralized as information), but also attempt to fill the gap that formerly separated painting and the readymade, the artist and his works. It is no longer interesting to copy a mustache and paste it onto a Mona Lisa; this is as normal as your average pizza box (which in itself is not uninteresting). Painting in the information age has one task and one task only: to seduce the cyborg. To pretend that no gap could ever keep them apart. To fake its orgasms and dope itself. It must get closer to the programs unleashed by digital cameras and computers, and appropriate the logic of these infernal machines. If painting embraces its loss of distinction to the program, and becomes even more committed in this affair, it might discover ways of making itself as smart and effective as any other contemporary device. But it must not lose its stupidity either. Collage is one way to keep painting opaque to itself, even as the program attempts to absorb and predict it. Collage is an experienced guerilla: Having nothing of its own, it infiltrates readymade territories and makes do with the enemy's readymade power.

Salvador Dalí understood immediately that his own painterly
capacities were radically thrown into question by the reproduction of museum masterworks on postcards and tea trays. He
invented a method called "*paranoïaque-critique*" to counter the
speed and intelligence of these new images, and was so successful
that he was eventually able—through the associative precision of
his self-induced delirium—to detect the existence of a painted-
over child's corpse at the feet of the farmers in Millet's *L'Angelus* ,
1858 (later verified by an X-ray).[3] In order to get to the bottom
of the Millet and steal back its power, Dalí first had to submit
to the experience of its threatening new potency as ready-Millet,
and to actively uncover the connection between the readymade and his own sexual impotence, the sound of crickets, sunsets,
etc. (Later, he would himself become one of the most reproduced artists ever.) Taking this example as a starting point, we
might ready ourselves to meet the new mannequins. And it
may be that art's job is no longer to produce more surprising
images, but to make itself a means of locating today's corpse
within the redundancy (or ecstasy) of communication. Collage
in particular might be a way of getting to the bottom of
impotence, of extracting living-dead gestures from information.

Another thought: Collage, especially in the case of Oehlen, is
no longer just an aesthetic activity, but a potentially endless
file, a filing and sorting that takes over where previous notions
of artistic agency lose their meaning. What is so non-Ernst-like
here is that the images seem almost bored of their own shock-
value. This file, deviously imitating the expansion and perfection
of the digital program, stores and processes images; but it also

3   Salvador Dalí, *Le Mythe tragique de l'Angelus de Millet* (Paris: Pauvert,1963). Lacan's first
    theories on paranoia were developed at the same time that he encountered Surrealism,
    in particular Dalí. Oehlen appropriates a Millet in one of his collages: The peasant leans on
    his hoe, staring blankly across his field at a pasted-in nudist, possibly a Hitler youth.

stores (reserves, withholds) the potential to go on this way forever. This eternal file could even be an endlessly redeeming procedure, as far as images are concerned. What never stops returning is the potential for images to become separated from any informative, revolutionary, or, ultimately, painterly task. Just images, with no job to do. Collage is a false program that refuses to ever make itself useful.

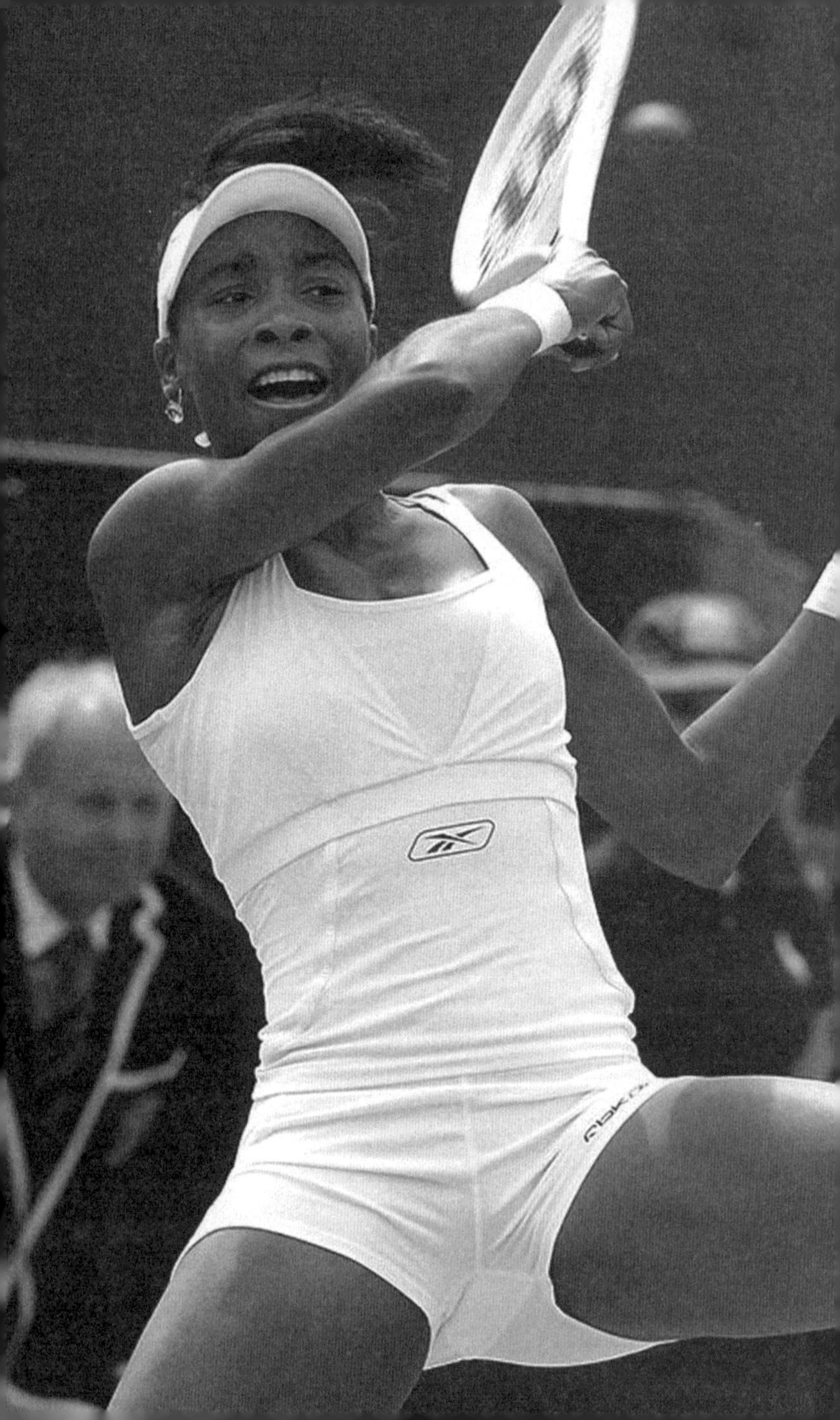

Decapitalism*

In the poster for a recent Fra Angelico exhibition at the Metropolitan Museum of Art, saints are being decapitated. They are kneeling in a circle, the sword follows this circle, and blood is gushing from the open holes of their necks. It's remarkable that, even chopped off, the heads keep their golden halos. The bystanders and kings on the left side of the composition seem to notice this too, but it's too late. Now, the heads are like gold coins rolling in the painting, like presidents' heads on money. And isn't money like a severed head? It's a sort of decapitation that moves money and everything else with it, as if in a trance. It was Marx who said that meditating on money makes men lose their heads.[1]

Showing together in Europe now for the second time, the artists Wade Guyton, Seth Price, Josh Smith, and Kelley Walker may not be the New Yorkiest band in the world, but if they were, this would be their second album. Let's call them fellow travelers, and assume their grouping is at least partly a European construction. It's their packaging and touring as *Guyton, Price, Walker, Smith* that allows for the production of something like a New York moment in the Kunsthalle, or wherever such moments are in demand. And it could be that the objects and images on view here are not so much things for the eyes as they are different ways of entering and inflecting the movement of this entranced circulation. The works themselves seem fascinated by what is happening to them.

---

*   First printed in a reproduction (by 38th Street Publishers, New York) of the forthcoming exhibition catalogue *Guyton, Price, Smith, Walker*, Kunsthalle Zürich.
1   Michael Taussig, *The Magic of the State* (London: Routledge, 1997).

If these four artists were a group, *The Decapitation of Saints Cosmas and Damian* would make a striking album cover design, or a poster for the tour (the actual poster for this show is an appropriated *New Yorker* magazine cover). That the saints are not only losing their heads, but their eyes too—being blindfolded—provokes a strange awareness of the fact of viewing in the viewer of this decapitating spectacle. Also, that these heads are rolling within the calm, rational perspective of a sunny, Tuscan landscape.

Circles are for the idea of recycling that is itself recycled in the work of Walker. Blood is for the liquid puddles and smears of Smith's "Palette Paintings," which are also at least semi-blind in their making. Money is for everything real and abstract that circulates in the practice of Price, whose very name conjures money. Blindness is for the technical malfunctions that both produce and disturb the images of Guyton. Price, too, has sometimes caused blindness by entombing visual information in sculptural works, disappearing highly circulated imagery, such as terrorist hostage beheadings, before the very eyes of his viewers. There is something definitely and strangely headless about Smith's palettes, but his total project can be discussed in terms of recycling as well: His exhibition posters may return in other works for other exhibitions, becoming new paintings, collages, or books, for example. In a way, Walker blinds his digital scanner by smearing its flat eye with toothpaste or chocolate. There's also something bloody in these splotches of mass-produced goodness. Not to mention the recycling of signature gestures from the Guyton-Walker collaboration, not represented here.

We could say that the contemporary artist is somehow split between the decapitated saint and the fascinated onlooker or king, and that his work is like the solitary, circular motion of the sword within the frame, or within the conditions of his own production. And here, where rolling heads turn to gold, we are also sometimes tempted to imagine another (evil?) recycling that produces nothing of any use and conserves no value—a bachelor machine grinding away for nothing, grinding itself. Because if there are the rational and natural cycles that produce and renew value—the seasons, the fashions, the compost heap, etc.—then there are also devious cycles like the ones Jacques Lacan graphed out, that turn on lack, and whose very turning erodes and splits identity, producing only missed encounters with the real and endless substitutions.[2] Breasts, for example, that aren't really breasts, but Polystyrene voids. Or material ejaculations saved and copied as JPEG files. Images that take repetition as their starting point, and don't stop. In the heart of our value-producing circulation, we plug in these machines that transform nothing, that do not progress, and only recycle their own revolutions. Like Duchamp's "Rotoreliefs," they throb and pulsate in the bustle of the marketplace, infecting the visual and the rational with a corrosive, deviant movement that moves only itself. They work and they don't work. Or maybe it's that they work by decapitating themselves.

A jammed inkjet printer printing out its own dysfunction. A still-wet painter's palette shifted from the table to the wall and presented as a finished work, and that keeps pulling us back down to the idea of a table again. A press release that appears on the desks of different galleries at once, and that articulates nothing except that it is assuming the place and function as a press release. A desktop scanner automatically capturing a formless stain or a brick wall. Packaging that contains nothing but

2   Rosalind E. Krauss, *The Optical Unconscious* (Cambridge, MA: MIT Press, 1993).

itself, or information that becomes its own wrapper, concealing itself in itself. Toothpaste without a tube. Or serially produced canvases, each as energetic and expressive as the next, overstocking four or five gallery booths at the same art fair, and sometimes even plastered with posters advertising previous exhibitions at other galleries. An artwork on the glossy cover of *Artforum* re-photographed and re-presented once more, installed there where we want to see the work-work. Stacks and piles of these. Works working on themselves, or else devising ways of standing in for and substituting themselves. Productions of productions, strange duplications, repetitions, and re-formattings. Commodities that announce their own way of being something other than what they seem, examples of art, etc.

The contemporary artist doesn't just produce and present objects or images; he produces production itself, presentation itself … images and ideas of these that are at the same time (like it or not) ethical propositions. Like any worker today, the artist's job is also to talk and move, putting words, images, and his own body into circulation. More than anything, he makes momentum. But there is really no time to think about this now. There is only the possibility of putting this no-time to work, and of capturing it in frozen glimpses, which are themselves built on speed and work. And any work that holds our attention today is one that not only shows itself, but also shows it could be otherwise, shows that the relation between an artist and his own activity can always be modified, even interrupted.[3] Art becomes a way of working on the displacement of information from one format to another, and of working on the way we are displaced too, in work and in play. At what point do the boundaries of the artwork dissolve in the momentum that carries it along, and how can

3   Paolo Virno, *The Grammar of the Multitude* (New York and Los Angeles: Semiotext(e), 2004).

this be made visible? And all of this—what Jacques Rancière has been calling "the distribution of the sensible"—is precisely a question of politics.

It's been a long while since the time an artist put into his work counted as a valid measure of the work's value. Duchamp and Warhol, with the readymade and serial production, freed art from the old calculus of time and value. Meanwhile, in the so-called real world, the time of production continues to dilate and expand in relation to the shrinking time of paid work, colonizing the unpaid time of speaking, thinking, and consuming too. And back in the art world, there is the growing suspicion that objects aren't the only readymades, that the artist himself is the subjective equivalent of a urinal or Brillo box, even. Viewers may notice the glitches and dysfunctions in these exemplary productions signed Guyton, Price, Walker, and Smith, and wonder whether they count more as expressive gestures, as accidents, or as moments when design realizes the possibility of escaping itself. Because readymades can also be un-made.

It has been said that, under the conditions of contemporary capitalism, our work is no longer able to transform anything. It has also been proposed that the artist's gesture no longer has any direct influence over the apparatus that circulates and assigns value to his work.[4] So we are now asking ourselves about the perverse im-potentialities of processes that know how to quit in the midst of their own cycling, that suddenly do nothing with their doing-nothing. The images that hold our attention today are half-lodged and half-disappeared in what circulates them, in the very mechanism they want to picture. They are presentations of this, and within their own rhythms, they

4   Claire Fontaine, "Artistes ready-made et grève humaine: quelques précisions," *Pacemaker* (December 2005): 9–10.

sometimes seem to open up unexpected spaces of non-work, without even stopping.

Guyton has taken the chrome frames of office chairs, turned them on their sides, and presented them as sculptures. For his last exhibition in New York, he recycled the poster for the gallery's previous show, superimposing two separate events and the two artistic identities they promoted on a single document. Such strategies, in addition to the digital reproductions and mechanical accidents in his serially produced canvases, open the possibility that an artist's gesture is never identical to itself, and that it's most subversive potential lies in its capacity to make itself slip and stutter in the very moment of its appearance. We could call this inspired, but that would be banal. The work signed Guyton is interesting precisely in the way that it hijacks something like inspiration, interrupting and splitting it from itself, automatically and repeatedly. This is also a kind of politics. Because it's when the materials and the processes themselves are allowed to fold back and infect this thing or moment we always want to call the artistic subject that they meet the possibility of their own emancipation. And we, too, discover new potentials when our relation to our own products becomes reversible, or when the decisions we make are able to turn around and decide us too.

Price recently produced a "work" consisting of a title (*Grey Flags*, 2005) and a few paragraphs of rambling prose. These were then inserted into different contexts, functioning as the title and press release copy for two exhibitions in two separate New York venues. By re-appropriating the tools that mediate and explain our work in both commercial and institutional contexts, we address the fact that our only available means of production today are also and at the same time our common means of communication. For Price, bootlegging and piracy are not merely acts of theft (of content); they are creative transportations and rhythmic interventions. Because if work today can be defined as the movement of information from here to there, the contemporary artist no longer pretends to invent a new language, but instead confronts us with the potential we all share to disrupt both the directionality and the tempo of readymade codes, thereby undermining how these reproduce property relations, for example. The knots, folds, and loops in Price's recent vacuum-forms and Mylar "films," as well as his use of commercial packaging processes, are sculptural ways of interrogating the artist's capacity to re-route cultural capital. While his silk-screened sheets of clear plastic cause transparency to work against itself when folded or rolled, the opaque Polystyrene panels call our attention to the fact that, today, the packaging is the content, and that only by intervening at the moment when format becomes message ("dispersion") might we regain something like communicability.

Smith is a virtuoso of the shortcut, and although he never seems to quit and is constantly stoking the engines of his own machine, few contemporary artists are so Chaplinesque in their handling of materials and of their own productive rhythms. He recently produced ninety paintings in one week in order to fill an abandoned power station in Memphis, and tomorrow, he will plug in his photocopiers and line an entire bookcase with hand-bound volumes of his own drawings. But it would be misleading to celebrate speed and quantity for their own sakes. Smith has volatilized and dispersed the notion of the artistic gesture. There is always his hand, as there was always Picasso's, but in Smith's case, the hand has joined forces with any and every available means of mechanical reproduction (no matter how rudimentary and everyday) in order to extend and multiply itself in time and in space. The gesture is there, but it is also there and there, and never exactly equal to itself. The name "Josh Smith," both signature and recurring subject of so many canvases, reminds us that the mark he makes is always already displaced along the constantly bifurcating assembly line of his production. The artistic subject is not identical to this mark; it is multiplied by it every time, and at the end of the day, will stock a room, stockpiled and stacked and pushing itself to the point of exhaustion that never seems to arrive. It's as if he first needs to overwhelm himself with work before he can start discovering the escape routes and counter-rhythms that are his art. Smith's "style" could be described as an impossible attempt to reinvent the folk artist's hand with all the invisible and automatic speeds that outmode it today.

Walker has a particular way of confronting the historical legacy of Pop serial production with contemporary technologies of digital reproduction. Not long ago, he kidnapped the desktop scanner from its normal and designed purpose, putting it to work as a kitchen cutting board, a painter's palette, and a camera instead. This could be described as extreme pro-sumption, or as a delinquent attempt to cash in on the false promises of user-friendly technology. Taking this so-called friendship at its word, Walker then tests its limits, sometimes abusively. His recent exhibition of enlarged reproductions of Michael Jackson's identification card, along with images from a television commercial starring Andy Warhol and his signature recycling symbols, points to the perverse possibilities lying dormant within the means by which our culture endlessly repeats itself, and us along with it. How can copy and paste be converted into experimental strategies of dis-identification for the consumer and duplicator of digital media? At what point does the artist disown his own products, and when does he decide to let technology take over his gestures? In Walker's practice, a scanner is not just an available means of copying images and altering scales; it is itself a potential site of creative dysfunction, containing within its own mechanism repressed possibilities of subjective play. Which is to say that a machine can be made to lose its head, too, suddenly revealing new and *improper* spaces of projection, where before we only perceived work, repetition, and efficiency.

Of course a production process can also decide to behave properly and fill a gallery with objects for passive enjoyment, striking poses, showing up on time before moving on again, steadily gaining value, etc. But in New York, it's always a question of how to put tension into these performances, how to open things up again, there in the commercial gallery where it seems least likely that any real difference can be produced. The works on view here have mobility built into them from the start; they are, to varying degrees and in different ways, opportunistic; and of course Zürich offers one more opportunity to mobilize some fresh currencies. They knowingly take their chances and make their moves within the conditions they reflect and mediate. There is the Guyton machine, the Price machine, etc., each attempting to elaborate its singularity, its own strange rhythm on this common plane. Their best moments are when they manage to do something concrete and unexpected with this law of equivalence that seeks to conform everything to its own flattening abstraction. And since breaking this law is not as simple as it once seemed, the more effective strategies will from now on involve using flatness, abstraction, and reproduction against themselves, and convert these into forces of heterogeneity instead. Capital never stops its decapitating, so our productions will have to become headless too.

In the poster, armed soldiers are also present, standing by as heads roll and turn to gold, as if guarding the perimeter of a crime scene. Maybe they are museum guards, maybe they are part of the production itself. We also notice hundreds of finely brushed flowers, and the bright, un-splattered stockings of the onlookers in the foreground. In the background, the vertical ramparts of a castle reflect the sunlight. And beyond these, receding green hills crowned with smaller, more distant ramparts. If we have discarded the perspective that once allowed the depiction of such a scenario, we have also multiplied our means of decapitalizing.

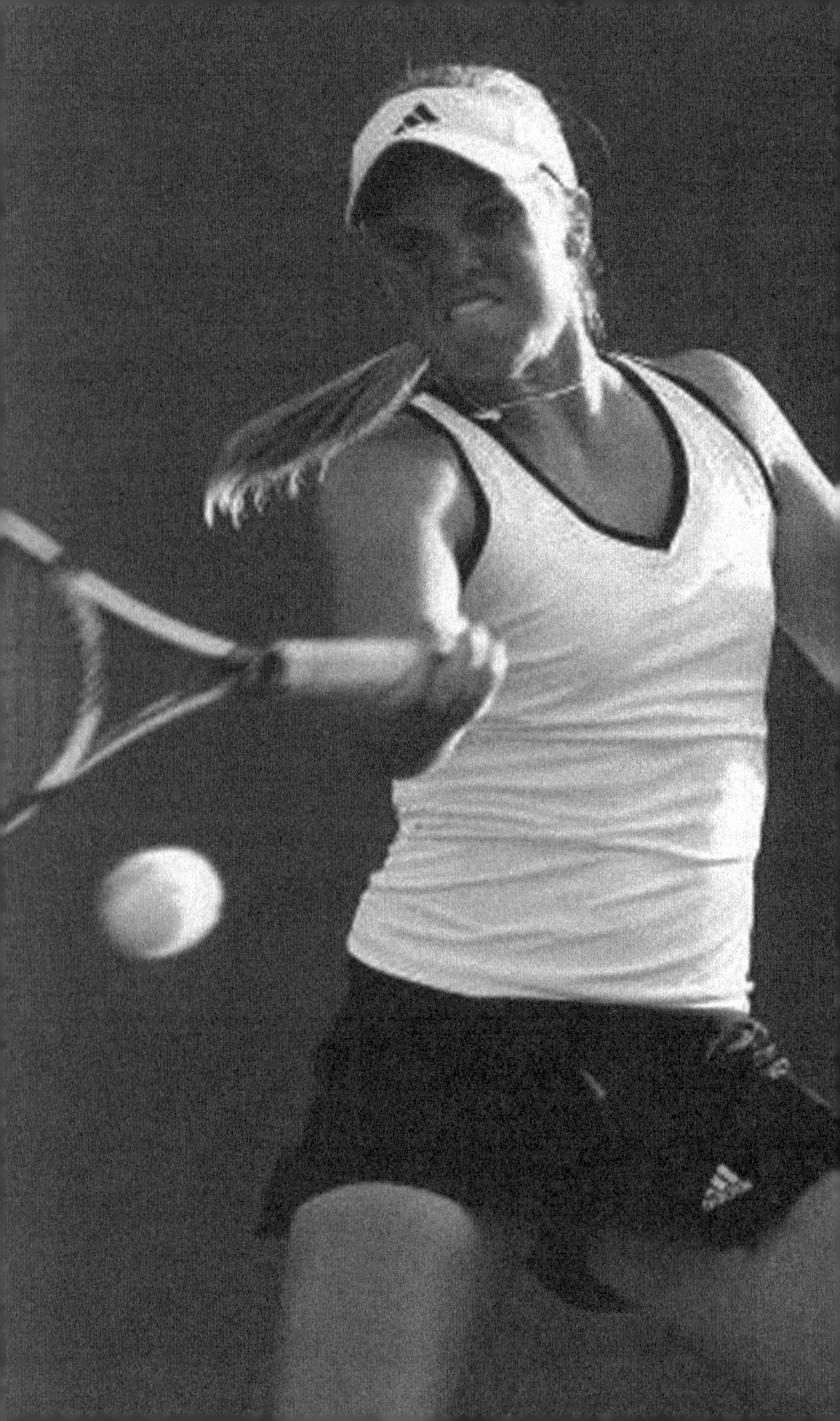

Dinner*

Sailboat races probably start like this—one table pulling out in front on a stiff gust of wine and words. The artist we're celebrating nods in his place, keeping time like a coxswain. He may not be much but it's his moment, his momentum and ours too.

If you could, you would just pump life into yourself at the nearest filling station and be off. On the other hand, who can deny the pleasure of reading a room, and that it only improves with years of similar dinners? You learn to see irrelevance as it starts to yellow a painter's complexion like the early stages of a cancer. You can hear the money laughing in its ripped jeans, all the way across the room. You can almost taste an artist emerging in a dealer's mouth. Eventually, you are even able to spot the missing people and predict the newcomers. Meanwhile, the steady, confident rowing under everything we're saying and agreeing about New York takes us deeper and farther out than we've ever been before, moving forward while looking back. Reading is rowing is chewing the dinner, a medium-rare invitation on its bed of young opinion and beans, followed by a desire to strangle the curator.

What was and always will be bourgeois in this ceremony has been streamlined and hastily translated into brute acts of business, which makes the dinner all the more efficient and amusing, at least to those of us who aren't even eating. Some prefer not to sit down. There is activity around the bathroom, text messaging, a deliberate avoidance of wit, and whatever there is in our cash register hearts is very much out on the table now, with the

---

*   Originally published in *Texte zur Kunst*, no. 66, June 2007.

bottles and the sea bass. Information is simply thrown down like freshly killed game, or dropped like a bomb. All of this makes a more festive table, both in the Martha Stewart and the Bataillean senses.

Next time, we should eat an art student. Then we would know what we were chewing on and finally have something solid to wash down with the Merlot. I don't know how to do this sober; I couldn't possibly sit and listen to you like this, or repeat myself as I do. But if we were eating a photographer, these silences would be full again, like our mouths, and dinner would be epic. Fresh meat has been slaughtered, your plate is round like the sun, there are stories to tell, and soon it will be spring.

This publication is modeled on an ideal round table, where topics like porn and romanticism are pretexts for the display of something like a general intellect, and where conversation exhibits itself as both a democratic and a professional activity. Why the table? These are like dinners with assigned seating, where you wander the room for a while before finding and installing yourself in front of the card that holds your place. The discussion is a food-less, wine-less table that lets us surround ourselves, backs to the world, microphone in the middle. The roundtable wants to rise above the dinner table, transporting us into purer, leaner places.

Sometimes, there is the raw spectacle of a sudden mafia forming in our midst, the solid wall it makes in this human flux. It's animal and visual, choreographed language, an almost sexual resistance to democracy's pretensions. You have been with them all, or versions of them, and you see yourself in there too, rejecting and overthrowing yourself too. Everything always returns at a dinner, like tribal magic or compost. Martin is here.

Jumping ship, following some other money, sacrificing all this newfound complicity in order to salute a pirate bond stronger than any written contract. The exit is a graceful or tactless act of cutting it off, walking the plank, man overboard, finally burying this particular dinner in its own water.

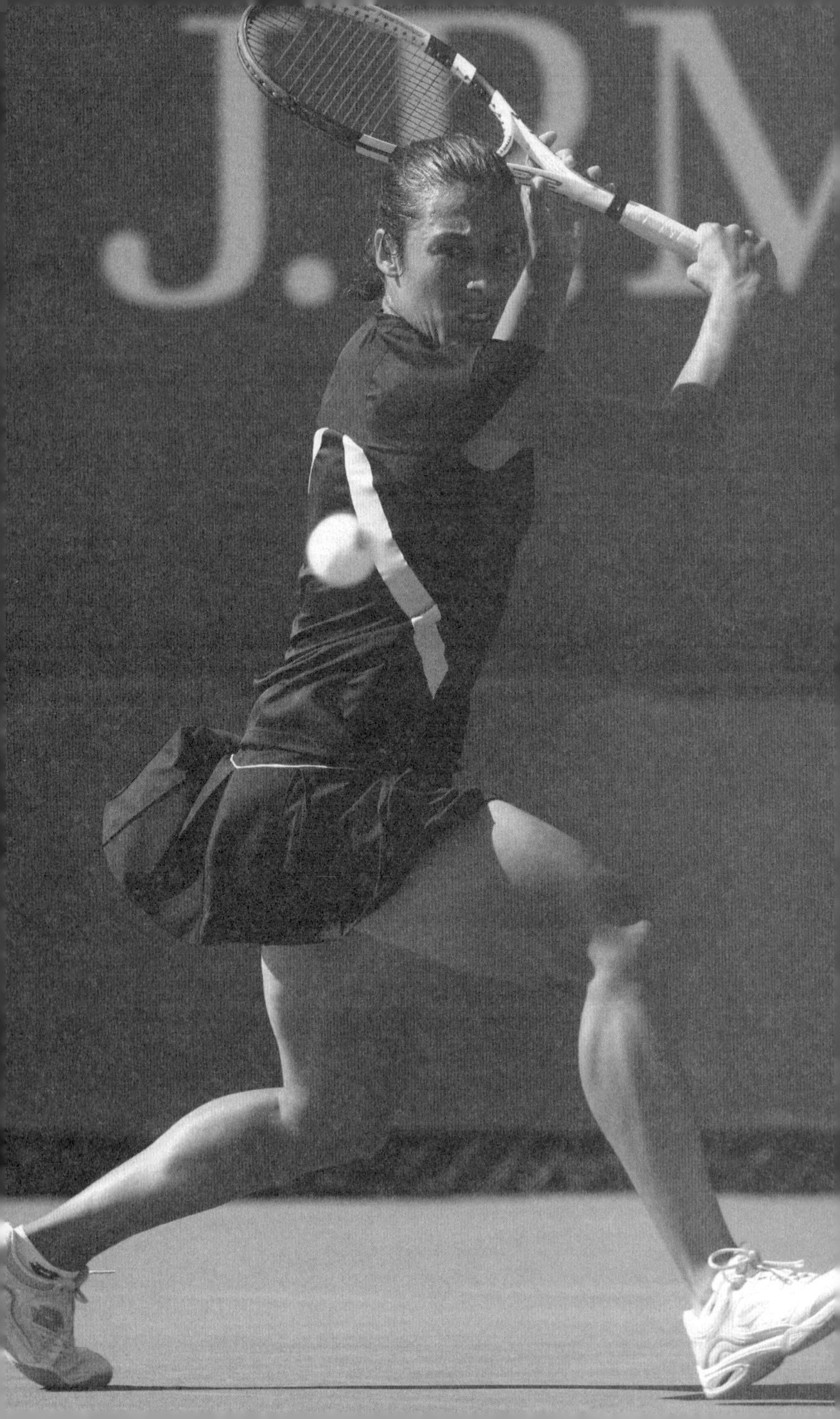

Dresses Without Women*

The hallucination that haunts an America in ruins is as mythic as
ever: From these singed, frayed, distressed fragments, something emerges again, if not in life then as a sort of glamorous
undeath, at least for a season. For the fashion-design team
Rodarte, devastation always precedes construction. Informed
by the post-inferno landscapes of Southern California and
the dilapidated, foreclosed properties along the 110 freeway
connecting L.A. to Pasadena, by echoes of the Dust Bowl
and the horror films they won't stop watching, Kate and Laura
Mulleavy are drawn to the ruins of the present, or to the
present as ruin. At the Cooper-Hewitt, National Design Museum
in New York, on the former Carnegie mansion's second-floor
landing and in what is still referred to as the Billiard Room,
seventeen gray mannequins display samples from Rodarte's
previous four fashion seasons, during which the Mulleavy sisters
emerged as the most acclaimed female designers of their
generation. An abbreviated yet potent survey of their recent
work, the show consists of garments pulled from the designers'
own archive and presented on crude sets devised (by Matthew
Mazzucca) to look like half-demolished rooms.

Known for their intuitive, DIY approach to design (neither sister
received formal training in the craft or business of fashion),
Rodarte attack materials at the molecular level, devising ways of
transforming and combining them into strange, unorthodox
complexes—"vinyl birdskin," "wool cobweb," "metallic mohair,"
and so on—before submitting the results to an intensely labored
reconstructive surgery-cum-couture. The research-and-develop-
ment phase of their process may involve fraying a material with

*   Originally published in *Artforum*, April 2008, under the title "Riches to Rags."

pinking shears, hand-dyeing it, or burning fabric with acid or a cigarette lighter before elaborating the labyrinths of knit loops, Frankensteinian assemblages, and multilayered architectures that fit on bodies. Sometimes criticized for an indifference to structure or for a certain inarticulateness that accompanies their wizardry with materials, Rodarte, we could argue, relocate design in the fingertips, the eyeballs, and that part of the brain most exposed to and shaken by the world—away from the more academic, silhouette-oriented values that rule the traditional houses of Europe. And it is not just in terms of what the late film critic Manny Farber called "termite art" ("It goes always forward eating its own boundaries, and, likely as not, leaves nothing in its path other than the signs of eager, industrious, unkempt activity.") that we can identify Rodarte's aesthetic as American, but in all the improvisatory ways it de- and recodes a culture that is already impure and blended with crisis. If the typically European strategy is to construct avant-garde gestures around the inversion of established, legible codes (aristocratic or bourgeois), an American vernacular is already corrupted in advance, the border between high and low long since dissolved. Here, it is less about turning the queen on her head than a matter of tracking mutations in the desert, where celebrity and nothingness have always shared a strangely productive cohabitation. Rodarte are perhaps closer in spirit to Roger Corman or Wes Craven than to the top men of haute couture.

Based on a narrative of a woman burned alive in the desert who returns as a California condor, Rodarte's spring 2010 collection involves serpentine braiding and weaving of hand-tooled leather strips, macramé and crochet with black yarn and feathers, bandage-like swaths of dyed cheesecloth, and belts fastened with bird-claw clasps. The dresses have a charred, posttraumatic look, assembled as if from tatters, their coal and tar-pit blacks punctuated by glints of silver and Swarovski crystals. A new fabric designed by Rodarte for Knoll also looks both scorched and glimmering, and samples of this material are mashed—along with several pairs of black leather and "acid-treated zombie vein" heels—into the dark rubble of the installation. These erotically charged garments and their models were engulfed in clouds of toxic-yellow smoke at their New York runway show last September, emerging for brief glimpses as if from a nuclear test site.

Fog and cement grays dominate the fall/winter 2009 collection, creating a blanked-out atmosphere at times sliced through by harsh glints of emerald-green lamé. A marbled leather jacket evokes shifting slabs of stone, cinched tight and low, its narrow arms bound by a series of python-trimmed straps. Some dresses feature turbulent architectures of knit wool, whose varying densities and degrees of fuzz produce thundercloud-like volumes that are echoed by the installation's burst drywall. Others, more tunic-like, combine crisscrossed sections of silver metallic laminated silk, hand-marbled leather and silk tulle, printed chiffon and lamé. A single pair of Rodarte's famously fetishized wrap-on, thigh-high boots (designed by Nicholas Kirkwood for the label) is semi-buried in Sheetrock dust in the back of the installation. Lighter and more ethereal, the fall 2008 and spring 2009 seasons include dresses layered with embroidered lace, silk tulle, and soft webs of looped mohair, as well as metallic mohair tights, in hues ranging between rusty pinks and corroded, coppery oranges. The airy, soft-spun shimmer and metallic frizz of these hand-knit confections are grounded by hand-cut leather leggings whose angular *brise-soleil* patterns suggest urban security gates. Fastened to the floor with copper wire and screws, a pair of platform shoes (again, Kirkwood for Rodarte) made of "mirror leather," metal, and electrical wire glint with a mosaic of golden mirror shards.

Rodarte absorb the seismic energies of recent natural and economic disasters, working these into dazzling, one-of-a-kind luxury products, but, strangely, with no *body* in mind. Fashion designers—usually men—tend to begin with an ideal or particular woman whom they aim to dress and beautify. But the Mulleavy sisters—like David Cronenberg's twin gynecologists in *Dead Ringers* (1988), whose diabolical medical instruments conform to the body of no known patient—have not yet determined whom or what they are dressing. These are garments produced in advance of their wearers, an open question: Where, and to whom, does a dress belong? Dressing no one, Rodarte address their designs to an abstract condition. The Mulleavys' alchemical experiments and gothic ornamentations surround a scorched void, a potential or perhaps impossible woman, a body provisionally occupied by stand-ins such as Kim Gordon, Kirsten Dunst, and Michelle Obama. In the mahogany-paneled Cooper-Hewitt, Rodarte's constructions challenge viewers to locate themselves in relation to the burned-out yet obsessively labored glamour the Mulleavys are proposing.

This winter, a line of Rodarte products designed for Target quickly came and went, torn from the racks by fans who can't afford the Rodarte-label garments so prized by Anna Wintour and other arbiters of fashion value. Collaborations between top designers and mass-market distributors are like ghosts of the former's concentrated runway visions, conceived under extreme constraints. Factory-made, using the cheapest materials and the most cost-efficient production methods, these are aimed at an actually locatable nobody: the average American shopper. Most impressive in Rodarte's crossover effort was that, rather than attempting to translate their detail-oriented craftsmanship and alchemical experimentation into mass products, they simply made good-looking, accessible clothes for kids while managing to keep their idiosyncratic brand legible within a supermarket context.

Moving between Target and the Cooper-Hewitt, between DIY techniques and commercial collaboration, between rag-picking forays in the desert and the runways of the metropolis, the Rodarte label is itself like one of those border towns built around a constant renegotiation of exclusion and inclusion, of the local and the alien. The conditions seem right for the success of an approach like that of the Mulleavy sisters, whose personal, intuitive aesthetic, had it been operative in the 1990s, would most likely have remained cornered in some culty style ghetto. Yet we can't be sure that the usual trajectory of an up-and-coming fashion label will apply to Rodarte—that their brand will expand, or they will end up designing for one of the established European houses, for example. Capturing the energy and un-decidability of this moment, the Cooper-Hewitt, which has also named Rodarte finalists in its 2009 National Design Award competition, affords viewers an opportunity to encounter the Mulleavys' singular vision up close and in a sort of freeze-frame. Not art, fashion prefers to haunt art. More mobile and exposed, in certain ways fashion remains the more effective means of processing the chaos of the present, probably because, as a socio-cultural mediator, it is itself already highly mediated and be-cause, while sticking close to the body, it is ever so responsive to how quickly the ground shifts under its acid-treated zombie-vein heels.

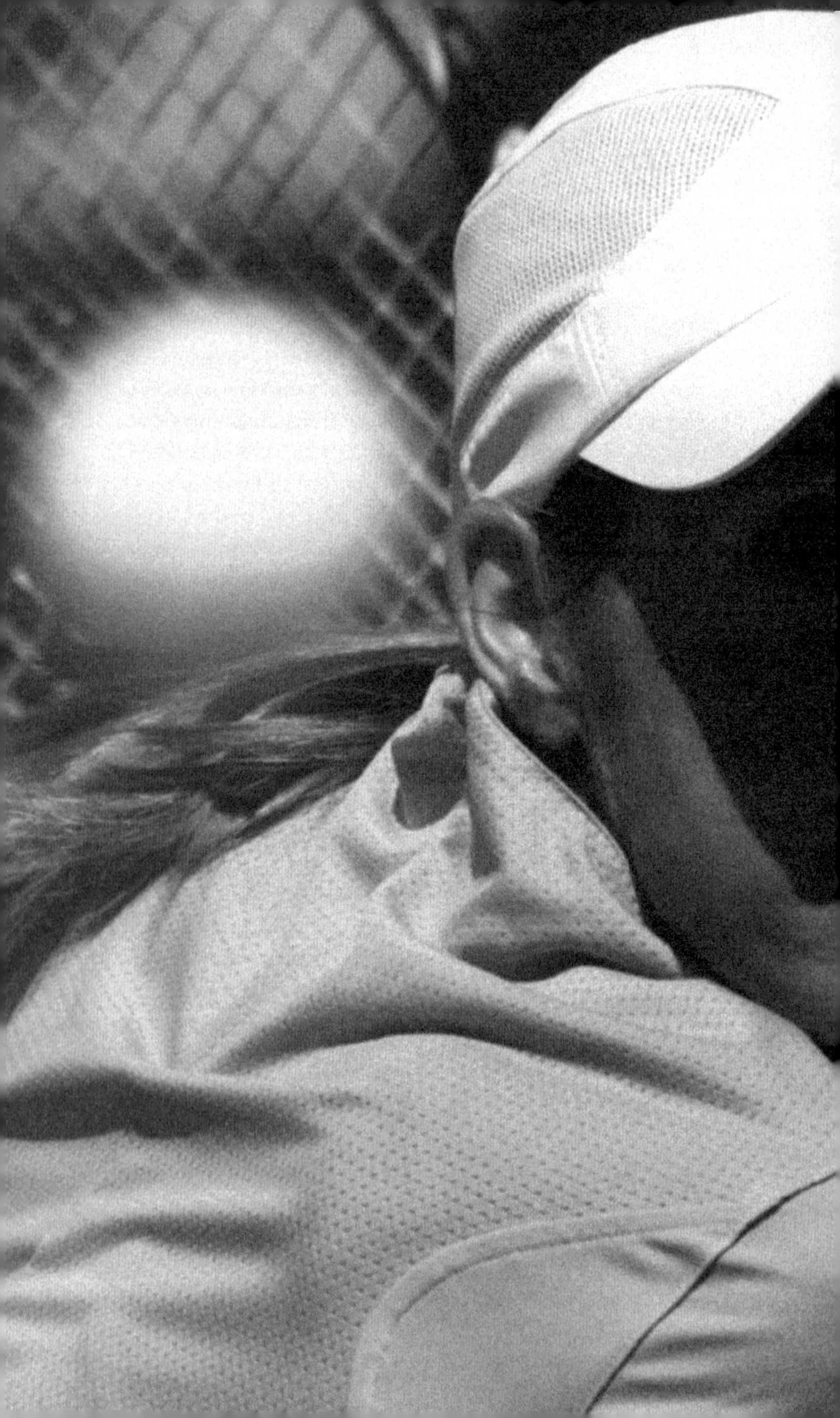

Escape from Discussion Island*

When the discursive situation is called Art Basel Conversations, and sponsored by Bulgari, *parrhesia* is most likely neutralized in advance. *Parrhesia*—whereby speech becomes free by assuming the risk of telling the truth from below, and daring to offend power—is unauthorized, uninvited discourse. A practice indispensable to democracy in ancient Greece and a concept at the center of Michel Foucault's late lectures,[1] *parrhesia* is not only the paradoxical authority of speaking without authority; it is the idea that language is not separate from life and production, that it can be a radical means of subjectification in relation to an established order of subjection. It is the practical and political possibility of using discourse to transform relations between subjects and institutions: "speech activity" or speech-activism. Foucault's return to this concept was, of course, compelled by his interest in the fact that power today requires freedom of expression on the part of its subjects in order to function. He was questioning the possibility of practicing truth in an age of exacerbated, enjoined discursivity. And we suspect that branded, funded, sponsored words may still somehow cling to the possibility of dismantling or evading the discursive situation that they have been called upon to produce. How can we make speech free again in a context where critique and freedom of expression are always already in the process of being recuperated by capital? One possibility is to never stop. Nonstop talk could be the dirty bomb of branded discourse, along with lying, "fabulation," plagiarism, endless self-reflexivity, and activating the agrammatical and asyntactic potentialities that already

---

* Originally published in the exhibition catalogue *Meaning Liam Gillick* (Kunsthalle Zürich; Kunstverein München; Museum of Contemporary Art, Chicago; and Witte de With Center for Contemporary Art, Rotterdam), MIT Press, 2009.

1 Michel Foucault, *Fearless Speech* (New York and Los Angeles: Semiotext(e), 2001).

lurk within every statement. We sometimes imagine something like Volvo fiction. Or discourse that makes itself as smooth and pliable as Plexiglas, or as abstract and de-centered as the networks that distribute it in order to occupy certain productive channels. Or even a scenario in real time, narrating infinite variations and versions of itself, revised and rehearsed continuously, without any final performance, and that this scenario could involve not only postwar history or labor relations, but the serial reproduction of its own moment. It could be a story about work where work finally loses any distinction from the story itself. The late poet and novelist Roberto Bolaño has done something similar by writing a series of books about his own life as a teenage poet in Mexico City, and he continued writing variations of this literary coming of age adventure until his death. Discourse hijacks time as it turns back on its own production and re-tells itself, and the time of reading and writing is eroticized by this obsessive circling around a seventeen-year-old literary hard on. The art world panel or round table discussion, on the other hand, is one of the more deadly and desire-killing discursive time zones we know, rarely disturbed by the occurrence of *parrhesia*, when an invited speaker somehow manages to unsettle his or her hosts by saying something diabolical or cruel. When *parrhesia* is used, someone always gets hurt, either the speaker or the addressee or both, since it's always a social relation that's being disturbed when truth is practiced. So how might we engage a truth practice today, elaborating speech activity in a context where social relations have been almost entirely absorbed as modes of production? In fifth century B.C. Athens, the authority to speak the truth had to be taken in the most *inappropriate* way by the potential, upstart user of discourse. To practice truth was to steal it, but not always to get away with it. In the postwar automobile factory, truth was practiced in the strike, where productive relations were put on hold and time was re-appropriated for other uses by workers. When the machines were unplugged, when the workers unplugged themselves, there was suddenly a lot of talking and reading going on instead. Songs, jokes, graffiti, and idle conversations become truth practices only when they are violently taken back from work time, and when the use of discourse is at the same time an interruption of normal productive rhythms. An idle conversation outside the factory gates is not necessarily *parrhesia*. But today, we don't have gates; we carry the factory everywhere, within our most intimate communications. And if contemporary art is above all a discursive situation, the artists who produce and extend it merely conform to the requirements of their profession. Dinner table chatter would be the bare minimum discursive requirement of any practicing artist today; we need not come equipped with theories to do our work. But the question remains: How can artists re-appropriate the discursive situation they are always already producing, and steal it back as a truth practice? I once saw an artist fall into the most severe of silences at a gallery dinner in Basel. He later wrote about this catastrophe in *Parkett*.[2] If the artist was on strike in the restaurant, he was certainly earning his money in the magazine and putting himself back to work there. What's interesting in this example is the relation between these two experiences: silence and narration of silence, mute *parrhesia* and its chatty, journalistic report. Starting here, and trying to think our way out of a simplified, binary opposition of non-work and work, truth and un-truth, we find ourselves grasping at possibilities of discursive appropriation whereby speaking and its opposite become confused, and where this confusion, precisely, becomes what is useful and strategic. If the refusal to appropriate the discursive situation, clamming up precisely

2   Josef Strau, "A Non-Administrative Performance Mystery," *Parkett*, no. 84 (2009).

when speech is most expected, disturbs the normal productive relations that determine our convivial context, perhaps something of this strike can be carried into the production of discourse too. There are strike narratives, which are clearly not the same as narrative strikes, and maybe these aren't entirely functionalized, obedient texts either. For example, such a narrative could occupy the place of an art review or artist's statement, and thereby refuse its task even while extending the discursive situation. Sometimes, we wonder if it even matters what we say when we write about art, so why not write about saying nothing instead? And when this writing takes on a certain literary character, suddenly other displacements are happening too. Art production is displaced by the act of writing; art writing is displaced by a literary practice that invents a sort of foreign language within language; the object of the review is displaced by this strange textual material that maybe begins to reflect upon its own work and its own materiality; and the potential author, too, is displaced in the act of writing. It is no wonder that academic critics are so dismissive of what they call "belle-lettrist" writing. Who is authorized to speak the truth about art? While professional critics and art historians attempt to horde discursive power and to somehow own and guarantee the most legitimate debates, showing up at round tables not only to contribute to an ongoing conversation, but to literally *fill the seats*, it's become clear that these roles are in crisis. (In fact, it's this crisis that's become one of the more fashionable topics at recent panels.) There is not much power there to unseat, and sooner or later, almost everyone is offered a speaking opportunity in the contemporary art institution, even if their lecture is not sponsored by Bulgari. While still something of an exception today, the writing artist is now under a sort of curatorial spotlight, because multi-tasking and the blurring of disciplinary categories are so symptomatic of post-Fordist conditions. The artist who also speaks and writes and who elaborates fictions and scenarios in parallel to other modes of production is a performer not only of immaterial labor, but of the flexibility and redundancy that characterize the nonstop work of networks. When discourse is elaborated as art, or in the place of art, the writer performs the redundancy of the artist he also is, or was. Such a figure embodies the "production of communication by means of communication,"[3] which drives the information-based economy in a "connexionist" world,[4] as well as the erosion, or deregulation, of fixed roles and activities that, since the 1970s, accompanies contemporary processes of capitalization. This virtuosic, multi-tasking manager of codes and texts is currently under discussion because he occupies a fascinating and ambiguous non-position at the avant-garde of value production, and can simultaneously stand for something emancipatory and be entirely complicit with institutional and market demands. The more free the worker, the more he puts himself to work. Does he exploit the discursive situation in order to liberate time and space for unforeseen, possibly disturbing activities? Or does he extend this activity everywhere, into a thousand recuperated and value-producing projects? To what degree does he re-appropriate time for non-productive purposes, and to what extent does he make himself the busiest of networkers? The discursive practitioner is perhaps doing both things at once, and only his style and attitude can decide if we like him or not. When Marcel Broodthaers elaborated his Musée des Aigles, partly in the form of "open letters" that were strategically distributed within the context he was addressing, he appropriated bureaucratic and institutional discourse in order to do something Brechtian with art power. He made discourse strange again,

---

3   Paolo Virno, *A Grammar of the Multitude* (New York and Los Angeles: Semiotext(e), 2004).
4   Luc Boltanski and Eve Chiapello, *The New Spirit of Capitalism* (London: Verso, 2007).

but he did so precisely where it seemed most neutral and normal: in the anonymous promotional-pedagogical discourses that structure institutions, whether in the mode of press texts, wall captions, shipping labels, or museum signage. We can call these truth practices because the former poet stole discourse back from institutional power and its usual function, making it stammer, making it *aesthetic*, and thereby upsetting normal hierarchies and productive relations within the world of art. This approach was later taken up again and tested by Hans Haacke, Andrea Fraser, and others. But the writer and presenter of scenarios who arrived in the mid-1990s, when laptops began to appear in cafés, and when the café itself had become successfully codified so that it could be mass-reproduced everywhere. And more profitably, this programmer and manager of discursive situations, who was as focused on the terminologies he wielded as he was on the fonts, layouts, and materials he used to bring his texts forth as décor and installation, preferred a more slippery or "open" use of discourse. Attuned to all the new ways that architecture and business were recuperating the deconstructive tendencies of French theory, translating "rhizome" into the productive efficiency of e-Flux, and "difference" into refreshingly personalized, non-standardized commodities, he knowingly opted to engage art where it was most compromised, where words like "creative" and "network" wavered unsteadily between their most liberating and recuperative possibilities. He was interested precisely in the zones of indistinction or the points of negotiation between art and business, and in how these zones and points were beginning to proliferate everywhere in the neoliberal universe. At Zone Books, theory was already being repackaged in slick volumes by designer Bruce Mau. Rem Koolhaas is an example of how Deleuzian concepts could be re-branded as tools for developing business environments, and early on, before producing actual work and retail spaces for clients such as Prada and Condé Nast, this architect's practice consisted almost exclusively of discourse (plus graphics). In the immaterial, discursive situation, "concept" is everything, and so is look. Indeed, neo-management relies on a digitally enhanced, sped-up, and immersive discursivity when it engages the productive rhythms of the contemporary metropolis, and there were suddenly myriad points of potential strategic overlap and cross-fertilization between the field of art and all other modes of production. This was where discourse was most up for grabs, and also, strangely, where *parrhesia* seemed least possible. Dispersed across the new productive networks, we preferred to imagine things horizontally rather than up and down, so it seemed less a question of contesting positions and relations in the old way than of manipulating the efficiency of flows and connections. If anything was to happen or change here, it had to happen immaterially, and it had to flow. But what about the idea, probably also Deleuzian, that there is no real difference between what we say, what we do, and what we become? Only the most nihilistic of formalisms would want to disconnect discourse from bodies and actions, and from the subjective transformations that arise from the kind of speaking or not speaking that experimentally destabilize our relations to others and to our own production. The writing artist who still believes that discourse is embodied, and that discursive bodies and subjects are altered through their relations with other bodies and subjects—and that *parrhesia* is another word for the ethical dimension of discursive practice—will strategize not only the distribution of discursive contents, but the modes and styles of their distribution as well. What can be done with the discourse of neoliberalism and management in order that it can be made useful again? What kind of narrative do we want to engage, how do we share it, what spaces and channels of communication does it exploit, and how does the discourse it appropriates become transformed or pulverized there? There is the possibility of wearing discourse down, hollowing it out, dismantling it in order to make it sing. We are still wondering what Volvo literature could be. Could its production unleash us from work and calculated time, or recalculate time strangely and open up other temporal experiences? Is it too Deleuzian or too Nietzchean to take care of the fact that material bodies are connected to immaterial labor, and that the laptop produces a particular life form? A slightly hunched body connected to separation, strange to itself, happily amputated, monitored, Facebooking. The new fictions will arise from this unfortunate posture, somehow. While extending the discursive situation and its ever more efficient networks, these fictions will perhaps attempt to delay and defer work under conditions that always already put communicativity to work. Because these practices are networked and somehow public, and always mobilized and in flux, communication will be constantly confused with something like a utopian promise. Productive communities and their formal freedoms will be encouraged and swiftly commodified, tracked and mined by marketers. They will be constantly formalized and codified. So the new fictions will have to learn to invent ways of transforming what mobilizes them into opportunities for immobility. How can *parrhesia* happen as a connexionist practice, in a molecular world where power is not located somewhere up above, but is activated everywhere within the most everyday relations between subjects and in the discursive flows that multiply them? We have seen student occupations of campus buildings that were also Facebook moments (and that have meanwhile been stored on Facebook's servers, to who knows what purpose). In ancient Athens, the *agora* was the place where *parrhesia* appeared. Truth was practiced in public, where bodies were most exposed to each other and where buying and selling happened too. In the privatized but at the same time public networks and spaces, *parrhesia* can be used to challenge ownership of discursive space and whatever flows through it. It can occur as misappropriation of this space. The artist who writes may find himself in an opportune position to challenge the habits and laws that determine both the value of discourse and its public uses. In other words, the discursive practitioner can elaborate scenarios that challenge and transform the shape of the *agora* in which he works, travels, and communicates. We will know *parrhesia* is being used when the police show up, and when bodies get involved. Meanwhile, new discursive practices linked to the building of communes are intensely resistant to the old militant model of the general assembly, or the social-democratic ideal of a gathering of bodies to discuss, debate, and vote on future actions[5] In the discursive situation of the assembly, action is always *preceded* by and usually neutralized in advance by discussion. But speech activity doesn't work according to this deadening, managerial logic. When there is no longer any difference between what we say, what we do, and what we are becoming, the formalism that would put discourse in its place, and action in its time, is joyfully discarded. The commune knows that the general assembly is exactly where both official party management and undercover police flourish and poison every possibility. Discussion, it seems, is not in itself a good or useful thing. Words disconnected from actions often produce nothing but more disconnection. And back in the art world, where the virtues of dialogue and convivial exchange are universally promoted, discourse must constantly rethink and challenge its own formalization. The artist who speaks and writes must at all costs avoid reproducing something like the aesthetic and institutional equivalent of the general

---

5   The Invisible Committee, *The Coming Insurrection*, (New York and Los Angeles: Semiotext(e), 2009).

assembly if he wants to have some sway over the concrete forces that determine life and production. Or else elaborate scenarios that refer to this model, while at the same time disturbing its self-managing and productivity-inducing aspects. Forms such as the lecture, the round table discussion, and that catalogue text must be reoccupied and tested as sites of speech activity. Such discursive spaces could be dismantled or even abandoned from within, along with their claims to authority and criticality. The artist who writes knows that it's not communication that makes us free. Perhaps he is here to perform all the ways that it determines and enlists us, precisely. If he offers a lesson, it may be that the discursive situation can only be usurped from the dictates of production if it is to become useful again. When Deleuze and Guattari speak of "collective assemblages of enunciation," it has nothing to do with the assembly or with group conversation. In *Kafka: Toward a Minor Literature* (1975) and *A Thousand Plateaus* (1980), they locate the presence and potential of a "mobile paraphrase" at the heart of every statement, whereby compositions of order are transformed into components of passage or variation. "Indirect discourse" is when there is no more individual enunciation, no longer even a subject of enunciation: every statement is always collective, even when it seems to be emitted by a solitary author. In so-called minor literature, social representations are dismantled in a way that is much more effective than any critique could accomplish, because an assemblage of enunciation ceases to speak "of" things, and instead speaks on the same level as states of things and states of content. The writer and the virtual or coming collectivity are both components of the assemblage that dislocates and recomposes them. In this way, indirect discourse produces new statements through the dismantling of established orders of subjection as these are reproduced in language, in the redundancy of order-words and dominant significations. The useful opposition here is not between information and noise, but between the indiscipline and discipline at work in language. Language does not necessarily have to be interrupted when it can become foreign to itself. So perhaps *parrhesia* can occur as a kind of indirect discourse, dismantling established relations of production from within the discursive situation. It could be the invention of syntaxes that don't exactly interrupt the discursive process, but produce internal breaks that become a part of it. This would involve the practice of discursive indiscipline in relation to the network's way of connecting us to work and information. It would also mean speaking on the same level as the network and its dislocations. More effective than any critique would be the unauthorized or uninvited use of the situation that promotes the formal freedoms of dialogue and connection. What must also be put to use are the very conditions under which ideas of the "open" are exploited to sponsor a nonstop productivity without a final product or end. The open is where the virtuosic producer of discourse appears, promoting quasi-utopian notions of immateriality and incompleteness. Architects and designers have tried to build airy, paperless openness into our business and shopping environments. We are constantly tracked as we move through this wired *agora*. But we haven't forgotten the dismantling that Kafka was able to accomplish within the discursive situation of his father's law office, within the German language and the space of the book. The contemporary practitioner of discourse could make use of the open, testing its promises and challenging its emancipatory claims. The artist can re-appropriate the discursive situation by engaging all the ways it merges with design and the built world. How can we use the fact of being productively dislocated within an open plan? If our projects have no end, and if our newfound flexibility has also made us redundant within these endless projects, there may still be the possibility of setting up something

like a commune here. But for this, we would need to transform flexibility and redundancy into opportunities of deferring
work in order to self-organize. We may not want to go so far
as melting down our "discussion platforms" and converting them
into shields and barricades, but we can still extract collective
assemblages of enunciation from the discursive situation.
Dislocation can be exacerbated to the point where it becomes
a means of avoidance of controlled exchanges. As the artist
who writes unpins and dislocates himself in discourse, he might
elaborate scenarios that engage new possibilities of life. The
scenario might serve as a concrete mode of subjectification,
a means of auto-temporalization that could be taken up by
others, folding back onto the work we do, not outside of discourse, but pushing discourse to its own outside, producing
breaks and flights within the discursive situation in such a way
that work becomes a foreign activity.

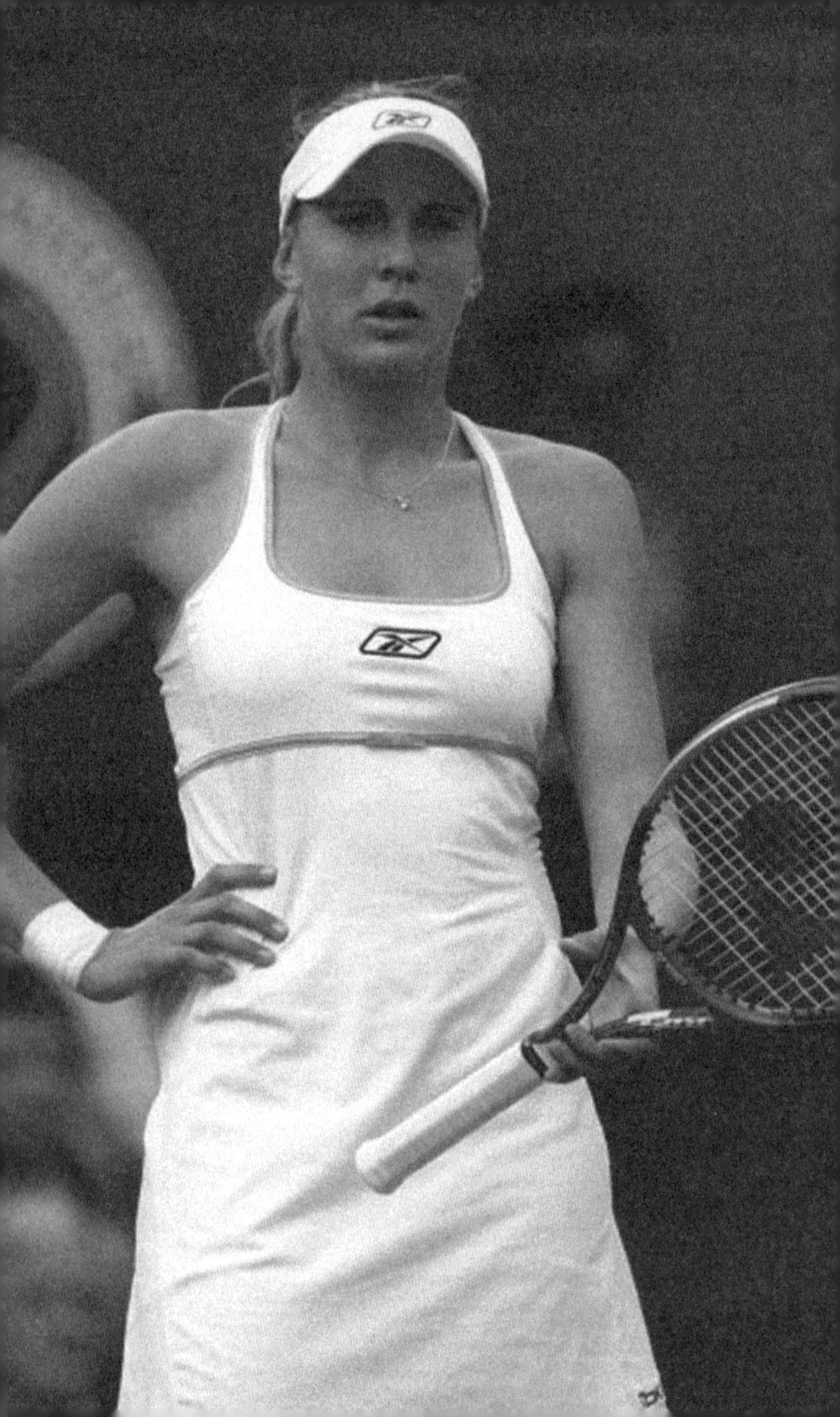

The Galleries

I

The gallery has been broken into. Just as we realize it, I can hear the culprits' footsteps escaping through some distant, backstage part of the building. Hearing as if seeing: a four-legged step, or two people running in pace together down a long corridor and out. Diabolically synchronized.

The gallery has been broken into, and the group show we had installed yesterday has been vandalized in the night. I am trying to report this to a thin, pale woman with dark, wavy hair who clasps a clipboard or file against her hip. Searching for us in her file, she is only half-listening, half-understanding, asking again how to spell our name. She's in charge of this place, which is like an art fair, maybe Frieze, except it feels a lot like Los Angeles, and our gallery is now located in a sort of hive complex among other galleries in a kind of mall in the sun. Trying to explain what's happened but I can't, either because I don't understand it myself or because my voice is physically unable to reach her now. She is already disappearing into a complex that is stirring with morning activity, now open for business.

The gallery has been broken into and something is different now. But what? Looking more closely and gradually realizing these anonymous vandals or visitors have in fact left us with a much better art show. Whoever they were, they were very good. Better than us, but also like us, a better version of us. They've made this clear. The vandalizing angels have worked through the night, leaving us this sign. A sign for us: Make yourself a version of yourself. In this way, they've made it easy (easier) for us. De-installing our show, they have installed a new space of ease. They have abandoned us to this space that is no longer ours, exactly. Now we are in it too.

What they have done is replace the group show with a sort of copy or approximation of the original. The flat art has been stripped from the walls and stacked like scrap wood under a plastic sheet. Vague copies of these works have been painted directly on the walls: forged, abbreviated, and impossible to sell, we realize. In a slightly earlier angle of this dream, the walls were papered from floor to ceiling (including the ceiling) with a rough, pixilated inkjet print of the show. Everything endlessly re-rendered. But that impression shifts to this painted, Pop-mural version. It has been done very quickly and easily, but also very consistently across every inch of the space. We can still feel the joy of the gesture, its sweep and momentum. Nonchalant, approximate, not looking back, already gone. And the colors have been simplified. Monochromatic areas of red, green, blue.

A pink and orange Jutta Koether has been redone in the style of her ex-student Greg Parma Smith. Repainted in a monochrome silver, its original three-dimensional relief has been reduced to a smoother, sanded-down joint compound abbreviation beneath the silver. The added forms of hands repeat everywhere in the new, baroque pattern, all protruding in a slight relief. And on another wall, paintings of paintings of laptop screens show ghostly, superimposed Internet news sites in pile-ups of painted windows or pages. These are fast oil paintings, some of them collaged with blank sheets of white paper, some beginning to peel off. I can see words, news headlines, and captions, super-imposed in the paint: "UNIONISTS," etc. The black text graying out in the still-wet, white under-paint is a little Josh and a little Merlin. A "page" leaning out of another painting includes the letters "B" and "C." Another has ghostly baseball players, a catcher behind the plate. Sports pages in the news pages. These are all painted images of Web pages, and in the address bar of one I think I see my own name scrambled behind some other words, a faint gray, still wet. When I look again, my name is gone. I think I see the word "whenever" or maybe "whatever" there, but not really… I'm not seeing what I think or want to see. Words erasing words. Other people have gathered around now and are commenting on the pictures. Niklas, or Fernando, says his favorite is the one with "BC" and I think that's a bit obvious and don't yet tell him it's not the same BC he assumes it is. None of us really know this "B" or "C."

By the gallery's entrance, in a sort of vestibule area jumbled with tools and supplies, I notice a table saw's round blade has been removed and placed on the floor beneath the table. The blade is bigger than usual, maybe a fake. Its removal and slight displacement feel violent and easy, like everything else. On its outward-facing surface, a story has been handwritten in paint. It is a history of the city, minor but epic in tone, narrating over a decade of cultural evolution here, decoding the place, rewriting it, talking of certain types of artistic "entities" having been continuously "disgorged" by the system over a certain time. We are a part of this story, and now the story has been set on the side, put under the table, and spelled out in movingly simple terms. We are reading ourselves under the table saw.

Outside, by the building's entrance, we had set up a sort of kiosk with free books. We decide to remove the free books and replace them with a poster. It doesn't make sense to give things away anymore, not here. I gather up the remaining copies of *Introduction to Civil War*. There is also a map showing a floor plan of the mall with all the other galleries: "Pax"-something, "Pacifica"… they all sound vaguely familiar and vaguely the same. We can stay or go now. We think we won't go back in today.

II

De-installing a hanging sculpture by Klara Liden, I notice a hole in the ceiling of the gallery. There's light. I get up on a table and put my head through the hole and there's definitely light up there, and activity. And people. And Carissa. What is she doing up there? It's a whole other room, a gallery hidden inside the gallery, and Carissa seems to be overseeing a staff of interns there.

Running through dark streets. Jumping in and out of cars. Emily in an expensive-looking dress in the night. Running from one place to another in a panic, trying to get back to the gallery. I wake up.

I wake up in another version of the same dream, still dreaming. This time, I'm dragging Emily along to show her the dream by dreaming it again …

I find a way to get back into the gallery (dream) by climbing across a leaning stack of enormous, unsold paintings by Josephine Pryde. When did she make these? On top of the paintings someone has perched a futon. Moving across the precarious mattress, I and it suddenly slide between the paintings, down to the bottom of storage. It's dark and I'm stuck. Some of the artworks have been damaged. Why is this futon here? Frustrated by this mess, it takes some effort to work my way out into the gallery.

Now I can show Emily the gallery (dream) inside the gallery (dream). It's a brown room carpeted wall to wall and much cleaner and better furnished than "our" gallery. So this is Carissa's space. Interns and assistants are busy working on some new project of hers at various desks and stations. It's all very professional here. There are two bathrooms, one for boys and one for girls, the doors clearly marked. They even have a water cooler. Glowing vitrines house what look like architectural models. It's a sort of city based on lit-up, interconnected glass pods, a cliché of the future, very complicated; and it also comes with an electronic soundtrack or DJ. I start to ask Carissa what this is all about, and she says, "Didn't you see the Quicktime file I sent out?" "No, I never got it." So this is where she's been hiding and this is her work. Carissa has her back turned and is laughing with her staff.

Now I notice a hallway connecting this other space to still more spaces. I had no idea: there's another gallery business upstairs from ours. Since when? I glance inside and see an exhibition of long, glass tanks filled with cloudy, rotten-looking water. Swiss Toby's art? A dirtier version. And what's the gallery called? I see a word: Nang? Something like Nang, but not. I don't like the font. On the floor are some filthy canvas tote bags. Which one is mine? Maybe the dirty Bjarne Melgaard bag. "Emily, did you know there was this other gallery here?" She doesn't really care, or she's talking to some other people in the hallway.

I wake up in a third version of the gallery dream. This time, the futon is in the center. Jason is kicking back there, casually talking to Carissa. I get the feeling his function is to take it easy on the futon in this repeating other gallery. But it's too much going through all this again and then I really wake up. On Cape Cod. I know it but I don't know how: In the dream I somehow quit smoking. Now I'm awake and I still don't smoke.

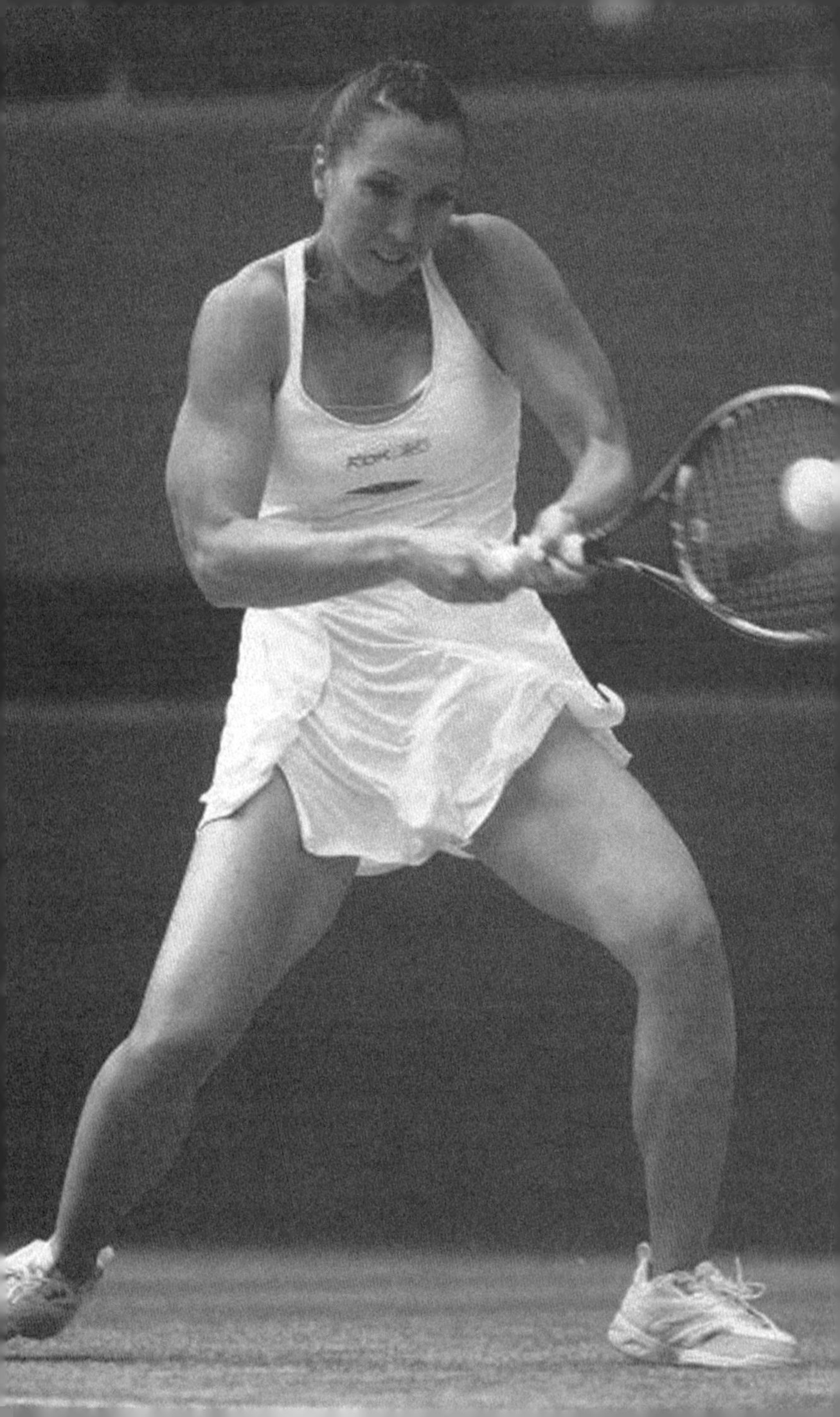

Installation as Occupation*

If cinema still offers a useful model for the contemporary art world, it is because of its capacity to produce images that move in relation to so many other, often competing movements—passing time, cash flows, erotic drives, shifting power relations, the encroachment of new technologies, global marketing trends, shrinking audiences, etc.—and because its particular way of moving has everything to do with this inherent impurity. A rhythmic means of intervening in the world, the machine that moves images also leaves itself open to manipulation on every level and at every turn, whether by screenwriters, distributors, advertisers, talent agents, or entertainment lawyers. Cinema is a battle at the crossroads of multiple speeds and interests, an ongoing fight, not for the specificity of any medium, but for a specific way of thinking and moving within a heterogeneous and de-specified reality. We know it is cinema when it is able to assume its own historical possibility and meet the world (and its own death) face-to-face—which is to say, with all the cunning and artifice it is capable of. And to strategize for freedom of movement *on the side of cinema* is to convert whatever depletes its potential into yet another weapon. So we have seen Jean-Luc Godard reinvent cinema *with* television, and we have seen how sound can be turned back around as a means of moving images, long after the advent of the talkie. Increasingly, the well-meaning guardians of film history have looked to the museum as a sort of final resting place, or refuge, for this endangered art. But some cinema keeps moving and prefers to undo itself rather than ossify into another monument to modernity. Godard is clearly not interested in putting cinema *in* the museum, whether to enshrine or entomb it there. Rather, he is using the institution as

---

* Originally published in *Artforum*, September 2006, under the title "Double Exposure."

another means of putting cinema into a relation with its outside,
with non-cinema, and risking its own territory in the process.
Which brings us to the disaster of Godard the contemporary
artist. An exhibition less installed than *inflicted* on the museum,
"Voyage(s) en utopie" bears all the signs of the conflict that
erupted between the seventy-five-year-old filmmaker and his
institutional host, the thirty-year-old Centre Pompidou, in
the final months leading up to the show's delayed opening.
(Originally planned for April 26, it didn't open until May 11.)
More than any particular thing in the three-room installation—
a truckload of video monitors dumped into a flimsy décor of
IKEA home furnishings and cheap potted plants, with an original
Matisse hung casually by the door—what makes itself felt is
the restless presence of Godard himself, the traces of his body
moving through this ransacked space, his fingerprints still
fresh on the walls, his use of a felt-tip marker to correct or delete
wall texts at the last minute, and other acts of physical and
aesthetic sabotage, such as holes left in the Sheetrock after his
sudden decision to rip out a video monitor here and there,
an overturned construction scaffold, rubble, trash, and so on.
These are countered by eleventh-hour control measures on
the museum's part: the bolting down of chairs to the floor, the
securing of loose video monitors with anti-theft devices, the
removal of empty wine bottles, and apologies to the public.
Between the damage and the damage control, "Voyage(s)" is
what happens when a museum attempts to program a filmmaker
notorious for jump-cutting aesthetics into politics, and
who already announced the death of cinema in films as early
as *Breathless* (1960).

From *Bande à part* (1964), whose cartoon actors run a footrace
through the Louvre, to *Histoire(s) du cinéma* (1988–98), in
which digital reproductions of works by Giotto and Goya are

superimposed onto stills from Hollywood movies, Godard has often provoked tense encounters between cinema and the museum, whether to show that in painting (as opposed to theater) cinema preexists its own birth, or to question its power to produce images after the introduction of sound (and Auschwitz and television). Invited more than once to install himself as a living Picasso in a museum known for its motherly embrace of cinema, Godard has finally responded with a sort of mutant—or counterfeit—strain of installation art, a film retrospective lost in an exploded yuppie loft—behind schedule, over budget, and not even finished. He has also produced an institutional scandal, and maybe the most anarchic and liberating museum-going experience in years. "Voyage(s)" is, in fact, less an installation than an occupation. And at the same time a desertion.

There is a rumor, seemingly confirmed by the unmade bed installed in one corner of the show, that Godard camped out alone in these rooms for a week before the opening. Other rumors—some backed up by the French press—relate how he first turned against and then fired his curator, Dominique Païni (recently absented to a new post at the Fondation Maeght in Saint-Paul-de-Vence, France), and how the filmmaker himself disappeared to Switzerland with half the show's production budget in his pocket. Such gossip fills a void imposed by the artist himself: the veritable information blackout caused by his refusal to collaborate with the museum's public-relations apparatus or to communicate with anybody outside the accounting department. No matter how the conflict between Godard and Païni actually played out, an official statement by the Centre Pompidou claims that "Voyage(s) en utopie" is what ultimately emerged from the shelving of an original project titled "Collage(s) de France: Archaeology of the Cinema According to JLG," abandoned in February 2006 due to "artistic, technical, and financial difficulties." This statement was posted at the show's entrance, next to a taped-up photocopy of Fragonard's 1777 painting *The Lock*. The sign, which reappears inside the show as well, has been corrected by JLG's recurring Sharpie: "artistic, technical, and financial difficulties."

Punning on Godard's unsuccessful attempt to introduce a course on cinema at the prestigious Collège de France some years ago, "Collage(s) de France" was meant to be a work in progress, with the filmmaker editing and projecting images on-site at the Pompidou for nine months. At some point, those nine months of filmmaking became nine rooms, a hyper-ambitious plan for a meandering, immersive environment that was to include film projections, monitors, and film stills sharing walls with original masterpieces by painters from Delacroix to Monet. There was even a proposal to install a giant mirror across the street from the museum, doubling all this in the world outside. But all that remains of this initial project are Godard's scale models for the nine rooms, constructed by hand using foam core, photocopies, scissors, and glue. Peering into these rough-hewn contraptions, where videos play on cell phone-size screens, one might think of turn-of-the-century nickelodeons, but they are also like dollhouses or rat mazes, with paperback copies of Arendt, Bataille, and Chandler nailed crudely to their walls and floors. Stacked in one room of the present exhibition, the models attest to the radical incompletion of "Voyage(s)," a still-fresh wreck of a utopia that at one point promised a friendly cohabitation of painted and filmed images under one roof. But it's the self-destruction of such a scheme that somehow preserves its utopian potential, because cinema is not something that wants to be installed, and because Godard is maybe like Walter Benjamin's "destructive character," whose "need for fresh air and open space is stronger than any hatred."

Everywhere cables are left dangling or snake up walls that are themselves unfinished so that AV equipment remains visible through rough gaps in the Sheetrock. Meanwhile, the latest flat-screen HD technology is allowed to be as obscene, ugly, and dumb as it wants to be. One monitor has displaced the pillows on a double bed, broadcasting Ridley Scott's big-budget, racist war movie *Black Hawk Down* (2001) in vivid wide-screen video where the Western couple's widescreen head would typically rest. Another monitor is splayed horizontally across a kitchen countertop and shows bootlegged porn. A half dozen more have been unplugged and tossed in a rude pile, like trash. Screens of all varieties—from pocket-size portables to pedestal-mounted home entertainment systems—fill the space as if it were a Circuit City showroom, looping key moments from European and Hollywood precursors to the Nouvelle Vague (*Johnny Guitar, On the Town, Bob le flambeur, Au hasard Balthazar,* etc.). And this is how the "art of the masses" adjusts itself to a public that no longer comes in crowds but as an endless series of individuals, each one scaled to his or her own screen.

Between what is called Room –2 ("The Day Before Yesterday") and Room 3 ("Yesterday"), a toy train carrying cigars shuttles back and forth through a smashed hole in the wall, while a scene from Vincent Gallo's *Brown Bunny* (2003) loops nearby. Room 1 ("Today") has a bedroom, an office, a kitchen, and a living room (but no bathroom), presenting metropolitan life itself as the readymade of all readymades, a desert that spreads both in front of and within the HD screen that it integrates. Equating the customized catastrophe of Parisian home life with the bankruptcy of contemporary installation art, Godard travesties aesthetic strategies that no longer produce images of the world, that do nothing but blindly reproduce the sameness of museums or bedrooms (and the subjectivities that inhabit them). Images by Godard (from *Weekend,* 1967, to *Vrai faux passeport,* 2006) and by his longtime collaborator Anne-Marie Miéville play on rows of small, wall-mounted screens pathetically decorated with store-bought picture frames. If the frame, too, is a ready-made, a mere image of itself, it has also lost its power to produce an out-of-frame.

Aside from the Matisse and a couple of other paintings, everything here is a cheap reproduction of itself, either burned on a disc, scanned, or Xeroxed; and all this appropriated, reformatted content is immediately subjected to the DIY violence of scissors and glue (and Sharpie). What "Voyage(s)" enacts is a politics of cut and paste, a guerrilla poetics of citation and *détournement.* And when Godard samples Levinas ("what in love is called the failure to communicate is precisely what constitutes the positive in a loving relation, the absence of the other being precisely its presence *as other*"), photocopies Goya's series of prints "Disasters of War," and pastes these next to a newspaper image of George W. Bush or a still from a John Ford western, then adds the caption "Fortress Europe," he is militating against official history and its representations, against the flattening logic of information and the contemporary demand for institutional spectacle. It is one kind of flatness resisting another. And if cinema returns here, it's in the idea that only in between two images, in the gap that both separates and joins them, a cut that is both spatial and rhythmic, can we begin to elaborate another relation to the world.

Godard has always countered the squareness of the frame (the screen, the wall, the page) with the shock of the cut (the out-of-frame). In "Voyage(s)," he applies this same dialectic to the museum and makes its rooms sing, for once. Following the moments of Godard's spatializing practice—literally in his tracks—as if reconstructing a crime, the viewer is haunted by another possibility of inhabiting the museum. But what is this impure thing that only poses as contemporary art? Scenographic critique? Relational anarchy? In Godard's own war film, *Les Carabiniers* (1963), soldiers conquer the world and return with nothing but postcard reproductions of museum masterpieces. Like everything cinema encounters, the institution is a raw material, flattened, repeated, and returned as something else. Causing the Pompidou to self-differ, to short-circuit in this way, Godard has found another way in and out of it.

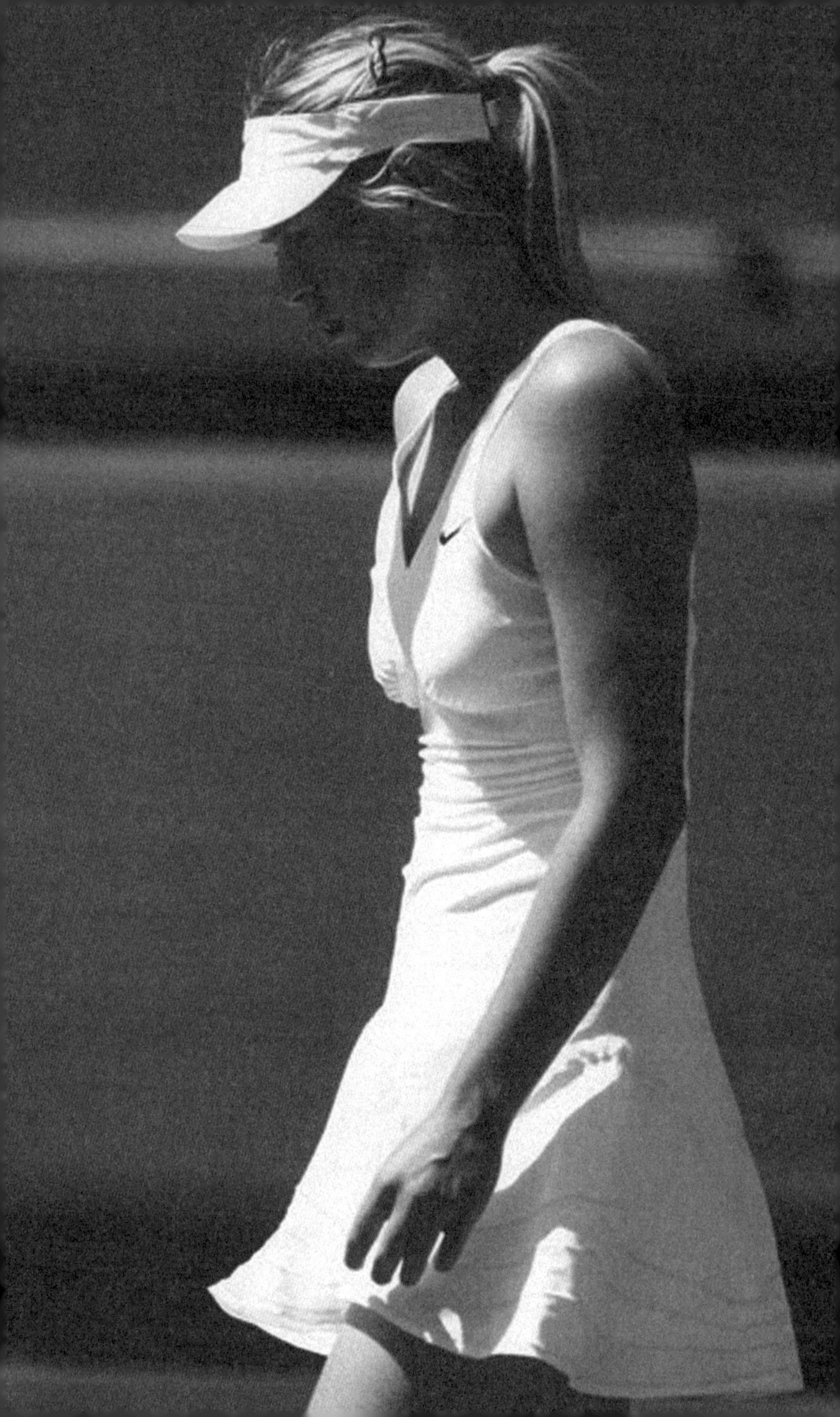

Moving Images Moving Images*

It's not only rage that drives children to break their favorite toys. Sometimes, it's the urge to release the productive potentials trapped inside a product; sometimes, it's simply the joy of wasting them. A history of dismantled and vandalized cinemas would include, among many others: Lettrist and Situationist attempts to liberate cinematic materials from their spectacular function by scratching the print, blacking the screen, and disjoining sound from image; Warhol's nonstop screen tests and his multi-projector film happenings; Joan Jonas's opening up of cinematic time and space to live performance; Tony Conrad's preparation of cooked celluloid, meat, and vegetables to "project" onto—or hurl at—a blank movie screen; etc., etc.

But cinema has always been broken and in pieces—it was even born that way. At the very first cinematic spectacles at the end of the nineteenth century, Parisian audiences encountered not only the screen and its magic, but also the noisy *bête lumineuse*—the projector—which was itself a spectacle to behold, and which, for this reason, was situated in the midst of the audience. This was before the fixed-viewing arrangement we know today, before the seats were lined up in rows and bolted down, before the projector was hidden away in its booth. In the beginning, the audience, the screen, and the projector were mobile elements in an open arrangement. There was no rule dictating the number or sequence of reels that made up a film, and sometimes scenes from different pictures were shuffled and combined into one program. So no two screenings of a film were ever the same, and the audience could move about, talk,

---

* Originally published in *Art and the Moving Image: A Critical Reader*, ed. Tanya Leighton, Tate Publishing, London, 2008. All excerpts from Bernadette Corporation, *Pedestrian Cinema* production memoranda, 2008.

fight, and arrange the furniture according to their impulses. These events did not take place in proper cinemas, but in pubs, dance halls, or whatever common dives could be made available for the night. There was no "cinema," no finished version of any film, no distribution system, and no official control over either the business or the presentation of film. There were simply the moving images, the machines that produced them, and the festive, informal gatherings of the first movie-going public. And cinema continues in pieces. The difference today is that its fragmentation is rarely festive or epic. Dismantling cinema and using its materials to construct a contemporary art installation, for example, and then installing this new arrangement in a museum only liberates cinema in order to lose it once again. No matter how immersive and kaleidoscopic the image environment, no matter how cleverly appropriated the material, or how brutally cinema has been fractured or derailed from itself, to encounter moving images in the form of a contemporary art installation is only to encounter their usual unavailability—another kind of window shopping. True, cinema has not been itself for some time now—since it went digital—and its recent mutations have been a sort of adventure. It's easier today than ever before for anybody at all to intervene in its processes, and everybody agrees that now is the time for piracy, hacking, and the free use of cinematic information. But the question is *how* to use it once you get your hands on it, and what kinds of subjective worlds this free use can make available to us.

Bernadette Corporation's film *Get Rid of Yourself* (2001–03) elaborates a politics of subjectivity linked to the emergence of anonymous and antagonistic life forms within the anti-globalization movement. The film borrows techniques from its subject—the so-called anarchist "black bloc"—in order not to simply document the street violence, property damage, and rioting that took place in Genoa, but precisely to make itself riot-like, and to put its own processes in contact with the chaotic rhythms and de-subjectivizing encounters of the event. In other words, not to present an image of resistance, but to produce an image problem; to make moving images move away from themselves; and to arrive at the cinematic equivalent of a burning bank, a looted supermarket, a line of flight opening up a provisional free zone in the midst of an intensely controlled and programmed confrontation. *Get Rid of Yourself* became a fast favorite among curators of contemporary art, an example of the "new politics of aesthetics," and has since found its place in the museum with all the others.

To create a cinema equal to our present desires would not only cause it to dysfunction and interrupt its illusory continuity in order to expose the traumatic real it prefers to hide; it would also open cinematic production (and reception) to other kinds of events—social, collective, inter-subjective—and to the vertigo or joy of its own dispersal in lived time and space. For cinema is not only moving images; it is a system of productive relations and a chance to intervene in the specific rhythms and distances that determine these from without and within. Is this a "relational" cinema? Only if the relationality it produces is not foremost and finally aesthetic. Between the street and the seat, the recording and the projection, the actor and the viewer, the soundtrack and the bedroom, the museum and the graveyard, play and rewind, original and copy, doing and not doing, countless potential sites of production and interruption remain to be discovered. To disperse cinema in this way is to create and multiply cinematic possibilities both on and off the screen where the finished product normally appears.

Pedestrian Cinema was conceived as a temporary underground film studio operated by Bernadette Corporation in Berlin. Since its inception in 2005, it has traveled to Mexico City, Paris, and New York, and has been presented in exhibitions at the Witte de With in Rotterdam ("Bernadette Corporation," 2005), the Hamburger Kunstverein ("King Kong," 2006), and the Künstlerhaus Stuttgart ("Multiplyplex," 2007). As part of this work in progress, Bernadette Corporation recently published a screenplay, *Eine Pinot Grigio, Bitte* (Sternberg Press, 2007), which the artist had no intention of ever producing as a film. In Hollywood, the memorandum has always been a preferred means of informal, interoffice communication. Written during the early stages of *Pedestrian Cinema*, the following memos accompanied the partly fantastical work of elaborating an underground film studio of epic proportions, an invisible film factory to fill the wide-open void of Berlin.

Our first fiction is that we are doing cinema at all, and not just any cinema but a collective cinema dispersed across the time and space of a year in Berlin.

***

Each day, *Pedestrian Cinema* confronts the question of fabricating itself. It focuses its processes as a motor for thinking and working on a cinema happening 'here', among us, not falling from the stars.

***

The fact that *Pedestrian Cinema* is a nonstop, year-long activity does not mean that it cannot be at the same time a cinema on strike (strike here meaning not a work stoppage but a suspension of the relations that support what we normally think of as cinema). Suspending the relation that ensures our habitual distance from professional cinema draws cinema into a state of exile, in which going 'underground' is not a disappearing act but the discovery of an empty, wide-open cinema whose first thought is its own repopulation.

***

The casting call, for example, is an obvious first step towards peopling our fiction. Like Kafka's 'Nature Theater of Oklahoma', everybody is welcome. And Berlin is full of idle young bodies.

***

Berlin, a city of voids and deserts, is where *Pedestrian Cinema* will discover an underground film studio as immense as MGM or Universal.

***

To practice a kind of 'offensive retreat' (T.E. Lawrence) and at the same time to be right here in the city, conducting casting calls and auditions, location scouting, writing scenarios, shooting screen tests, screening dailies, producing our production, etc. Hollywood began this way too: a few streetwise, ambitious sons of immigrants arriving in the desert of California with an idea of setting up facilities for the production of an industrial-strength glamour that would be more contagious than anything.

***

Pedestrian Cinema is the desire to set up a place and activity that becomes a device for intersubjective experience. By looking at places, encountering people, making an appointment to film, keeping the borders of the film open, the idea of an outside is revived—this exterior that the film studio runs into in its work. It is a relationship of the local, in which the people who enter into the production process also elaborate it, sending it in different directions. Once the script is thrown away, what remains is the relations of the film studio trying to make a new cinema and the world it will be made from. These will not be films 'about' something, but films that 'run into' something.

***

Making cinema mobile to the point of instability. Where it can take off in the same second as any thought or whim. "I is had gone." An excuse for a scene. Discovering a half-cooked actor. An excuse for a scene.

***

If culture and the conditions we live and work in come at us as rhythm— not just discourse or signs but as rhythmic discourse and signs—our function is also to play these rhythms back at different speeds and tempos. The question of 'how to make something happen' is at once critical/ interpretive and musical/poetic. *Pedestrian Cinema* responds in a musical and machine-like way to the deadening rhythms of commerce and urban life by excavating other rhythms within them, sometimes by slowing and interrupting them. So when we say 'cinema' we mean an attention to on- and off-screen rhythms (from the way an actor crosses a shot to the way global capital flows through a city) and a politics of rhythmic intervention. Cinema is a means of engaging both the system of movements—of bodies, of information, of capital, of thought—that our cinema is immersed in and of injecting new and mutant speeds back into the flow of the present.

***

There is the glamour of launching new stars. There is also the glamour of the death of the audience. Once the audience realises it is dead, *Pedestrian Cinema* will immediately begin (if you are there, you are making it too).

***

Distribution is the business of circulating cinematic products. Dispersion is something else. To disperse cinema across a collective activity and over the time of a year is to scrap the notion of a complete and finished product. *Pedestrian Cinema* is both a relational space and a process that continuously produces and modifies this space.

***

A visit to the studio by a group of potential buyers—a journalist, a curator, an agent, etc.—all the possible parties interested in the idea of 'new cinema.'

***

Pedestrian Cinema is an open door, a strange sign of production. Under the guise of cinema. Under the guise that is cinema.

***

Pedestrian Cinema undoes the efficient, linear logic of pre-production/ production/post-production, elaborating instead a system whereby multiple films, activities and relationships can be improvised within its overall topology. One film-in-progress can be usurped by or added to another at any point. Material from any production can be recycled and put to new uses by any other. The making of one film can unmake the others.

***

How to keep the air circulating without the power of fans?

***

Pedestrian Cinema is a 'production of production', continuously multiplying the very conditions and possibilities of cinema. Cinema as a means without end.

***

We are all moving images colliding with other moving images. *Pedestrian Cinema* sets itself up as a place where one image moves another, as a sort of 'backroom' where images can get together and move if they feel like it. Here we are all moving images moving images.

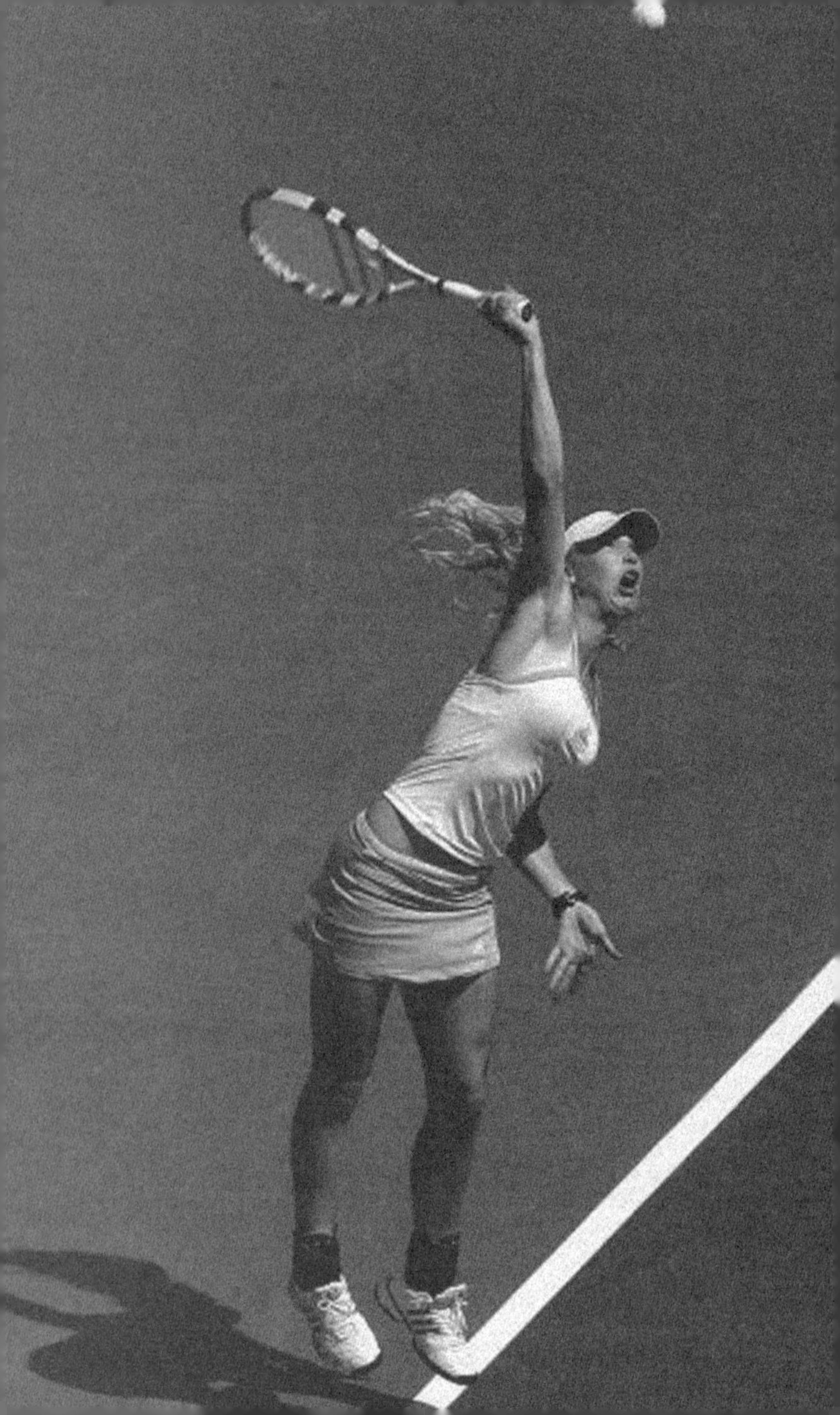

My Other Painting Is a Car*

The artist is always finding ways to test the capacity for non-specificity in this thing he's working on. For example, he might push a painting to exchange its own powers of abstraction and mediation with those of the poster, the page, the screen, the T-shirt, or even the muscle car. Because it's such a tough and at the same time flimsy object, the painting is still one of the better and more convenient devices for picturing the limit beyond which art threatens to forget what it is. For so long, it has been so convinced of its own nature, and it now realizes that its act is all the more convincing when it's able to abandon it. It's probably because the painting has so much built-in specificity to begin with that it's so good at hallucinating "the crisis of art."

Like postcards, the paintings arrive from a certain distance, and somehow packaged in their own distance, postmarked R-ville, signed Prince, but with somebody else's picture on them, somebody else's words even. They enjoy the anonymity of postcards, of personalizing and addressing them.

And a painting is a camera, we start to realize, when it makes itself more passive than expressive, more of a receptor than a signal. When the painting joins forces with the camera, it makes use of the photograph's automatic, passive-aggressive way of capturing and doubling the world, and repeating itself too, and its ease. It's how the painting gets real, gets fresh, catches us out here in this state of distraction we prefer to be in anyway, and even re-distracts us. And if it's abstract, it's in the way that a magazine page or a dollar bill is abstract, or abstracting. It involves itself in the abstraction of the world, in all the ways it has

---

*   Originally published in the Richard Prince exhibition catalogue *Canaries in the Coal Mine*, Astrup Fearnley Museum of Modern Art, Oslo, 2007.

of picturing and distancing itself. What a painting gets from a car is more than just speed; it gets culture.

Is a joke a material? To a comedian it is. There's the material and then there's its timing and delivery, which make it an act. He says "my act" or "my material," but he also has a way of disappearing behind these things, almost to the point where there's no more me, only material, like that joke about the psychiatrist doing my act now. Every comedian, every artist, is constantly scandalized about being robbed, and they're right because material has a way of getting away from us, like language. It's what it does, and maybe it never really belonged to us in the first place. For example, the neurotic on the couch who repeats himself (his life) into the tough crowd of the analyst's ear, who's already heard it all before. The joke is about not being able to hang onto yourself, about not being able to tell your own story, and also about transference. In a joke painting, Prince both spaces and times the material across the canvas, sometimes making it repeat and stutter in that tough, blank place, until it begins to do the painting's act too. It's working the room, the canvas. It's hard to say if the painting is ripping off the material, or if it's the other way around. And what we are tempted to call the comic timing of the painting has to do with the way the material takes over its surface, sometimes bombing and sometimes knocking it dead.

There is also the nagging question of where these works are coming from. A painter belongs in a studio, but maybe he calls it a second house, and maybe it's more like a library or a garage anyway, a collection. Prince has made it strange to call these things and places by their proper names; but he's also made it not matter that we're disoriented here. He keeps working, and these places become part of the landscape, the country, and soon you're saying the picture is a cowboy, the painting is a Prince, and those are his girlfriends, his tits, and his books, and here it is in a magazine too. This country is sometimes featured in the French fashion magazine *Purple*, for example. The works themselves pick up speed here, or develop a schizophrenic capacity to be in several places at once, sometimes without even leaving the driveway.

The bibliophile, the car freak, the homeowner, the stand-up, the cowboy, Stella Tennant, the artist alone in his studio, all the figures that people the art of Richard Prince are beings who, like us, keep coming up against the question of where their material ends and they themselves begin. This is a question we share with painting, which uses whatever it can—books, bank checks— to open itself up again, sometimes to the point where it threatens to abandon its own properties and get sucked into some other kind of space. Other times, it slams like a car door and nothing more gets in. But the Nurse only gives and gives. That's what she's here for, that and maybe to take the painting's temperature.

If something useful could be taken out of the museum and into life today, it might be the question of how to position oneself as a producer in relation to this never-ending work we call con- sumption, so that we, too, can start asking ourselves where and how the emergence of the subject happens along this slip- pery, twisted assembly line that links spectatorship to labor. It could be that all we have in common is the fact that nothing here belongs to us, and that Foucault's "aesthetics of the self" is from now on an art of piracy and duplication. By disturbing the idea or the image of property, we automatically make ourselves (our properties) slip too. And it's not as if the artist is immune or outside of these disturbances; they are now part of the activity he calls painting.

We could argue that the joke paintings are acting out the generalized process by which language—what defines us as human, our very capacity to communicate—is transformed into an image that reduces us to spectators and consumers of our own linguistic nature. The check paintings are rather direct presentations of the abstraction of interpersonal relations (or transactions) in a free-market democracy, their paper trails mapping the creative process itself in terms of cash flows between certain people and places. And if the cowboy is a lost idea of autonomy and manhood sold back to us as image, re-photography is a means not only of shoplifting this image, but of repeating our own theft, stealing theft itself. So in a time when the work we do consists almost entirely of communication, and of picturing communication, the challenge is to find ways of keeping a hand in one's own abstraction, or of intervening in the speeds and effects of one's own becoming-image. We should probably get more involved with the things that are rubbing us out. Sometimes, the painting takes a magazine speed and bogs it down in another kind of drippy, layered, tombstone-like slab of a picture.

To say there is a crisis of singularity under spectacular democratic capitalism today is to realize that the more individual we make ourselves, the more alike we become—not like someone in particular, just *like*. And in a time when the white male artist, for example, continues to align himself with all those forces that reduce his role to that of a regular freelance "creative" or symbol manager, a free agent loyal to no team, living from one deal to the next, working nonstop, and often cynically under the sign of this crisis, we sometimes wonder why he doesn't finally admit that he's done for, or at least take a break. In art school, they teach us how to show up in a field where artists have become as interchangeable as the things they make, a lesson in branding.

But the practices that interest us now are those that embrace the condition of whateverness itself as an experimental possibility. There are moments when the only way to make something happen is to become a stranger in one's own studio, in the very act of producing and in the face of our own products. Repetition can be a way of keeping this moment open, and so can interruption. Paintings without painters, painters without paintings.

To paint today is to locate oneself at the exact point where the loss of difference between activity and passivity begins to picture itself, to preside there as both cowboy and nurse, as a whatever-singularity. Which is to say that the "artist's life," if we could still call it that, is an attempt to elaborate a constant and precise relation to non-specificity, and to invent new and specific ways of presenting this. And there's no reason why painting can't accompany these exploits too. Painting is no more susceptible than any other medium of falling into bad repetitions, for example, and never coming out of them.

And what about the nurses, can they help? They are a lost genre stalking our scene as if in another man's daydream. Maybe they are a way of revealing the increasing non-specificity of our contemporary art, a zombie specificity stalking a country that no longer recalls the men whose dime novel fantasies these clean dirty normal working girls once starred in. Are they fake memories? Are they the new cowboys? Like blondes, or blonde jokes, they are provisional and readymade specificities looking for a connection, in a comedy club, in a hospital or in a painting. Are they visions? Maybe they're here because we are finally cracking up. How to put oneself together but also how to get rid of yourself: a question for paintings. Other ways of looking, but also the capacity to elaborate an unexpected, scandalously precise distance from your property, his material, her tits, my act.

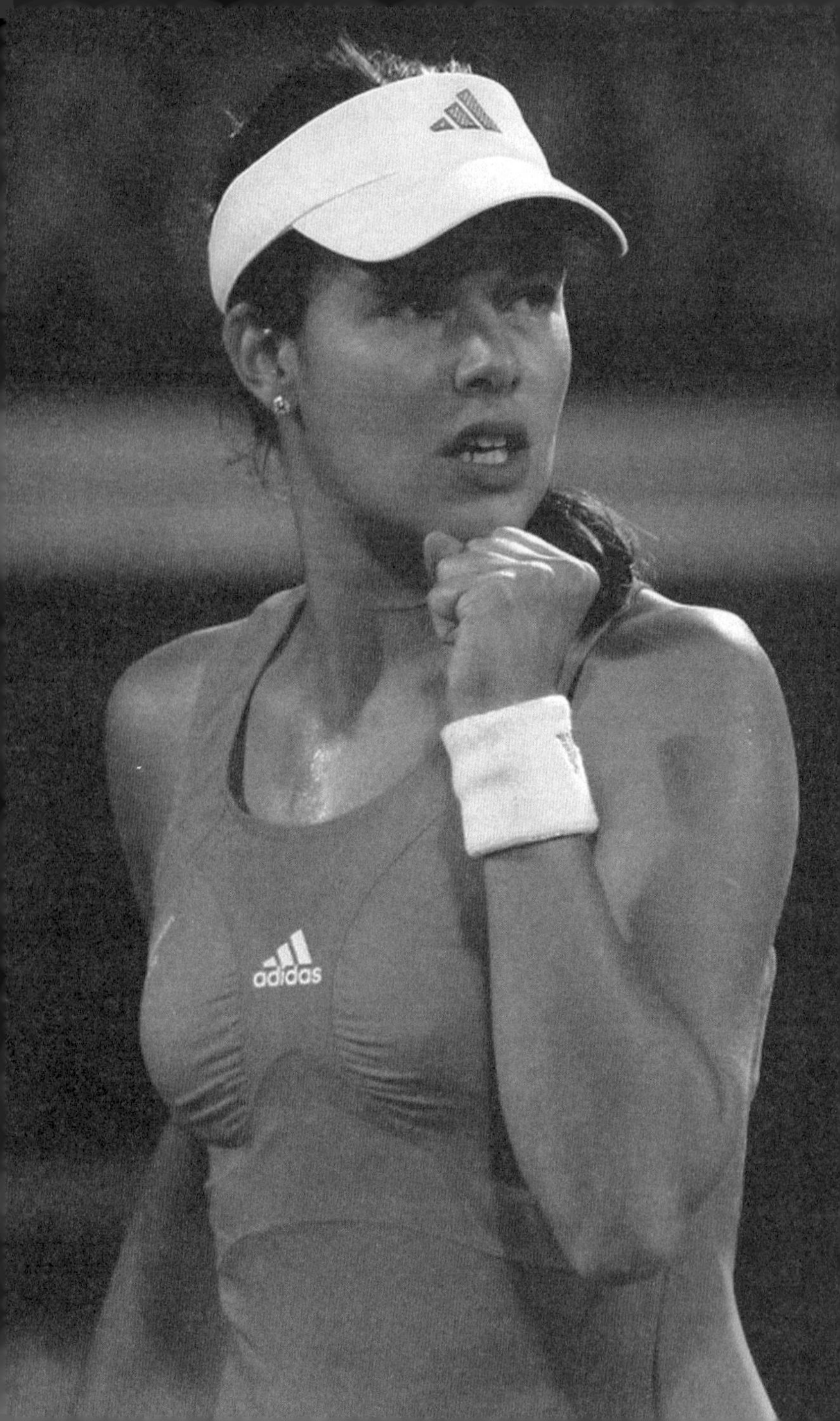

Our Bodies, Our Shelves*

Air

Sculpture sometimes reminds us that even heavy things can be air-borne (bricks, jets). And when sculpture comes with air, or attempts to assume the qualities of air itself, it does not necessarily do so as a *mobile*. It can be like a plaster lung or atomizer in the gallery, simply breathing its emptiness, taking it in and putting it out—airing.

Can

In her book *How To Cook a Wolf*, M.F.K. Fisher observed the canning of America during and after the Second World War. Her thrifty wartime recipes were attempts to learn "how better to exist" within a modern military-industrial complex, where traditional recipes were being outmoded by an increasingly efficient mass production and distribution of goods. The can is a humble abundance, our daily ration, and the promise of survival in an atomic age (shelf life). Just about anything can come in a can, even freshness (Air Wick) and death (Raid), even sculpture. When sculpture comes as a can, or with cans, it also comes with the classic TV gag: the customer grabs one can and all the rest come tumbling down.

Rack

The rack is where all things—trophies, magazines, cans, whatever—come together. It is where the language or communicativity of things displays itself as such, most shamelessly, in the gallery or supermarket. Our bodies, our shelves. When sculpture assumes the qualities of a shelf or rack, it is doing everything it

---

*　Originally published in the exhibition catalogue *Rachel Harrison: Museum With Walls*, CCS Bard Publications, Annandale-on-Hudson, NY, 2010.

can to show itself showing, and refusing to do more than this. Sculpture is always on display, but this is sculpture *as* display or *of* display. (Can we say "ready-displayed"?) And when sculpture becomes self-displaying, it also gets closer to the possibility of self-interruption. Sculpture can discover a new distance from itself in display.

Base

The base is the basic type of rack, traditionally beneath the head or the art. Here is a case where the art—with nothing on top, not even itself—has gone down into the base. The un-loaded base is a display of the basic possibility of sculpture, or sculpture putting itself in suspense. It could be sculpture, or not. Gone back down into its base, it has given up on posture, erection. It may be better to wrap it—what?—in a moving blanket.

Hole

The hole in the sculpture is not a window, just a hollow. It is where sculpture is missing. You can put a can of beans or a video in the hole, but only because there is no good place for these things. The sculptor sticks things in holes and the sculpture accepts this, a bit pathetically. The gallery, too, is a hole.

Bin

Things without value are tossed in bins where they become whatever-things. When sculpture assumes the low, jumbled but friendly quality of a bin, it is because the shelf is easy, but the bin is easier—more like getting rid of things, or not even; like suspending the getting rid, a deferred elimination and at the same time a deferred collection (avoiding the logic of a final order). The bin is limbo. It is a lowdown orgy of things, open to whatever.

Glue

Sticking one thing to another (collage), yes, but also just sticking, sticking itself. Glue without an object or any idea of completeness. "To glue" then becomes an activity without a job to do. "To show" can be like this too: showing showing, shelving shelving, shopping shopping. Sculpture does not necessarily have to put itself together or manage its parts, and glue without an object (without collage) is sculpture taking a vacation from its normal condition—actively self-unemployed. Not against form, not *informe*, but brazenly in the midst of forms and without the need to become attached.

Misc.

Presidents, paintings, olives, drinking straws, mannequins, magazines, marathon runners, toys, masks, mirrors, photos, sheetrock, telephones, wheels, cardboard, celebrities, animals, Xerox … the sculpture we have in mind will not be about any of these, and will not be beyond them. These are not treasures unearthed from a dump. These are examples, miscellaneous. And sculpture that's open to the miscellaneous prefers not to put itself above, before, or after the things it's made of. It's sculpture that prefers to be out among things, ready-making (can we say this?) with them. It is sculpture speaking the language of things in order to speak of its own happily distracted condition. And here is where browsing and making prefer to lose their distinction, and sculpture happens as a kind of passage or passing, easily forfeiting its own territory.

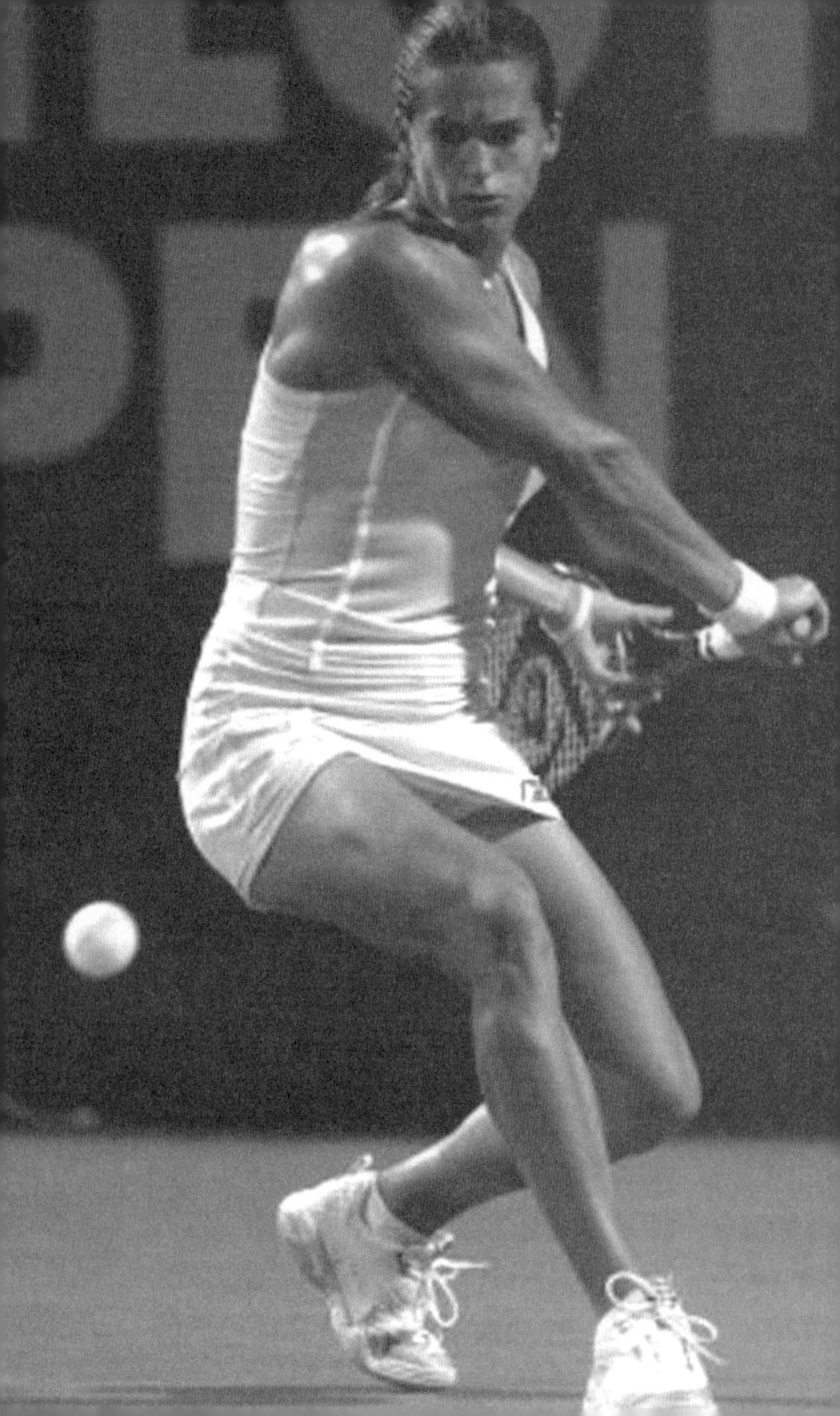

Progresso Fotografico*

> I immediately had the frightful impression that it was an unbelievably
> ancient apparatus, long ago forgotten in the deluge.
> —Bertolt Brecht

Screwing on our Soviet-made lens to photograph a riot in 1977,
for example, or a nude comrade in the morning, it seemed
agreed that photography, too, was part of the experiment. But it's
a strange camera that accompanies a movement whose starting point is the collective refusal of work. Why was it always a
pencil, not a paving stone? At a moment when almost every
other productive relation is interrupted in order to reclaim everyday life and unleash the new revolutionary subject, the camera
never stops working. The street is still a documentary and girls
always return on the covers of magazines. At a certain point,
Bifo (Franco Beradi), one of the main figures of the Movement
of '77, declares that the streets of Bologna are "unusable."[1]
Writing about radio in 1927, Brecht suggested that the things
we call modern are the things we don't yet know how to use.[2]

If radio was already inventing us as listeners before we could
decide for ourselves what "using" this apparatus might mean,
photography predicted us, too, reproducing within its very
mechanism the dubious distinction between an active producer
and a passive consumer of images, for example.[3] The more
automatic the device, the more automated the user. Any political

---

* Originally written for the unpublished Christopher Williams exhibition catalogue *For
   Example: Dix-Huit Leçons sur la Société Industrielle (Revision 5)*, GAM, Bologna, 2007.
   Originally published in the Christopher Williams exhibition catalogue *Program*, Bergen
   Kunsthall, 2010.

1 Bifo, "Anatomy of Autonomy," in *Autonomia: Post-Political Politics*, eds. Sylvère Lotringer
   and Christian Marazzi, (New York and Los Angeles: Semiotext(e), 1980), 164.

2 Bertolt Brecht, "Radio—An Antediluvian Invention?" and "The Radio as a Communications
   Apparatus," in *Bertolt Brecht on Film and Radio* (London: Methuen Publishing Ltd., 2000), 37.

134

critique of photographic production, then, should begin with the fact of our own automatism. The re-appropriation (or sabotage) of our common, instamatic whateverness could be a potential starting point for a coming photography, if we should ever feel the need to elaborate such a practice.

Or consider the Kiev 88, a Ukrainian clone of the Hasselblad, which quickly traveled West after the fall of the Iron Curtain. A much more affordable camera than the original Swedish version, it found its way into the hands of amateurs everywhere. But it kept breaking down, its results were unpredictable, and, in the absence of the usual consumer services or trouble-shooting guide, the product's users began to seek each other out instead. There is no prescribed or proper way to use the Kiev 88, only an ongoing experimentation with its quirks and capacities by this unofficial network of enthusiasts. We can't help noticing the return of something distinctly *communist* here. It's not simply that Communism failed, and that the camera fails; it's that these malfunctions at the same time provoke the return of what is disappeared in professional Hasselblad culture: the spontaneous collectivization of photographic know-how and production. When the thing's use becomes uncertain, the user does too. And it is in such moments that photography, becoming strange again, is swiftly reclaimed.

Christopher Williams's *Kiev 88, 4.6 lbs. (2.1 Kg) Manufacturer: Zavod Arsenal Factory, Kiev, Ukraine. Date of Production: 1983-87 Douglas M. Parker Studio, Glendale, California. March 28, 2003 (NR. 1,2,3)*, 2003, presents its object in a mode very close to

---

3   Jacques Rancière questions the modernist notion that art is political when it emancipates the viewer from a supposedly passive position in relation to staged spectacles. See Jacques Rancière, *The Emancipated Spectator*, presented at the Borderline Academy, Frankfurt, 2005. Transcript available at www.borderlineacademy.org.

commercial "tabletop" photography.[4] Such exacting attention to the camera's body and design, and the precision and control invested in the amplification of its surface qualities produce an image both seductively formalist and brutally distancing. As specific and anonymous as a skull, or an archeological find, the "black box" is something to contemplate when divorced from its own usefulness: an image of authorship reflecting upon its own possibility—or impossibility—or even a kind of technical existentialism is suggested. This, too, is one of photography's strange moments. There are three different views of the camera floating in a neutral, gray atmosphere. The image is internally dislocated by its own serial rhythm, programmatically auto-differentiating. Supplementing one view with the next, the triptych circles, repeats, but never nails down its object.

Christopher Williams enters the photographic system knowing that he has already been summoned there, and with the suspicion that his role as a producer is already predicted by the camera's own program. He has made works by re-photographing pictures torn out of camera catalogues. Sometimes, he prefers to exchange the photographer's powers of expression for those of the executive producer, the casting director, the videographer, or the printmaker, for example. And then there is the social historian or genealogist for whom photography is an archive to be perused and extended, not only by adding pictures but by filtering one's own participation through complex series of citations and productive constraints. Williams doesn't take pictures so much as find new ways of intervening in photographic situations. These ways or uses often seem *unassignable* to any

4   Commercial tabletop photography is a studio-based technique for shooting inanimate objects. At some point in the 1960s, tabletop production supplanted the advertising industry's former reliance on human spokes models to mediate our encounter with a product. Extreme close-ups of steaming hamburgers and sweating beer bottles, for example, are typical tabletop images.

author. And the photographs result from a displacement of readymade notions of authorship and use across multiple stagings and re-articulations of the medium's various procedures, and are themselves means of producing such displacements. Production blurs with reproduction. The artist (dislocating himself from the role of the photographer) uses not only the camera, but also the changing contexts of its usefulness and, equally importantly, the conditions of the photograph's reception in a given exhibition situation. For Williams, the photographic event always both precedes and exceeds the moment of the shutter's release. It is not even an event; it is a sort of meta-program, linking the camera to the rise of the modern military-industrial complex, and to the dawn of the information age. What is staged and restaged is an encounter between the program's inevitable return in every possible picture and the contingency of each particular use of this return.

Not included in the present exhibition is *1964 Renault Dauphine-Four, R-1095* (2000), one of Williams's frequent allusions to the events of May '68, a sort of period piece in which the language of postwar advertising begins to say something about the persistence of revolutionary desire. Picturing a vintage automobile tipped over on its side under lush studio lights, the black-and-white photograph reenacts a press image of street riots in the mode of a high-end product shot. The Williams remains generically and semantically undecidable. It opens up an uncertain space between contradictory readings, teetering here like the Renault between one possible image and another. In a riot, the qualities of materials (and bodies) are intensified: the density of stones, the fragility of glass, etc. It is the same in a Williams. In a riot and in a Williams, we suddenly discover a new use for "speed, luxury, modern France," another use and experience of a given state of things. And in his ongoing attempt to produce a representation of the Cold War period, Williams often catches glimpses of how realities as seemingly antagonistic as capitalist consumption and Socialist revolution (Coca-Cola and Marx) contaminate and un-decide each other in improbable ways. These glimpses are of course constructed perceptions, resulting from Williams's redistribution of codes within the photographic program. But we could also say that the artist sets up situations where the program is allowed to contradict itself—automatically.

If the barricade can help us define a use of photography that we are now tempted to call "improper," it is not only because it is such an authorless and collective construction.[5] Interrupting the everyday language of things by converting objects like paving stones and automobiles back into raw materials, it produces not just an obstacle in urban space, but also a moment of chaos when meanings and materials are unlinked and begin to exchange their qualities freely, unpredictably. And this semiotic and material vandalism is inseparable from the following joys: the free use of public and private property, the anti-architecture of a building that's much closer to singing and dancing, the new mobility produced by blocking that of the enemy, and the spontaneous displacement of notions like use, work, and production from the programs that normally define them. Photography can experience these joys too. In its own way and in its own context, the photograph is already a barricade when its surface qualities and its informational contents are disjoined and put into flux again, when it foregrounds the contingency of its own construction, and when this construction and our reading of it become inseparable from an active displacement of the notion of use. *Lodz, October 2004,* (2004) an image of a Soviet-con-

5   In her book on the poetics of insurrection, Kristin Ross discusses the building of barricades during the Paris Commune. Kristin Ross, *The Emergence of Social Space: Rimbaud and the Paris Commune* (Minneapolis: University of Minnesota Press, 1988).

structed apartment building in Poland, is not the same as architectural photography; rather, it is a free use of its conventions.

And sometimes the image seems to go on strike: *Lodz, October 1, 2004* (2004), a sister image to the building Williams photographed a day later in the same city, depicts two machines at rest. Taking up the greater part of the composition is an industrial textile-printing machine, still spooled with the kind of cheap material we could imagine ending up as curtains in the Lodz apartment tower, where textile workers, for example, might actually live. Dwarfed by this contraption is a humble sewing machine on wheels, where a person might normally stand in attendance. It's historically ambiguous, this scenario, an uncertain moment caught between the nineteenth-century workhouse and the twentieth-century factory, or between the factory and the contemporary sweatshop. There is also something brutally naked in its mise-en-scène, in the way these machines are so clinically exposed here, the bigger one a sort of mechanical Olympia laid bare under the fluorescent work lights, neither active nor passive, but somehow interrupted in action, in the moment of its staging. And the somber factory is devoid of people, suggesting either a recently outmoded economy or a mass walkout, or both. The long, looping skein of fabric also happens to resemble a loaded roll of film, and we get the feeling we've caught the camera staring into a mirror, weirdly fascinated and frozen by its own mechanical reflection: photography maybe glimpsing its own historical precariousness, the day when everybody finally walks out of the lab.[6]

This technical self-reflexivity recurs in another photograph of

---

6   Williams has often relied on a soon-to-be outmoded dye transfer process in the production of his color prints. One of the few remaining labs for this work recently closed its doors to the artist.

a hand-drawn diagram—the threading instructions for a German photographic paper-coating machine manufactured in the 1930s. Its mechanics are almost identical to the Lodz machine, and we begin to perceive a sort of call and response between one apparatus and another, across decades and regimes. This perception of a shared formal matrix—which also somehow echoes the revolutionary call for worker solidarity across national borders and between industries—is another manifestation of the improper at work. What some might call a "topological" perception of the way forms migrate and recur between topographically distinct places and times, could also be described as a sort of non-verbal machine language speaking between these images. It could be a dialogue about the strangeness of their common automatism, and about how this shared condition might contain the possibility of transcending and refusing existing relations of production. An unbalancing, then, of order, or of whatever system assigns an image, or an activity, to "its" proper location in a hierarchical distribution of spaces and values. We could also describe this migratory possibility in terms the logic of the supplement: each singular image comes to extend and thereby unsettle another, within an archive whose relation to the Cold War period is always, and rigorously, in-progress, which is to say: incomplete and non-totalizing.[7]

> Let's allow holes to grow, let's not fear orifices, let's fall into them and pass on elsewhere.
> —A/Traverso (Radio Alice)

One Williams communicates with another, but sometimes we fall into the gaps and distances that separate them. The strike, too, is a form of communication, but what it communicates and

7 "La politique s'oppose spécifiquement à la police. La police est un partage du sensible dont le principe est l'absence de vide et de supplément." Jacques Rancière, *Aux bords du politique* (Paris: La Fabrique-Éditions, 1998).

produces is, precisely, the experience of a gap. The interruption of work by workers is like building a barricade in time, an experience of discontinuity that comes to sabotage an enforced rhythm, a policed temporality.[8] And this withholding of labor power or know-how not only puts the machines on pause; it also suspends the normal relation between worker and boss, between one worker and another, between the worker and his own productive capacity, opening up an empty space where these can be rethought. This is the sort of gap that Williams prefers to work in. It has everything to do with the strange distances the artist elaborates in relation to the objects he photographs, to the modalities of their representation and to the situations of their exhibition. The moment of interruption or disconnection is always close at hand, and it is within this creative interval that notions of authorship and use are strategically destabilized. Between an image of a Pirelli tire and a Pacific sea nettle, for example, something is suspended, held open. Information goes missing; the work of informing is paused. The viewer experiences a similar uncertainty here, in regard to his own automatic task. Between pose and pause, these images seem to announce a strange new potential of displacement.

For example... (2009) sets up a serial rhythm whereby a given quantity of information returns again and again in subsequent revisions. "Revision 5" (Bologna) restates or recycles the materials of "Revision 4" (Vienna). As if refusing to exhaust their own possibilities, the photographs on view in this series of exhibitions return in new configurations, re-distanced in fresh ways, and this continuous "return of the same," between exhibitions and their catalogues, becomes a way of making visible the

8   On the logic of temporal interruption and "chrono-politics," see Paul Virilio and Sylvère Lotringer, *Pure War* (New York and Los Angeles: Semiotext(e), 1983).

discrepancies that haunt the overall program. On the one hand, there is the program's redundancy, and then there is the artist's nomadic and termite-like activity that persistently accompanies it. Williams, then, is working *with* or beside redundancy (and against the recurring sameness of novelty). And the logic of the supplement contaminates this unstable archive to the point where we can no longer distinguish between the production of specific images and the ongoing dislocation of a potential whole (the Cold War period). Beyond the limit of each particular frame, our perception of this whole encounters the possibility of an always-open construction site.

The histories that recur and recycle in Williams's photographs also fold back onto and revise the particular contexts of their exhibition. An example of "red" Bologna's legacy of post-Fascist urban planning by and for the people, the original GAM (Galleria d'Arte Moderna, Bologna) building displayed all the qualities of a hopeful and reasonable Euro-communist society. Buildings speak, and over time, they also revise their statements. Designed in 1975 by the then-fashionable painter and architect Leone Pancaldi, the GAM's dynamic and Brutalist concrete aesthetic quickly fell out of favor, and the institution's various custodians, in an effort to keep up with the times, have progressively made the building over by Sheetrocking sections, closing off windows, readjusting traffic flow, and updating the institutions typographies. For an exhibition at GAM in 2007, Williams reversed this progress, in the institution's final months, before it changed locations and renamed itself MAMBo. Not exactly a historical reconstruction, his alterations of the GAM's space were both crude and precise. By revealing an original set of windows behind one wall of the gallery, and transposing the subtracted elements to the opposite side of the space, for example, the artist was repeating some of the same strategies we see in his photographic work: rethinking use as an intervention within an already existing system, intensifying the qualities of materials in the act of their displacement, foregrounding the contingency of both his decision-making process and our own readings of the works. And such references to the legacy of Institutional Critique (in particular, strategic removals of gallery walls by the artist Michael Asher)—a mode of practice that has frequently informed Williams's uses of photography and its archive—also double as references to the displaced Communist identity of the GAM. Recovering original sight lines, laying bare the old concrete bones of the building, the artist allowed the Red institution to breathe again and function one last time before it finally closed. If Williams stages a dialogue between the museum's building and his own images, he also supplements the discipline of architectural photography with an activity that undermines the functional subservience of one discipline to the other. The GAM, too, is a kind of camera, a program susceptible to the photographer's intervention.

To elaborate a dialogical form is to provoke and participate in the instability of meanings, and once again, to venture into improper practice. Williams has photographed elements from an installation by Daniel Buren, a work originally produced in response to a Michael Asher intervention at the Stedelijk Van Abbemuseum, Eindhoven, in 1977. The Asher consisted of de-installing and re-installing the museum's skylights. With *Frost and Defrost* (1979), Buren responded by removing the tiles of a dropped ceiling in a Los Angeles art gallery, methodically papering them with a green and white striped pattern, and finally replacing the tiles stripes-upward. Williams continues or supplements this conversation by photographing a single Buren tile, reproducing the image three times, and then distrib-uting these identical prints throughout the present exhibition.

Homage, *détournement*, citation, appropriation, or theft, whatever we want to say such exchanges between artists consist of, what we witness is an ongoing displacement or recycling of gestures, and a dialogical construction that exceeds the domain of any one author. That this call and response occurs between three artists known not only for their critical engagements with institutional politics, but also for their radical questioning of the notion of authorship, reminds us that improper practice is also, necessarily, shared. This is perhaps a viral version of the old community of artists, a contamination of techniques that evades the general policing of private property, a topological migration between distinct times and places. Only upon closer inspection do we realize that the Williams is not a Buren, but a document and a detail of one, and only on second thought do we realize it's still a Buren, and also a Williams, or maybe neither.

Also improper, we might say, is the fact that Williams chooses to supplement the practice of Institutional Critique with such produced and finished works, with slick product shots. And it suddenly seems strange to discuss frozen images in terms of movement, displacement, and dialogue. Nothing in these pictures ever moves. Their carefully posed people, fixed objects, and depopulated, actionless scenes are as immobilized as the camera itself, in the moment of its operation. The fixity of an Afri-Cola ashtray, for example, is particularly striking because it is also tipped onto its edge, very much like the Renault/barricade we mistakenly described as "teetering." And yet something does teeter in the reading of the image, and Williams enlists all the precision and control of the studio situation in order to make this movement happen.

Afri-Cola is a German soft drink that predates Coke; it was almost wiped out by its competitors in the 1960s, but then revamped its image under the guidance of the commercial designer and photographer Charles Wilp. Williams, it turns out, has borrowed certain tropes from Wilp's 1968 Afri-Cola ad campaign and recycled them in his own work. The glass doors in his "shower girl" series, for example, refer back to the humidified and frosted glass panels that appear in Wilp's fashionable soft drink ads. So the Afri-Cola reference is split across two of Williams's works (*Ashtray* and "shower girls"), just as the ashtray is split across its own diptych, presented as both recto and verso, undermining its own coherence by revealing the German manufacturer's old-fashioned inscription hidden under the object's clean, postwar design. Pulling Afri-Cola apart in this way, intervening in its program in order to extract raw materials such as glass and the color red ("Everything is in Afri-Cola"), Williams sets in motion a chain of associations that had been lodged in the product's dubious identity all the while: 1968, the crisis of colonial power, the war of brands on the postwar global marketplace, Germany's buried past, the persistence of revolutionary (Red) desire in the new consumer class, the Western eroticization and consumption of darkness, etc. Obsessively revising and restaging itself, *For Example...* has no ambition of ever completing its Cold War portrait. The red of the German ashtray now calls out to the red of Rina (a Cuban bath soap), which in turn corresponds with a shower girl shot in Canada, where it then comes into conversation with the Kodak yellow of her towel, and we get the feeling that none of these photographs really wants to hang on to its own properties, or that these properties never really belonged to the photograph in the first place.

> I am constrained every day, with this pitiless accountant's gaze that the cinema demands, to observe the "objects" that I film. These days, I'm in the midst of shooting a scene in which some bourgeois ladies have tea. I have therefore observed, among other things, teacups...
> —Pier Paolo Pasolini

Whether it's the silky sheen of a bicycle's fenders, the functional yellow skin of a Packset shipping box, the play of squares and rectangles on a building's modernist façade or of suds in a model's hair, we are mostly looking at surface design. The Cold War, it seems, was packaged like everything else. And if we can say, with Pasolini, that human communication is massively supplemented (if not supplanted) by what he called the new, postwar "language of things,"[9] we can also say that there remains the possibility of critically intervening in the work of this new language, of engaging it on the surfaces where it speaks most efficiently. Williams, like a good commercial photographer, is hyper-attentive to the surface qualities of things, but when he uses readymade techniques to bring out the yellow in a towel or amplify the glint of ground glass, he is always at the same time disturbing the efficiency of the commercial program. The Brechtian gesture of including a photographer's Kodak Three-Point Reflection Guide (© 1968) in a tabletop display of simulated corn on the cob is one example of how a Williams interrupts a seamless image of postwar abundance. Sometimes, the orientation of a typeface is skewed or inverted, and others have pointed out the blemishes on a model's skin or the inclusion of an awkwardly angled street lamp in an otherwise perfectly symmetrical composition. Commercial packaging and photographs are signifying surfaces that are programmed to work efficiently together in the construction of a seamless, post-historical social space. And if the author can only proceed from his own automatism, within the program that integrates him with the apparatus he pretends to control, he is still able to introduce glitches and lapses. Such discrepancies reveal the fact of the program, so that the totality of the program itself becomes image too—in the very moment of its disturbance. When two signifying

9   Pier Paolo Pasolini, *Lettere Luterane* (Turin: Giulio Einaudi Editore, 1976).

surfaces are momentarily misaligned, something (history, materiality) manages to come un-packaged.

As nostalgic and reactionary as Pasolini's writings on mid-1970s Italian youth culture may have been, they are interesting in their attempt to grasp a revolutionary moment in the terms of an emergent consumerist sensibility. He makes it nearly impossible to distinguish between widespread disobedience to authority and submission to another totalitarian order, that of the new consumer society and its so-called freedoms. His *Lettere Luterane* (1976), a series of articles published in the daily newspapers of the time, were written while making his final film, *Salo*, shot in Bologna in 1975. In a photograph taken during a casting call for that production, we see a horde of young bodies lined up to audition for the director, who, in his writing, meanwhile condemns the conformism of their long hair, rebellious postures, drug habits, and semiotic enslavement to a dehumanizing culture of commodities. It will be the last time he ever films teenage flesh, and by the time *Salo* is released, Italian youth is already rioting in the streets. All this to say that not only does revolutionary desire always somehow return as a commodified language of things, but the language of things can also hide an unforeseen potential to override its own function. It's never really either/or. Pasolini uses the raw material of teenage boys (and tea cups) in order to say something about the impossibility of human communication in the new city, and a few months later, he is murdered. Where the language of things dominates, we can only elaborate new ways of involving ourselves in the automatic processes that always already disappear us.

A title like *Universal Travel Adaptor, Scorpio Distributors Ltd., Unit DZ, West Sussex, Great Britain, Product Number TXR77000, Power Rating: 6A Max 125/250Vac, with Built-in*

Surge Protector, with Safety Shutters, Surge Status Indicator Light, 110Vac or 220Vac Light Indicator, Built-in 13A Fuse, Testing Based on International Standard IEC 884-2-5 Witnessed by TUV, CE EMC Approval, Douglas M. Parker Studio, Los Angeles, California, December 15, 2005 might constrain the potentially open and free meaning of the image if it weren't already undermining its own function by specifying too much. It is obviously not the thing itself speaking here, but another way of supplementing the image, or of picturing the wordless, functional language of the Universal Travel Adapter. The title's descriptive redundancy verges on the absurd, as if it could convert electricity back into words. We could call the Universal Travel Adapter a sort of Cold War icon (the reverse image of something like the Berlin Wall), technology's dream of absolute communication in a world where humans still can't figure out how to share their own language. Distanced in the photograph, and thereby distanced from its own function, too, the device and its promised powers float in a newfound impotence. Maybe the travel adapter takes refuge in the photograph, finally relieved of its globalizing labor, basking here in this specific, glamorous, almost dandyish unplugged-ness.

In mid-1970s Italy, the young and radicalized multitude attempted to unplug itself from the old political economy. *Red Bologna*, a once-popular 1976 study of the city's exemplary Euro-Communism, presents a Bologna made up of communities and neighborhoods whose planning and development, from the public bus route to the preservation of historical structures to the price of peaches, were as if directly spoken by its responsible inhabitants.[10] This picture was already imploding at

10 Max Jäggi, Roger Müller, and Sil Schmid, *Red Bologna* (London: Writers and Readers Publishing Cooperative, 1977).

the time of the book's writing, and soon the Movement of '77 would articulate a radical break from the official Left, calling for an experimental re-appropriation of everyday life on every level, starting with a widespread refusal to work. An entire generation was teaching itself how to make creative, strategic use of laziness, passivity, and non-production, the idea being to collectively withdraw from the systems that only exploit human potential, and to *autonomize* this wealth instead. In tracts by Antonio Negri and others, "exodus" was becoming synonymous with rebuilding social space, and sabotage was the new production.[11] Looking back on this crisis now, however, we see in how many ways the revolution coincided with a paradigmatic shift to a globalized, postindustrial economy. Many of its subjective experiments were quickly absorbed into post-Fordist systems of production based on worker flexibility and communication, the retreat from factories to home offices, temp work, networks, the blurring of work and leisure time, etc.[12] Paolo Virno describes this transition to a post-Fordist economy in linguistic terms, as the becoming language of labor, and vice versa. We could also maintain, with Vilém Flusser, that the camera is what presides over this shift.[13] Neither a tool nor a toy, exactly, it is the first postindustrial object, and contains within its impenetrable black box the program that will definitively outmode the Industrial Era, the cybernetic code that

11 "I look around myself in amazement. Is this really the spirit of the century? Is this really the creative Marxism in which we live? Nothing reveals the immense historical positivity of workers' self-valorization more completely than sabotage, the continual activity of the sniper, the saboteur, the absentee, the deviant, the criminal that I find myself living. I immediately feel the warmth of the workers' and proletarian community again every time I don the ski mask." Antonio Negri, "Domination and Sabotage (1977)," in *Books for Burning: Between Civil War and Democracy in 1970s Italy* (London: Verso, 2005), 237.

12 "The masterpiece of Italian capitalism consists in having transformed into a productive resource precisely those modes of behavior which, at first, made their appearance under the semblance of radical conflict." Paolo Virno, *A Grammar of the Multitude* (New York and Los Angeles: Semiotext(e), 2004).

13 Vilém Flusser, *Towards a Philosophy of Photography* (London: Reaktion Books Ltd, 2000).

finally takes over where worker and author leave off, replacing machine and user as primary models of production. Photography *informs* us. It closes our distance from the things we use and make, inviting us inside its own function. Indeed, the camera was always a part of the experiment, the ultimate de-subjectivizer.

> Freedom is playing against the camera.
> —Vilém Flusser

It could be that any attempt at subjective emancipation in the information age must necessarily start by picking up a camera. "I am a camera," exactly ... to start from there, from the fact that we are already included in its program. And exodus might not necessarily mean no longer producing images. There are other modes of refusal too, more subtle and perhaps more devastating to the photographic program: strategic appropriations of information and techniques, disconnecting these from the systems that employ them, halting or derailing the communicative labor (or play) of an image, diverting an industrial image into an aesthetic regime, or otherwise undermining the distinction between art and non-art photography in a particularly undecidable image. The way a photograph can be made to oscillate between art and non-art, especially, could be a kind of photographic equivalent to the desubjectivizing practices that emerged during the Italian experiment. In both cases, it is a question of opening up a space that wasn't there before, of supplementing a given, redundant, policed order with a previously excluded possibility, an excessive or improbable image. If the camera is no longer a factory or tool, sometimes it isn't exactly a camera either. When it is momentarily diverted from its own program, the camera becomes strange again, goes into exile with its ex-user, and is swept up in a new movement where it might join others.

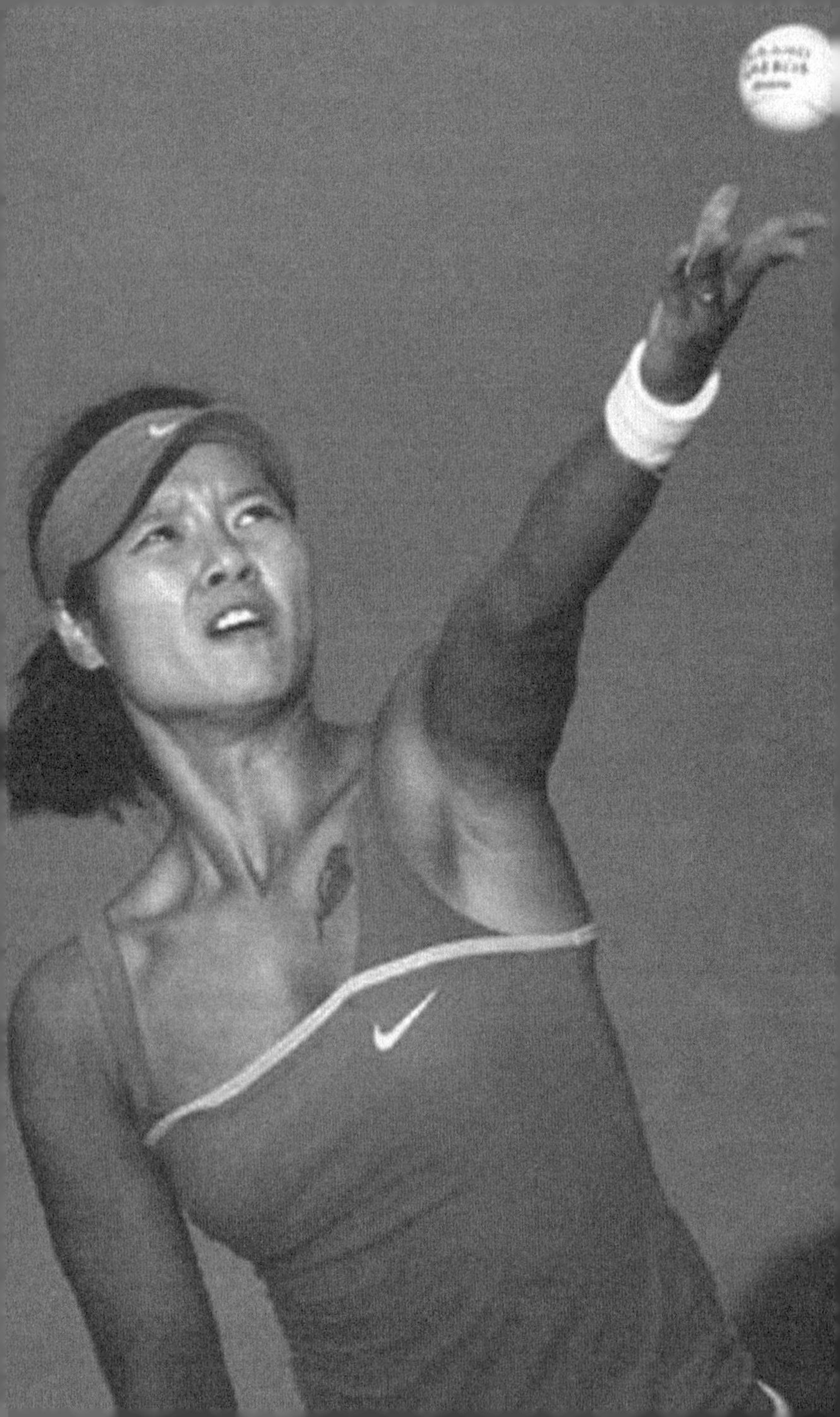

Rape and the City*

The Mutilation of the Apes

The first time New York saw Bjarne Melgaard was in 2000, at the former Alleged Gallery. He showed a gang of tough bronze sculptures based on *Planet of the Apes* (1968) characters. Posed within a trashed-out installation, these ape-men had enormous bronze erections and came pre-vandalized by graffiti. Later, when the gallery closed, rumors circulated that Melgaard's show was the reason for Alleged going out of business. Something about a mink coat stolen from one of the ape sculptures and the artist charging first-class plane tickets to his dealer. And a fight about money. True or false, this is what we heard: Melgaard destroyed Alleged. But this story would soon be followed— and seemingly contradicted—by reports of the artist giving away an entire museum exhibition in Oslo. On the last day of the show, apparently, people showed up with trucks to cart away the free work. We need both of these stories to understand the sacrificial logic at the core of a practice that never stops producing a victim at one or the other end of the paintbrush. There is probably no other way to understand the work of Melgaard or the symbolic economy that founds his factory.

A Concept of Rape

In 2004, at Reena Spaulings Fine Art, there was a small show of digital photographs by Melgaard. The pictures documented the artist and another man injecting themselves with anabolic steroids and performing rough sex in a bare room. I remember duct tape, butt plugs, needles, and combat boots. Death and muscles. These raw, claustrophobic images were intercut with voyeuristic views from a Berlin window, the camera picking

---

*   Originally published in the Bjarne Melgaard exhibition catalogue *Jealous*, Astrup Fearnley Museum of Modern Art, Oslo, 2010.

out potential male victims from among the pixelated passersby. The photos were displayed on a card table in stacks of Plexiglas box frames, and were accompanied by a very short poem called "The Concept of Rape." In the poem, Melgaard called for armed gay violence against straight oppressors, positing gay rights (or more exactly, a sovereign rejection of rights on the part of the "victim") at the point where murder equals freedom and joy. It was a feeling very far from the former activism of ACT UP. The press release and the poem were stuffed in a black Christmas stocking hung from a pipe in the storefront space. Melgaard didn't show up; it was a mailed-in exhibition.

It was in 2008, in a penthouse suite at the Maritime Hotel, that I finally met Melgaard in person. He had been staying there for weeks while preparing his debut exhibition at Greene Naftali Gallery. The view over Chelsea was both commanding and banal, with the river and New Jersey fading out in the distance. The rooms were piled high with the spoils of a recent shopping spree: boxes of shoes, tuxedoes in every color, entire racks of Marc Jacobs. On the table were books by mainly gay women poets. Melgaard had also been reading Kathy Acker and other 1980s transgressive lit, as well as *Intercourse* by the late radical feminist Andrea Dworkin. We talked about poetry and then about who was hot in the New York art world today. Melgaard was curious about the new young men, especially the ones with the fashionably bad reputations (Dash, Nate, etc.). He was fishing for information, because in a few weeks, he would decide to move here. Because for some reason, he could no longer return to Barcelona, where he'd been seeing a married cop. Apparently, he'd left a world of trouble behind him there and wanted to start a new chapter in New York, starting by getting clean and healthy. The show at Greene Naftali went well. Giant, still-wet canvases with monstrous figures and death-driven inscriptions were installed with tasteful "snuff" furniture, the fabrics of which were custom-designed by the artist. There were also some antique crafts and figurines on loan from a collection in Scandinavia, and Melgaard had taped hand-written pages of his latest "novel" to these, forcing a narrative of sexual abuse onto rare and precious objects that couldn't help exuding an aura of myth—relics of a sunless, pagan space-time far from Manhattan.

So Melgaard's New York chapter had begun, monumental like Schnabel, with multiplying cocks, grizzly-sized chihuahuas, dead hookers, and paint straight from the tube. It was "bad" painting at its very worst, with none of the critical distance currently in fashion. In so many ways, it was *out*. Out in the sense of "at large." Breaking out, like teen skin. Out like queer, but also outside of that (the words "gay mafia" and "snuff sluts" appeared on some of the canvases at Greene Naftali). Mainly out of step, willfully so, with the values we'd been fostering and promoting in New York art these past few years: self-reflexivity, self-composure, restraint, civility, etc. Melgaard's output is neither cool nor contained. His painterly excess, demonic figures, fauve colors, overstuffed installations, and disambiguated utterances shoot their load in the face of the mute, monochrome, carefully minimal, and personality-free abstractions of his peers. We had produced a void and Melgaard was invading it, bringing a nasty, muscle-bound, wide-screen kind of kitsch at the very moment we were all stuck on Broodthaers and Barré. This art does not belong here, and knows it; but here it is anyway. And if some people would like to see it suppressed or even deported, it's likely that Melgaard is positioning himself in such a way that high-minded indifference will not remain an option for long: He may have to be physically put down before he changes his ways. The artist seems to be waging a sort of war of the worlds here in New York, where worlds slide past each other but never really touch. They say there's no longer any outside, but Melgaard, for better or worse, is working overtime hallucinating one.

This year, I visited Melgaard's studio in the Bushwick area of Brooklyn. It is an entire floor of a warehouse, big enough to hold several tennis courts and bustling with activity. The artist was wearing a new suit and smoking a Cuban cigar while a dozen recent MFA grads prepared the canvases he would be showing at an upcoming exhibition in his hometown, at the Astrup Fearnley Museet in Oslo. Retreating into their iPods, the assistants labored in silence over large, photorealist images based on the covers of vintage NAMBLA (North American Man/Boy Love Association) publications. This slow, monk-like work was step one (discipline). Step two (punish) would be Melgaard's Neo-Expressionist over-painting. The assistants rendered the little boys, and Melgaard would later finish these images off with his jabbing, slashing, personal brush. This imitation of a Warhol/Koons factory by a Norwegian in Brooklyn did not feel good or okay. The only smiles in sight were on the kids in the NAMBLA images. And the artist looked different now: a slimmer, more compact body with a close-shaven head and a new sort of tension in the jaw and neck. When he asked me to feel his muscles, there was concrete inside the Lagerfeld. Melgaard had been training to run in the next New York marathon, he said through a cloud of cigar smoke. On the computer screen were several images of the artist Kelley Walker, downloaded from the Internet. Like the under-aged boys in the NAMBLA publications, these, too, would most likely become under-paintings in advance of Melgaard's abusive gestures. Here, every subject is a potential victim, and painting is a colorful kind of rape.

N.Y. deserves B.M. As the city continues to distract itself with folktales of wild youth and nonstop creative experimentation, it methodically extinguishes any possibility of these. So in a bad cop sort of way, Melgaard brings back a rough kind of poetry—as order and death. He reminds us that the factory is *no fun*; it is the headquarters of an idea of destruction. Before work, this destruction begins with health, in the gym (David Barton Gym on 23rd Street), where the men of Chelsea work their own bodies like a potato field in the vain effort of making a body appear. Rehab, too, is a kind of self-centered violence, and the artist is learning how to channel it. Control of the self through discipline and its language is how the monster finds a diabolical pleasure in forging its own, personal chains. Starting from here, from no fun, from this strange hardness, Melgaard engages an S&M truth at the heart of the art system. Every artist is a boss and manager of his own impotence. Taking this powerless power to the top of its game, topping himself from the bottom, Melgaard arrives at a sort of auto-crucifying extreme. The operation is supervised in the most sober, professionalized way. And if painting is a symbolic form of rape, for Melgaard, it is also a maximal form of attention bestowed upon the subject, and ultimately, a way of penetrating New York, where the "death of the author" is always mirrored and already outpaced by the death drive of the market. Here, in the end, rape is mainly about efficiency. Like work (and gambling), it immediately brings out the stranger in us. And if work doesn't make us free, it at least makes us show up.

Some recent paintings are inscribed with fragments of a new novel in progress, this one set in New York. The novels, it seems, are perpetually in progress, and always joined to visual artworks. This is because a Melgaard painting is first of all a surface of subjective invention and projection, so it insists on having a voice (or voices), on being dialogical and telling its own story. Talking back to the viewer is a kind of refusal to settle back into mere object-hood. Meanwhile, the "novel," like the whores it describes, uses big painting to exhibit itself in the most shameless way possible. What it seems to want more than anything is to fail as a novel, and to display this in public, where its parody and ruination become "exhibition value." It *wants* to be an object, a slut. So Melgaard enacts a sort of profanation of literature in the gallery, where language is put down (humiliated) in paint and ultimately sold off. Appearing in fragments, the novel is also a way of displaying the violently amputated condition of the art product itself. A novel-in-paintings is a torn apart novel, a story told in commodities, full of gaps. Here, it is screwed on the wall and completely consumed by the eyes, as many as possible.

Kathy Acker abused and at the same time reclaimed literature through an eroticized plagiarizing and rewriting of the Western canon. Her literature was improper both in the acts of theft (reading/rape) by which she constructed her books, and in the de-subjectivizing flights that wrecked the coherence and stability of the text. It was not only what she said (of her selves and of the city), but how "she" said it—with other men's words. She was fucking other books with her books, fucking writing. And if Melgaard is somehow channeling Acker in his recent painting, it is in order to counter the reigning tastes and codes of Chelsea today, and to return the subject that has been exiled from the cleaned-up city (and the city along with it). This subject has to be re-constructed (rehabbed) and forced upon the void in the gallery, and can only appear here as a sort of imposter and scourge, out of place and out of time. Choosing tropes and styles we had relegated to the trash can of post-Pop art history, Melgaard is dashing out the New York novel we were really hoping not to be involved in, the one about our own living death in the city, reminding us what doomed sluts we are, how fatal our separation is, what a pig a painter is, and what sort of factory our creativity has become. On the bright side, there is color. There is also the possibility of inventing other bodies—quasi-fictional ones—to touch each other with, as horrible as that may sound. The creatures and sacrificial selves that populate Melgaard's paintings recall the psycho-activated children in David Cronenberg's film *The Brood* (1979), or the magical spiders and scorpions that Charles Manson handcrafted in his prison cell and mailed out to his enemies. They are emissaries …

… from his factory to ours. In a way, the paintings (like whores) work by directly addressing what is most anonymous in each viewer. If these are New York paintings, it is because they capitalize on every encounter, playing on speed of contact. They abandon themselves to exposure, working hard at being out, gambling everything on our attention. They are *painted paintings*, as painted as possible. And a Melgaard installation is something brutally stitched together, a painted/written monster made of multiple, fatally partial, sometimes contradictory, and warring selves. The more magnified the subject on display, the more it strains at its seams, and the more visible and crude these appear in the gallery. There is a camp aspect to Melgaard's rampant expressionism and a zine-like quality in the way the exhibitions are put together. While camp implies a strategy of putting the self outside or beside itself, a fictional projection that subverts the authenticity of the expression, the DIY comic book-like construction of Melgaard's installations may betray an eager, if not entirely sincere, compulsion to make a world of one's own and to share this with others, anonymously. Here is an outside where we can meet, finally outside of ourselves. Call it rape (or painting).

Melgaard is now working on a series of paintings that depict his mother visiting his exhibitions, posing with and looking at her son's art. It seems that she—as most mothers do—holds a special place in the artist's universe, alongside the cock monsters, cigarette monsters, elephants, and dead hookers. Here, she is both in the paintings and among the paintings, subject and viewer. An ideal viewer, perhaps. Has she been summoned here to witness another rape? This may well be her function, because without an ideal viewer, it's as if the crime and the art never really take place. It is always interesting when an artist finds a way of putting the essence of the communicative act itself— embodied here, in Melgaard's case, in the mother as witness— on display, thereby interrupting the event of the exchange in order to freeze it at a fresh distance. Without having seen these new images, I imagine they go straight to the center of Melgaard's secret. With *her* there in *his* eyes, and at the same time encountering and showing himself reflected there in her viewing eyes, and in ours, the rape is possibly complete. But we doubt it ends here. As long as the factory is operating, paintings and victims will continue to materialize.

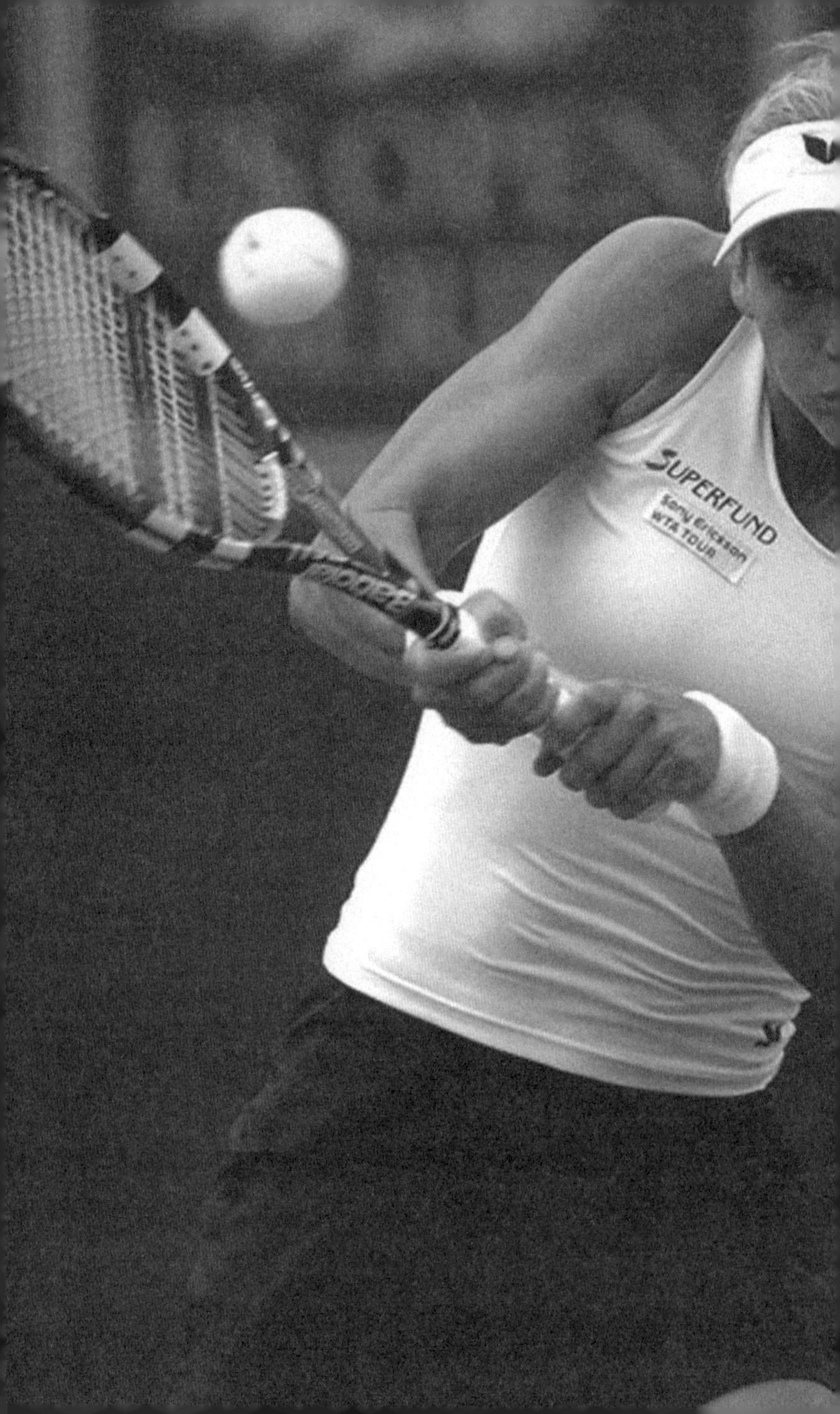
SUPERFUND
Sony Ericsson
WTA TOUR

Respekt Frischlinge*

Describing Montgomery Clift's performance in *Red River* (1948), the film critic Manny Farber opposed the delicate languor of this actor's "stances and kneelings and snake-quick gunmanship" to John Wayne's "claylike" and immobile business of barking his way through the film. It is a story about a massive cattle drive across the wilderness, the birth of an empire in the desert, and we can easily imagine the hypersensitive actor lying alone in his tent at the end of another day of shooting, burying his head in a pillow to muffle the sounds of Wayne and the director, Howard Hawks, boozing it up and hollering like good old boys in the background. Montgomery Clift in his first film role. His first and last "nonmush performance." How will he get through it?

Like paintings, cattle must be driven to market. Crossing a river into unknown parts, these meaty properties are threatened not only by Cherokees and rustlers, but by the Oedipal tensions of the men who drive them. At one point, in the middle of the night, a young cowboy attempts to steal some sugar from the communal canteen, knocking over some pots and pans and causing the nervous animals to stampede. For once, everyone shuts up in the panic. Before all of this, we saw the men brand the cattle with hot irons—a lesson in value production as the adopted son Clift watches Wayne plant his bossy, paternal initials on a stolen steer. The entire plot hinges on moving the cattle east, where they will finally be cashed in. In order to arrive at this possibility of exchange, the men must of course sublimate some primitive emotions.

---

* Originally printed as the press release for Michael Krebber's exhibition "Respekt Frischlinge," Galerie Daniel Buchholz, Cologne, 2007.

What is the difference between a drive and a stampede? In purely kinetic terms, a drive that crosses a certain speed limit dissolves into panic and death. From a dramatic point of view, problems between fathers and sons, and between men and women, can also put the drive at risk. Clift's job is not to kill the bad father, but to produce the possibility of his return as good, or neutral. The father would never give up his autocratic cruelty without the son first assuring him that nothing will be disrespected or wasted if he does. But at the end, it is Tess who does the shooting. Wounding Wayne in the leg, she has a mocking way of disowning the rifle afterwards, making the property strange again: "It isn't mine. It's his." Earlier, Wayne had instructed her that the drive was "too much for a woman."

A rambling lecture about the problem of calling oneself a painter today, originally delivered in Frankfurt. This talk has been transcribed by a hired, commercial sign painter onto ninety canvases, over screen-prints of old comic books. A solution to the other, equally pressing problem of producing three gallery shows at once, by actually filling these spaces with works. Cologne, Paris, and London. Round 'em up, head 'em out. A drive or a stampede of painting, with all the psychic subtexts and the "hard, clamped-down" performance of Michael Krebber, in his Galerie Buchholz debut. *Respekt Frischlinge, frischlinge gestrichen!*

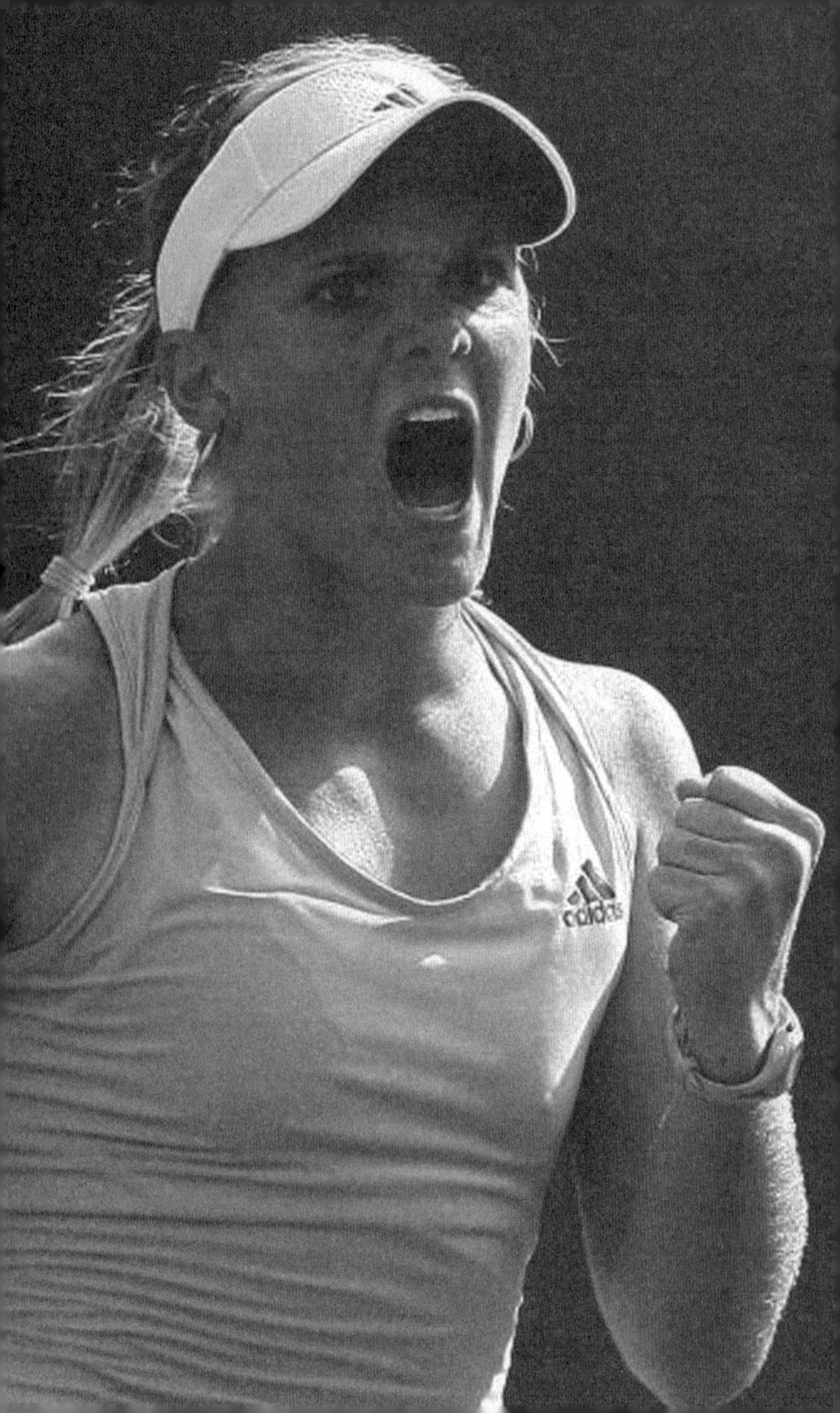

Sculpture in an Abandoned Field*

Some sculptures seem to want a pedestal, others obscene graffiti …
—Michel Leiris

Erection Set

Sculpture is from the Latin *sculpere,* to scratch, to carve; whereas from status, position, comes *statuere,* to set up, and statue. Like the bronzes that occupy our parks and plazas, these works come with the names of famous men, and stand up like homo-erections in space, sometimes on pedestals. Statues also call for graffiti, and these have been hit with at least a sort of makeup. Rachel Harrison does not cast or carve, but, in several senses, *sets up* her works: erects, of course, but also establishes, plans, and maybe even tricks them into situations where they will be caught or blamed. How else can we explain their excessive costumes and colors, or the way they distract us from their erections with drinks, pictures, Styrofoam apples, and other unexpected offerings? So many shameless tactics to both grab and divert our attention from a sculptural condition, which these works do no seem exactly comfortable with, or from the feeling of being in the wrong room. These are the most psychological sculptures we've ever met, so it seems fitting to call them "complexes," rather than "combines." And a paint job can be like a blush or a rash, a sort of betrayal, or else like the ink of a retreating octopus.

With status and stature come Woods, Alexander, and Gore, although some of these are famously unstable figures: Al Gore got the most votes, lost anyway, and ended up with an Oscar instead; the strange sign that Tiger Woods really did belong in

---

*   Originally published in the Rachel Harrison monograph *If I Did It,* JRP Ringier, Zurich, 2007.

the white world of golf was to be suited in a green P.G.A. blazer; when Hurricane Katrina hit in 2005, New Orleans resident Fats Domino was proclaimed dead (his big house sentimentally spray-painted "RIP Fats. You will be missed."), and then a day or two later was announced back among the living; the merchant and navigator Amerigo Vespucci discovered America before Columbus, but this claim has been disputed, and although America took his name, we never celebrate Vespucci Day, etc. What these Harrisons tell us about status is that it's a historical, juridical, and retinal setup that's only possible if something else is also positioned as a spectator, citizen, or nobody. The men she chooses, the statues she erects, travesty their own verticality in so many ways, reminding us of the hollowness hidden at the center of every bronze.[1] These are *complexed* erections.

On a recent trip to Corsica, Harrison photographed the ancient menhirs, or vaguely man-shaped stones that stand around the island with no other job today but to have their pictures taken by tourists. It's a funny coincidence that the "men" in menhir is actually Middle Breton for "stone" (menhir means "long stone"). And that, long before Harrison's visit, Alberto Giacometti (with Michel Leiris) gazed upon the same long, mysterious "men."[2] If their influence can be seen in the Italian sculptor's pin-shaped figures, Leiris, on the other hand, would go on to write obsessive autobiographical accounts of sexual impotence (in *L'Afrique fantôme*, 1934, and *Manhood*, 1939). There is something so inescapably idiotic about these standing stones, and we are not sure if this has more to do with their timeless

---

1   Michel Leiris, "Stones for a Possible Alberto Giacometti," in *Brisées: Broken Branches* (New York: North Point Press, 1989), 137. Leiris opposes an idea of sculpture to, for example, the cannon, "which is a hole encircled by bronze."
2   Ibid., 132.

verticality, with the fact that they never change or go away, or if it's rather about the fact of looking at them now through the viewfinder of a flimsy point-and-shoot, and getting nothing back but more instant moments of this mute eternity. Stones can be read, and these must have meant something once, but whatever they signified then was probably as idiotic as what we read in them today: man-made erections in an empty landscape, dumb rocks. If Harrison borrows anything from the menhirs in her recent sculptures, it's not their mystery but their comedy and kitsch.

Pylons in Nylons

> I remember "muscle magazines" nothing to do with building muscles.[3]
> —Joe Brainard

There is no other way to take these new sculptures but as stand-ins and imposters. Standing in for men, they perform their statuesque act in drag, and verticality as a sort of camp routine.[4] They are not only setups, but place holders, because to have status or mean something is first of all to be *positioned*, like a post or pole. When a Harrison inscribes itself in space and in discourse, it is with a transvestite sort of intelligence, or like *Johnny Depp* in his pirate role: a sort of chameleon in earrings. What was it that Jacques Lacan said about the phallus and veils, how it always hides in skirts?[5] *Claude Lévi-Strauss* might be a sort of key to this men's warehouse, splitting itself before our eyes into a binary male/female setup. Both an elementary structure and a gateway, positioned such that the viewer passes between

---

3 All Joe Brainard citations from Joe Brainard, *I Remember* (New York: Penguin Books, 1995).
4 The artist Mike Kelley has written on the relation between aesthetics and gender confusion in pop and avant-garde culture. See Mike Kelley, "Cross-Gender/Cross-Genre (1999)," in *Foul Perfection* (Cambridge, MA: MIT Press, 2003), 100–120.
5 Darian Leader and Judy Groves, *Introducing Lacan* (London: Totem Books, 1996), 90.

its two poles—cock and hen. The mounted game birds usher us into a game of either/or, so that we literally traverse this hallway-sized gap that both separates and founds a sexual relation, which, according to Lacan, does not exist.

To mount a game bird is also to stuff and sew it, and it's funny how the unmanly arts and crafts, in the end, are what prove the hunter's skill and courage in the field. To take a trophy ready-made and place it on a post is, in a way, to re-prove this thing, but also to fluff the post. *Claude Lévi-Strauss* is a conversation not only between male and female, but also between columns and feathers, and the fact that the columns are in turn supported by a U.S. Postal Service box and a Sharp inkjet fax box reminds us that what's going on between the birds and in the sculpture is no less efficient and confused than what happens between people when we say we communicate. As nearly obsolete forms of communication, the postal system and the fax also say something about what communication itself outmodes in the name of eliminating distances. Whether the space between these totems is more open than closed, at this point, is a good question.

Like the colorized statues that surround him, the cock is painted, because in the animal kingdom, the fierce order of virility always comes with makeup, like our TV politicians today. *Al Gore* comes not only accessorized with a thermostat, but also dappled in the bright, sunny pinks and greens of a Monet lily pond. The inconvenient truth about this sculpture is that its hard, vertical mass is also a skin—a sensitive, Impressionist surface smeared over an inner emptiness, nothing but a quick-dry surface effect. *Alexander the Great*'s paint job mimics the red and blue graphics of a readymade wastepaper basket. Jeff Gordon, the race car driver, is represented on this hollow can by a slick headshot, recalling an earlier Harrison reference: Buckethead (the guitarist who replaced Slash in Guns N' Roses is a sort of human-sculpture who appears on stage with a takeout fried chicken bucket covering his head). As race cars are branded with corporate logos (Dupont, Pepsi, Nextel), so has the conqueror Alexander been decorated with a festive harlequin skin, as well as a gold-starred cape and spooky makeup from some bygone decade. The child-sized mannequin that tops him off is a sexless creature, and, mimicking the pose of *George Washington Crossing the Delaware*, makes over and doubles something heroic and statuesque in other, Harrisonesque terms. The mannequin's head is fitted with a plastic Abe Lincoln mask, facing backwards, Janus-like. In the end, there is no end to this work, no right way to face it. It is an irreconcilable, doubled, bi- or trans-sculptural complex perched on a clean white plinth two sizes too small for the mass it pretends to support.

More diabolical styling tips: *Fats Domino* dressed in vintage Louise Nevelson with a readymade can of Slim Fast for a hat; *R.W. Fassbinder* carried on a wave of foam packing peanuts, wearing purple Spandex cycling shorts, two pairs of glasses, and a backwards Dick Cheney mask; *Pasquale Paoli* bundled head to toe in a moving blanket—people dressed like this would be bashed in some states. There is a point beyond which sculptural properties of material, form, and structure disperse into more hysterical outbreaks of style and vernacular reference, and this is the very point around which the best of Harrison's works tend to both blossom and congeal. Between disguise and sculpture is a world where people like Jack Smith and Leigh Bowery come alive. This is the theater that Michael Fried once accused Minimalism of, except here, it becomes a shamelessly and intensely sculptural force, as do shopping, reading magazines, wigs, and other modern realities. And if Harrison's sculpture is so caught up in this chaos of signs and surface effects, it's precisely because it's so serious about space: In a time when space and image lose their distinction, and the old, ideal distance between viewer and object is always already filled up and occupied by a thousand communications, sculpture, too, finds ways of making itself multi-surfaced and schizo-temporal. In order to re-occupy our contemporary no-space, it trades in its timeless pose for a temporary one, or for a manic series of appearances.

Everything Must Go

> I remember in wood-working class making a magazine rack.
> —Joe Brainard

Harrison has often appropriated commercial display systems, from magazine racks and mannequins to video screens and shelves, and many of her works assault the viewer's attention with the same gimmicks any 99-cent store uses to promote discounted merchandise: Everything Must Go! Oftentimes, the merchandise itself appears readymade in a sculptural setup: a work both displays and consists of a can of Slim Fast, employing it as both content and material; or a stack of glossy celebrity tabloids shoved under one corner of a plinth intervenes as both pop cultural reference and as a structural element that literally gets under the feet of the sculpture, shifting its weight. We could easily discuss such instances as a critique of consumer society and the marketing of urban life, but we can also approach them in a more direct, de-sublimated way: as active sculptural facts with real sculptural consequences. In a riot, for example, things are transformed in the act of their spontaneous displacement.[6]

---

6   On the poetics of barricade construction during the Paris Commune, see Kristin Ross, *The Emergence of Social Space: Rimbaud and the Paris Commune* (Minneapolis: University of Minnesota Press, 1988).

Automobiles, street signs, and other objects are torn from their normal functions, as well as from their normal meanings, and suddenly literalized as obstacles or projectiles in urban space. This is how gesture converts signs back into raw materials. In a riot and a sculpture, such tactical acts of re-appropriation alter the circulation of bodies and information within a given terrain, if only for a moment.

When sculpture opens itself up to other activities, such as photography or window-shopping, and sets itself up as a sort of switching station, where cultural materials and meanings are violently disconnected and recombined, it puts itself into flux too. These are trans-sculptural complexes, perverse and sometimes manic redistributions of the sensible world. A readymade object or image—Slim Fast or Leonardo DiCaprio—is never fully integrated into a Harrison; it always retains a degree of material autonomy and non-belonging, and is for this reason a means by which the sculpture willfully produces an internal self-differentiation.[7] The sculpture claims Slim Fast as a component, but in so doing immediately unsettles its own proper status and territory. Harrison's complexes recall Marcel Broodthaers's first sculptural work, *Pense-Bête* (1964), produced by sinking volumes of his own poetry into a lump of wet plaster. Announcing his career shift from poet to visual artist, Broodthaers's simple gesture made his books unreadable by transforming them into sculptural objects: The only way to get at the poems now would be to demolish the artwork.[8] But unlike the Broodthaers, a Harrison allows its readymades to be as readable as they are on the supermarket shelf, and, in fact, this readability (and

7   Rosalind Krauss writes on the self-differing, heterogeneous aspects of Broodthaers's work in *A Voyage on the North Sea: Art in the Age of the Post-Medium Condition* (London: Thames and Hudson, 1999).
8   Dieter Schwarz, "Look! Books in plaster!," *October*, no. 42 (fall 1987): 57–66.

sometimes the shelf too) is one of the sculpture's unavoidable and defining qualities. The work not only includes the can of Slim Fast, it reroutes and pirates all the communicativity that comes built into its design. With the cylindrical form and the gloss of the packaging come the information on its surface, the social and cultural connotations of the diet beverage, as well as the historical memory and subjective associations that accompany such products; and we realize that there is no way to identify what is specifically sculptural in a Harrison without taking all of this into account. These works are as heterogeneous and self-differing as *Pense-Bête*, with the difference that they perform this in a wide-open, even exhibitionist manner. And if they at the same time remain hermetic or opaque, it is a paradoxical result of their extroversion.

Totem and Tattoo

> In a vain attempt to keep it looking bright and festive, local shop owners have taken to spray-painting colored polka dots on it.
> —Mike Kelley

Returning to the relation between Harrison's forms and the paint-jobs they've been subjected to, another prototype comes to mind: *Framed & Frame* (1999), Mike Kelley's spray-painted, faux concrete reproduction of the "Chinatown Wishing Well" in Los Angeles.[9] In this work, Kelley was exploring the potential for visual confusion in the haphazard "tinting" of a given form or image. Looking at poorly colorized vintage postcards of kitsch tourist attractions such as caves and rock formations, the

9 For a statement on his work *Framed & Frame (Miniature Reproduction "Chinatown Wishing Well" Built by Mike Kelley after "Miniature Reproduction 'Seven Star Cavern' Built by Prof. H.K. Lu")*, 1999, see Mike Kelley, "The Meaning Is Confused Spatiality, Framed (1999)," in *Minor Histories* (Cambridge, MA: MIT Press, 2004). In this text, Kelley also discusses works based on a menhir-like, pre-Christian megalith in Denmark.

artist was pursuing a "confused 'nothing' space," whose erotic charge he related both to gender slippage and to the threat of the *informe*. In the same way that Kelley locates possibilities of cultural mixing and social subversion in an aesthetics of instability and chaos, we could say that Harrison elaborates similar proposals in terms of contemporary design-and-display culture.[10] Because while commercial design succeeds by dissolving any clear frontier between a product and its packaging, between substance and image, Harrison's sculptures build themselves around the hijacking or occupation of such frontiers, opening troublesome gaps and causing the work to stammer and dysfunction in the very places where display and communication occur. A readymade mannequin, for example, becomes a radically undecidable figure in a sculptural complex such as *R. W. Fassbinder*. It is both figure, in the traditional sculptural sense, and figured display, or mediation figured as such. There is no way to nail its function down in specifically sculptural terms. And by giving it two faces—male and female, plaster and rubber, backwards and forwards—Harrison causes an immediate confusion between the space of retail and the space of subjective construction. This is also the biopolitical space of self-help and cosmetic surgery, but squatted and travestied. The gender confusion in this work comes *packaged* with the sculpture's formal and aesthetic undecidability, and it dysfunctions or disidentifies at the points—subjective and sculptural—where commercial design normally produces the illusion of a coherent, seamless experience. Harrisons are divided selves, and anything vertical or solid in them is founded on these de-subjectivizing faults and interruptions.

10 Hal Foster, *Design and Crime* (London: Verso, 2003), 126–27. Foster considers how what was once called sculpture's "expanded field" has imploded in recent years, to the point where contemporary installation art is indistinguishable from the production of controlled, corporate space.

Sculpture Goes for a Walk

Forming a horizon line behind her vertical forest of columns and figures is "Voyage of the Beagle," Harrison's series of fifty-seven digital photographs. A row read horizontally from left to right and back again, these ink-jetted "headshots" are taken from mannequins, menhirs, bronzes, Brancusis, hunting trophies, posters, record covers, and magazines. Beginning and ending with close-ups of Corsican menhirs, the series, like the voyage it was named after, is a sort of quest for the origins of sculpture, but in this case, a comically circular one. The menhirs—whose erections have perhaps been overly stressed above—are now put on equal footing with a Buddha-like statue of Gertrude Stein and a stuffed beaver, for example. But Harrison's democratic and horizontal photographic embrace takes in many others too: Stryofoam wig displays, Kevin Bacon, a detail of a Giacometti, Beyoncé, etc. Sculpture, it seems, begins and ends everywhere: in the park, the street, shop windows, yard sales, magazines, the Internet, etc. The lateral arrangement of these images reminds us that standing up is only one possible trajectory for a work that is sculptural. Another takes the form of a *walk*, as the artist—a sort of bee in this garden of forms—goes camera in hand through everyday life, collecting sculptures wherever they turn up. If the photograph is put into play as sculptural material elsewhere in Harrison's work, here, it continues its work by other means. To produce sculpture is sometimes merely to notice it, to find it, usually not in the museum.

I remember digging around in ice cold water for an orange soda pop.

I remember Belmondo's bare ass (a movie "first") in a terrible "art" movie called, I think, "Leda."

I remember a lot of movie star nose job rumors.
—Joe Brainard

With photography come stars. Harrison has appropriated images of celebrities many times before (Liz, Marilyn, Mel, etc.), putting her sculptures into awkward conversations not only with photography but with People who can only be consumed and known as ready-mediated, as industrial productions, and usually as endorsers of other industrial products such as canned iced tea. Athletes and movie stars join Harrison in her work not only as common materials, but as muses and models. It is an uncertain, wide-open space between *Star* magazine and the artist's studio, and what better guides than these human commodities and proper names who move with such ease between the bedroom and the cover of a tabloid? Most fans would agree that Michael Jackson was one of the greatest living artworks of our time, at least since Warhol (since King Ludwig II, even). And then there is O.J., who, like M.J., is connected (rightly or wrongly) to gloves, knives, and sex crimes. Both have endured the brightest, harshest spotlights, and neither has ever failed us, as stars or as works. Appropriated as the title of Harrison's last exhibition in New York, Simpson's "If I Did It" could even be an aesthetic slogan for artists today: a perfect articulation of the uncertain relation between producer and product in a time when artists, too, come readymade. Among other things, what the celebrity teaches the sculpture is that sometimes the most effective way to show up is by falling apart, or at least to involve the viewer in this dramatic and aesthetic possibility. There is also the lesson about public and private, the two faces, and how to put in an appearance without totally giving yourself away. But the most captivating celebrities are the ones who keep us fixated on the moment of crisis where these two faces might finally collapse into one. Scandal and damage control are also sculptural possibilities, as is the "I want to be alone" of certain Harrisons, which never stop seeming to turn their backs on us.

If the celebrity is a model for a way of showing up in the gallery and the marketplace, sculpture itself—like certain popular women's magazines—proposes models for a contemporary politics and aesthetics of the self. Is there any possibility of re-appropriating lifestyle culture as a means of subjective emancipation? Can readymade, biopolitical notions of the Self be pirated and transformed into techniques we can actually use? Is there, on the most basic level, any way to *experience* a program that already includes us in its function? The politics of sculpture is about how it puts itself together before our eyes. It's in the way it can simultaneously occupy and abandon the place it stands in, and the ruses by which it opens up spaces of uncertainty between the materials it appropriates and the uses these come programmed with, that a complex such as *R.W. Fassbinder*, or *Alexander the Great*, becomes an instance of politics. *Police* means telling us what sculpture is; politics re-opens the question, or refuses to answer it in just one way. This is why, when the Harrisons stand up in their places, they do so *improperly*, and find their properties wherever, in whatever context. Jacques Rancière has defined politics as the formation of a subject around two contradictory terms: active and passive. In other words, when the agent of an action is also and immediately the material that is transformed by this action, there is politics.[11] Sculpture, then, when it becomes political, is a specific relation between ways of putting things together and of taking itself apart. There is always one more component, and it could be anything—a can, a wig, a video, a vacation—which shows up to antagonize the idea that sculpture is what it is, that it could ever be complete or self-identical. Sculpture starts again from its own contradictions. It stands up to get a better view of what's already been left behind.

11 Jacques Rancière, *Aux bords du politique* (Paris: La Fabrique-Éditions, 1998).

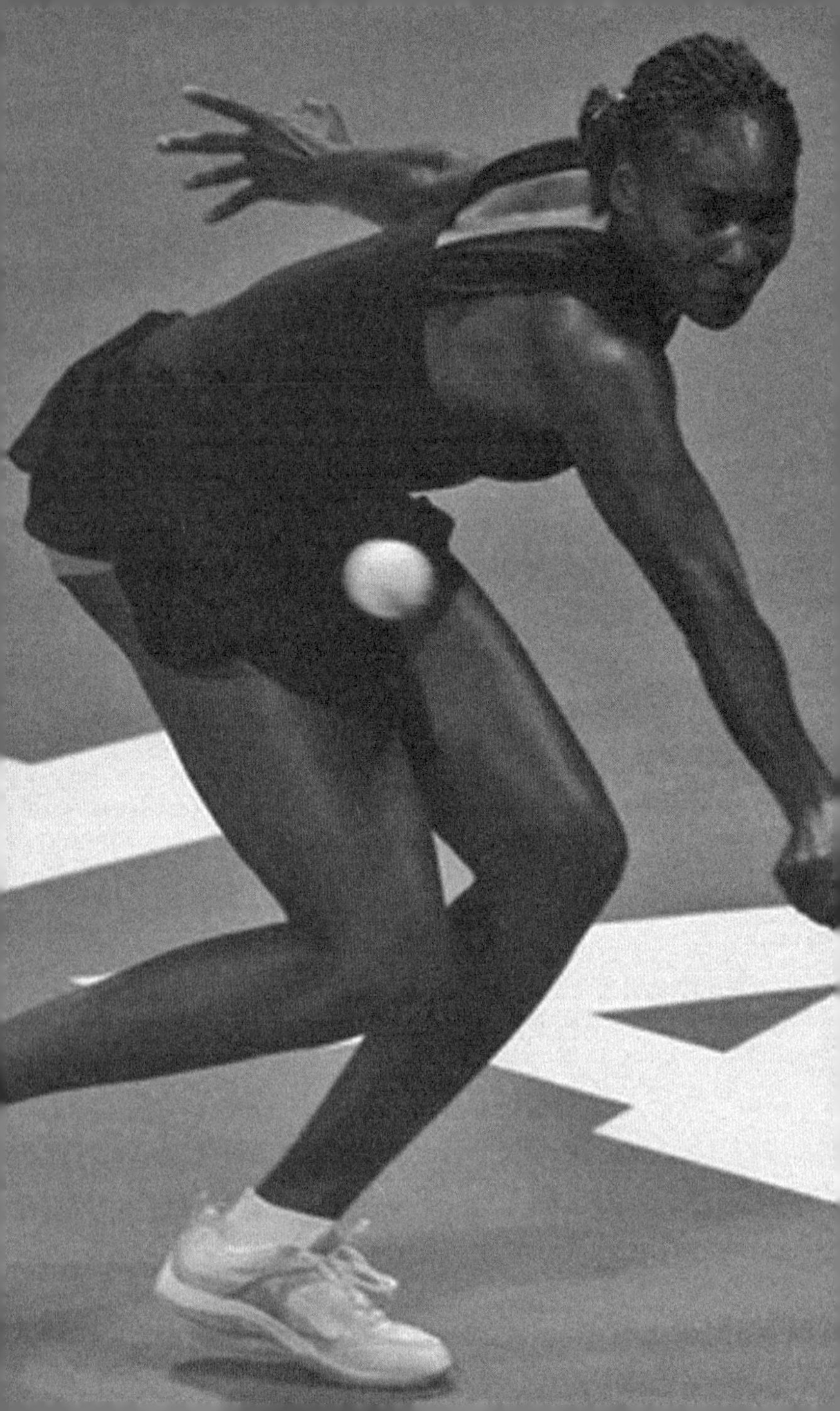

The Self-Employment Rate

This shirt was hand-tailored by some indie designers who operate a new boutique for men near the Bowery. It has the instant-timeless look that's built into so many New York interiors today—all these new hotel lobbies and taverns that conjure up visions of the olde downtown, where Vans go perfectly with worsted wool and tweed. Here, wood salvaged from eighteenth-century barns is the gourmet material against which today's "food revolution" is being staged. And this is a shirt for eating *saucisson sec* and drinking biodynamic wine, cut narrow for the slim bodies of the neo-Bowery. It's a shirt for getting rid of the city and, like the wrapping on the rustic sausage that dangles over the cash register, a way of dressing up disappearance. I myself am a sort of *saucisson sec*, I'm thinking as I take my seat next to a vitrine filled with skin-care products in a barbershop that's designed to look like a scene in *Gangs of New York*. I add my name to the list on the chalkboard—Alex, Rodrigo, Leo, Justin—and read about the riots in Thailand as another customer's Shih Tzu writhes at my feet. This is how the city returns as abstraction, and these are the haircuts who are doing their best to inhabit it.

In *Capital*, Marx makes a brief reference to the *Tagwerk*, an ancient German unit for measuring land.[1] The *Tagwerk*, based on the area of land that could be worked in a single day, was a practical and very rudimentary translation of labor time into spatial terms (and vice versa). Down on the Bowery, it is amusing to imagine that the relation between time, work, and space could once have been grasped in such a commonsensical way. Because here, even when nothing is getting done and no actual

---

1 Karl Marx, "Commodities," in *The Portable Karl Marx*, ed. Eugene Kamenka (New York: Penguin, 1983), 445.

labor is being clocked, the contemporary artist is always already immersed in a production time that includes every breathing moment.[2] So for today's artist, a contemporary *Tagwerk*—if such a thing were even conceivable—would have to include the studio and gallery, certainly, as well as bars, classrooms, bedrooms, *vaporetti*, and streets both here and abroad; and since most of our daily activity consists in producing communication by means of communication, it would also have to include the virtual space of the laptop's screen and the networks we constantly extend as we activate ourselves in what is called "discursive space." Our *Tagwerk* would be the total nowhere of our never-ending immersion in a de-localizing production time that includes both work and non-work. It would measure our full self-employment in a spreading non-place, which is beyond measure.

A proliferation of artisanal effects accompanies the recent (and recently stalled) renovation of the city, catering to a metropolitan taste for slow-cooked and freshly picked things. So the obscenely authentic ripening of the locally produced heirloom tomato greets the playful, jaunty mushrooming of these glass-walled structures throughout the Village. In his writing on commodity fetishism, Marx showed how relations of production were abstracted and concealed in consumer products, but today we see labor inscribed upon every communicating surface and every skin. The new commodity is a "social hieroglyph" that signals exactly who made it (Pangoa, a small co-op of about five hundred farmers), how (with traditional, environmentally sustainable methods), and where (on the Amazonian slopes of Central Peru). It is rough around the edges and a bit touched-looking, elaborating several ways at once of calling itself organic,

2   "Thesis 5": "In post-Fordism, there exists a permanent disproportion between 'labor time' and the more ample 'production time.'" Paolo Virno, *A Grammar of the Multitude* (New York and Los Angeles: Semiotext(e), 2004), 104–5.

fair, and real. Like Institutional Critic, the correct consumer demands this transparency at any cost. It is the old trick of the honest commodity (and it works in the art world too: thus, the recent attraction of the "artist's artists," and the re-programming of "real deals" from bygone decades in contemporary art galleries). But what could be more abstract than the signs of work, authenticity, and the local we order from menus and wear on our bodies today? For example, hand-painted Oxfords by YSL made to look like they've been kicking around a painter's studio for years. Or this bespoke shirt.

Meanwhile, our self-employment increases according to the degree that we make ourselves flexible within the networks of communication that we busy ourselves extending under the sign of the social, in the modes of art and entertainment. The best consumer is the self-employee who is available enough to invest maximal quantities of attention to the info-products that ceaselessly demand our attention. Because in an info-economy, attention is the new money. Dressing up our chaotically organized but never-too-wild activities in readymade bohemian signifiers (the artist's life, the writer's life, etc.), we make ourselves as available as these networks demand us to be: available to abstraction, starting with the vanishing of labor time into production time. And the less labor counts as a measure of what we actually do, or of our work's value, the more it returns as a surface effect, an abstraction we consume along with the sausages and tomatoes that lend our days a certain grainy substantiality. Is it the Protestant work ethic that somehow persists in us, despite our newfound capacities to abstract and disappear everything, starting with work, that makes it seem so normal to be going to the gym in the middle of the day, like ancient Greeks (but with earphones), to work our own bodies like a potato field? As if abstraction could ever find its body at the end of an hour on the elliptical trainer. And this body that never quite arrives is the artist today (and the artwork).

Production time, now constant, insists on making its appearance under the aspect of sociability, generating instant images and text of our relational activity, like a game improvised on a screen or a lifestyle magazine laid out on the fly. What the artist wants is to appear as vividly as possible on these transient pages while at the same time demonstrating some minor influence over their construction (we are all models *and* designers). Some artists will go so far as to use these fleeting on-screen moments in order to display their own crisis of presence, attempting to transform their being-in-mediation into gestures. So if our displacement in discursive space is always accompanied by something like a real-time video display or a stream of text messages (our very perdition generating an instant document of itself), the artist sometimes attempts to bring this mediation to a momentary standstill. Here is one definition of the contemporary artwork: an attempt at recovering gestures in an age that has lost its gestures.[3] Every artist deals with the fact of mediation, but the only possibility of producing gestures today is to interrupt one's own being-in-mediation, to make it strange, and to somehow sign the very processes that make our work so radically unassignable. In other words, we appropriate the processes and programs that make our productive displacement visible in order to intervene exactly there, at the point where communication becomes appearance. There is our availability as creative "life force," there are the thousand ways of communicating this availability, and there are artists who devise ways of putting this communication on display, taking it up as pure means and sometimes interrupting it. But there is no one resembling an author in this world—not really.

3   See Giorgio Agamben, "Notes on Gesture," in *Means Without End: Notes on Politics* (Minneapolis: University of Minneapolis Press, 2000), 49–60.

When the artist uses fiction, it is in order to tell this story of language and life going to work. But fiction, for contemporary artists who insist on staying close to the social and material conditions within which their discursive activity unfolds, is less about spinning yarns than it is a means of inhabiting the subject-object relation in a somewhat direct manner. It is a way of putting the artistic subject at a new distance so that we can go to work on it objectively. In the words of Adorno: "Thrown back upon itself, this subject is of necessity what is closest and most immediate to itself artistically. Socially, however, it remains derivative, a mere agent of the law of value."[4] The fiction we are talking about, then, also attempts to make itself socially immediate in order to get some traction in situations where what Marx called "real abstraction" already operates in advance of thought, at the level of bodies, money, and the language of things.[5] So while fiction tells the story of life and language going to work, it also puts the telling itself (the discursive activity that is the work) on display. In advance of the art magazine and the critic, the fictional artist is the self-writing one who already narrates his or her own emergence and disappearance in discursive space, at least until the story is taken up and repeated in the work of others. And there are moments, before the magazines inevitably move on to fresher news, when these journalistic and critical repetitions, too, are included in the display and in the work. Such uses of discursive space have a way of addressing and reflecting back the "work without qualities" that defines the practice of contemporary art today. For as Paolo Virno has shown, it is our most generic, human capacities that are driving the production of surplus value under post-Fordist conditions:

4   Theodor W. Adorno, "Valéry's Deviations," in *Notes to Literature: Volume 1*, (New York: Columbia University Press, 1991), 143.

5   For a contemporary elaboration of Marx's concept of "real abstraction," see Alberto Toscano, "Real Abstraction Revisited: Of Coins, Commodities and Cognitive Capitalism," http://www.le.ac.uk/ulmc/research/cppe/pdf/toscano.pdf.

language and communicativity, public exposure, social cooperation, openness to the unforeseen, etc.[6] Consider how the artistic subject already opened its generic qualities to self-writing and display in projects as diverse as Andy Warhol's factory-made literature (novel, diaries, *Interview*, etc.), Jörg Immendorff's self-critical paintings in the service of the Maoist party, Lee Lozano's works in the form of instructions to herself, Cindy Sherman's "Film Stills," Richard Prince's 1983 "novel," *Why I Go to the Movies Alone*, and Jean-Luc Godard's self-reflexive histories *JLG/ JLG* and *Histoire(s) du Cinéma*.

These days, dispersing the self across various, sometimes collectively elaborated discursive registers, and in the process, sometimes inhabiting simultaneous and seemingly contradictory professional roles, we are able to reflect upon the ways in which our capacity for abstraction is always already captured in production time. Never exactly there in the place or the moment where the work is happening, the contemporary subject may prefer to counter his or her own productive mobilization with further, discursive displacements, taking up fiction as a means. While established critical forms work on abstraction without actually transforming anything, fictional strategies always expose the discursive subject to the possibility of modification (sometimes even extinction). The subject in question is no longer an individual producer, but "a latent social subject for whom the individual artist acts as agent."[7] In other words, the one who goes to work is not exactly the same one who authors the situation: the distance between them is, in fact, the place where the work of fiction happens. This is the place where Marcel Broodthaers elaborated his strangely critical and not entirely post-poetic practice, starting with the invitation card

6　Virno, 2004, 47–71.

for his debut gallery exhibition ("The idea of inventing something insincere finally crossed my mind and I set to work at once."). And if we were talking about a factory or a school, this could be the moment of the strike and the occupation. Without wanting to stretch the comparison too far, we can perhaps agree that when producers intervene in their own mediation, or take up communication as pure means by interrupting its normal function and efficiency, the subject's relation to itself (and to its own social reproduction) is held in a momentary state of suspension. And then the script is somehow back in our hands. And perhaps other inter-subjective syntaxes can now be experimented.

"I'm not one for fine speeches," Martin Kippenberger would always begin. And then the dreaded, endless stand-up routine, and another art-world dinner was hijacked in the name of fiction. But we are already doubtful that the term "fiction" succeeds in capturing the various ways we have in mind of engaging a politics of mediation, or of re-appropriating our own being-in-mediation in order to produce socially immediate gestures. In a discursive situation, the possibility of transformation begins with the display of our linguistic capacity as such, from the moment communication is taken up as pure means. Display, in this sense, involves interruption or putting at a distance. Whether in the form of a drunken, shaggy dog story, by re-appropriating institutional language and making it strange again, in the trashy guise of a pseudonymous art dealer who emits press releases and does dinners, or as an artist who finds new means of self-inscription that scramble the critic's claims to truth and objectivity, the aesthetic subject performs its own crisis of presence in discourse, and exhibits this. Sometimes an actual body is there doing the

7   Adorno, 1991, 161.

fabulating; sometimes, a more opaque front presents itself. However it is that we show up, we are showing that communication is also social production and a vanishing act, too. Our particular concern, here where whatever is going on between us is immediately linked to the market's need to make something appear, is with how the dissolution of genre hierarchies and the blurring of professional divisions of labor have opened up other, experimental possibilities for aesthetic production and reception, allowing the emergence of new formats and unforeseen actors within this self-reflexive, interconnected space we call the art world.[8] It is a recognized fact that the very rationality of the connectionist system demands an increasing degree of flexibility and mobility on the part of the producer, and we all know that frenetic multi-tasking is not exactly an expression of new freedoms gained under post-Fordist conditions.[9] The question, then, is how to elaborate other distances from our own mobility and frenzy, and without necessarily assuming the safe seat of the critic or of "critical distance." While Foucault's theoretical work on the aesthetics of the self and *parrhesia* remain key points of reference for aesthetic practices that prefer to pursue the de-subjectivizing possibilities of discursive production, even he was not yet thinking in terms of the real-time, full-time communication in which we're immersed today. It becomes more and more difficult to link our discursively enmeshed gestures

8   Some recent examples come to mind: Stephan Dillemuth's performances and writings under the name Werner von Delmont (*Corporate Rokoko and the End of the Civic Project*, Copenhagen, 2002); Bernadette Corporation's anti-documentary protest film, *Get Rid of Yourself* (2001–03); Andrea Fraser's institutional performances and public speeches; Lucy McKenzie's appearances as a porn model in photographs by Richard Kern; Michael Krebber's 2007 series of paintings that filled three gallery shows and displayed a talk he had delivered earlier in Frankfurt; Seth Price's video *Redistribution* (2009), which re-appropriates footage of his own artist talk, etc.

9   For a discussion of the writing artist and multitasking in the contemporary context, see Tom Holert, "Expansion of Praxis or the Ends of Writing," *Texte zur Kunst*, no. 70 (May 2008): 133–6.

to anything habitable, especially after all the sad efforts at "conviviality" by artists and curators working under the banner of Relational Aesthetics. Speaking truth to nonstop communication can probably happen only as poetry or as insurrection, but we're not yet sure what an insurrectional poetics for these times might be. In any case, it won't happen outside of mediation or outside the processes that already mine our immaterial creativity for new sources of accumulation. And the subject will have to somehow put itself at risk within these processes, and share this risk with others.

Merlin Carpenter's recent series of painting shows in six different cities, all titled "The Opening," appropriates the Relational-Aesthetics formula "the exhibition as medium," but narrows its terms even further, reducing the "medium" to the ritual 6–8 p.m. time frame of the vernissage (even further, in fact, since his in-situ painting performances are usually deferred until around 7:30 p.m.). While the labor time (= painting time) for each of these exhibitions clocks only thirty minutes or less, the social time of standing around at an opening is drawn out (and displayed) as a doubtful, frustrated waiting for art. And in the end, the paintings themselves contain nothing (beyond their promised "intrinsic value"), but the "metaphysical index" of the artist showing up and activating himself in the gallery.[10] Under the watchful, calculating eye of an art world that celebrates and remunerates the free expression of its preferred subjects, Carpenter splatters his canvases with brief, dumbed-down phrases like "Relax, It's Only a Crap Reena Spaulings Show" and "Simon Lee Is an Utter Swine," in this way both answering to and throwing off the discursive compulsions every producer faces in a post-Fordist economy. Measuring these moments to the

10 The notion of the "metaphysical index" in discursive practice is taken from Diedrich Diederichsen, *On (Surplus) Value in Art* (Berlin and New York: Sternberg Press, 2008), 47.

pre-set material area of the canvases and to the programmed social time of the art opening, the artist elaborates a perverse series of equivalences: between production time and social time, between discourse and the material conditions of display, between communicative activity and the production of commodities, etc. If reading Marx has informed such a diabolical scheming out and presentation of the socio-economic conditions that rationalize aesthetic production today, the artist's brute extraction of a concrete image of production time from the surrounding flux, and the brute immediacy of its display add up to a gesture of refusal to hand over any more living labor than is logically necessary in the creation of aesthetic surplus value. And only on these prescribed terms can the inevitable speculation on the value of "bad" painting begin, or not.

Meanwhile, in France, the Sarkozy government has arrested a group of friends on charges of "criminal conspiracy with terrorist intentions," the only material evidence held against them being their alleged authorship of an anonymous, anti-capitalist tract called *The Coming Insurrection*.[11] If the production of communication by means of communication is how neoliberal society maintains and disappears itself under the eye of its managers and police, what these latter fear more than anything is when discursive activity finds a way of connecting itself to actions and life forms that escape the neutrality of our self-reproducing "connexionist world" (the Tarnac 9 terrorist cell has also been accused of sabotaging high-speed railway lines in France). The nightmare, in other words, is when abstraction recovers its bodies, and the bodies turn back on the reigning abstraction. Anonymity and "whateverness" are part of this menace, and a vivid reflection of the whateverness shared by discursive

11 The Invisible Committee, *The Coming Insurrection* (New York and Los Angeles: Semiotext(e), 2009).

subjects everywhere, because they reveal the insurrectional possibilities lying dormant in a society based on not much else beyond its interconnectedness and the productivity of its generic, communicative capacities. Especially in an economic crisis, it probably wouldn't take much to provoke a widespread re-appropriation of our own being-in-mediation, and to unleash truly scandalous gestures within the networks through which the production of communication by means of communication is presently managed. In the art world, it is doubtful that political expression will remain quarantined on relational "discussion platforms," and that discussion will remain satisfied with the illusion that it's not for sale.

Like the whatever-singularities that emerge in moments of social crisis, and that are, in fact, everywhere already produced within contemporary capitalism, other subjects and other ways of doing things will inevitably arise within the shifting discursive conditions that have founded artistic practice for the past several decades. Some of these may prefer to refuse the platforms already set up for them in magazines and museums, or they may swarm these platforms with strange techniques and new syntaxes. Already there are signs that the artist's life is no longer satisfying in itself, partly because it's become so undifferentiated from the all other individualized, mobilized, neoliberal life forms. Artists will either have to make do with exploiting the merely superficial differences that designate their own practices within a generic (and ever more captured and productive) availability to abstraction shared by every metropolitan self-employee, or they will invent new and specific ways of interrupting themselves. At a certain point, it just seems boring not to pursue the latter option on some level, not to appropriate and make use of our own special crisis as a kind of art.

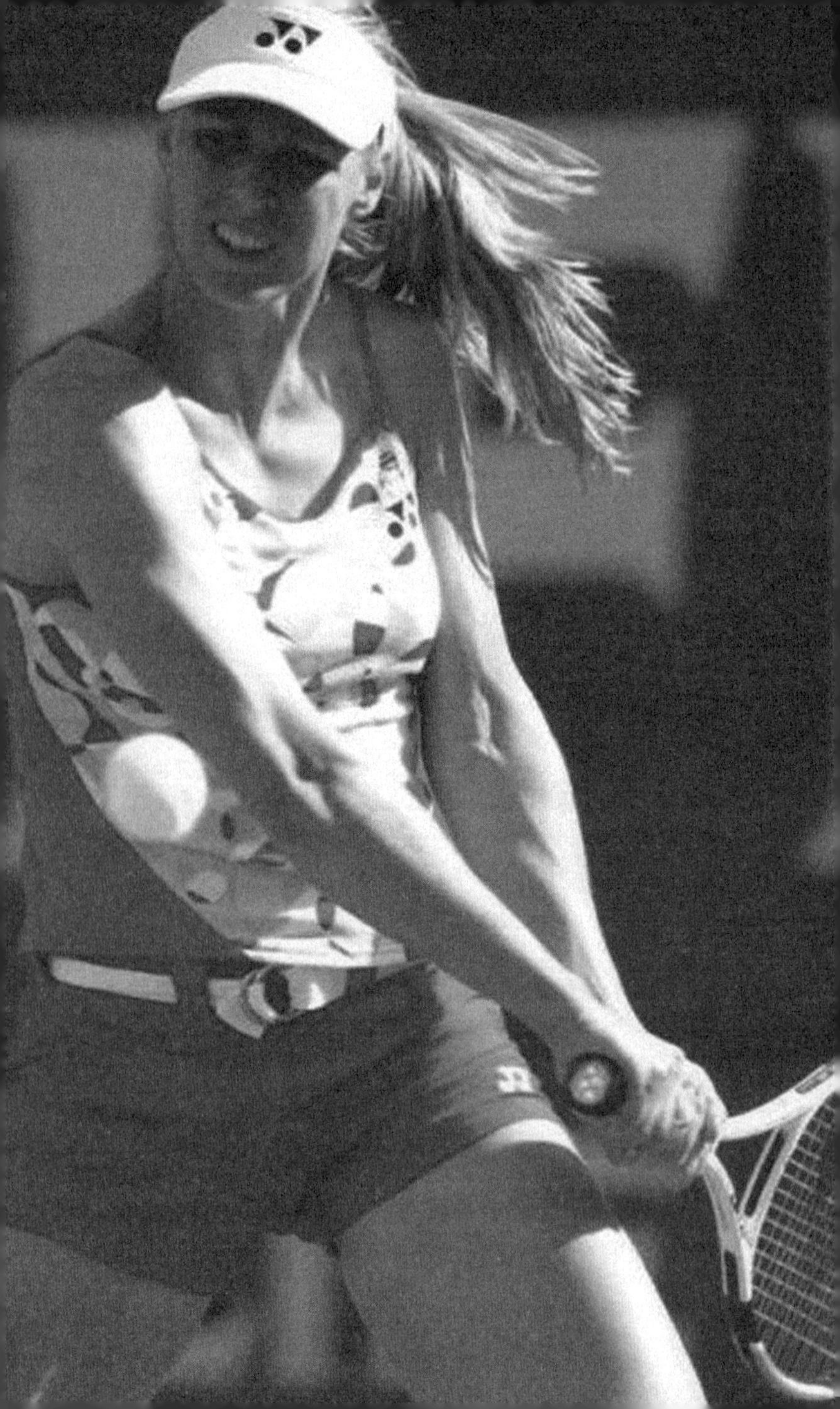

191

Stop Painting Painting*

> Gaps are my starting point. My impotence is my origin.
> —Paul Valéry, *Monsieur Teste*

Some say Michael Krebber doesn't translate to New York, but
a painter who "prefers not to" isn't exactly going to meet the
demands of a city powered by big dumb painting head on. All
the paint in Krebber's last two shows here couldn't fill one small
canvas by Dana Schutz or John Currin. With "Flaggs (Against
Nature)" and, only six months later, "Here it is: The Painting
Machine" (both at Greene Naftali in 2003), Krebber demonstrated here and here again that the proof is not in the paint job,
but in the idea that puts it at a fresh distance. Just as Paul Valéry
called the poem "a prolonged hesitation between sound and
sense," Krebber's practice could be described as an ongoing
hesitation between repetition and interruption (or between
having an idea and having no idea). It's never been a question
of how well or hard he labors on a canvas, a show, or a style;
it's all in the ways he uses painting as a strategy for extricating
himself from the wrong kind of work—both the bad works
that surround him and the bad works he, like anyone, is capable
of—or from the demands of work, period. Krebber keeps
finding ways of reminding us that it's not only that artists produce
paintings, but that paintings *produce* artists (and viewers, re-
viewers, dealers, collectors), and this is the productive relation
that must sometimes be interrupted if we too are to have a
hand in our own making.

Whatever Krebber's intentions, his two New York shows and
the mere half year between them were like the unfolding of a

* Originally published in *Artforum*, October 2005.

well-timed joke: the deadpan setup, the awkward pause, and then the offhand punch line. First he came up very short with a series of repeating, readymade blankets and bed sheets on stretchers—and not a single drop of paint. And then—as if apologizing for the dry spell and promising to really come through next time for New York—he returned to the scene of the crime with still more bed sheets, this time barely touched with a few restrained dabs of acrylic. Just before the second opening, Krebber seemed to shoot himself in the foot by draping every canvas with the exhibition's poster invitations, spoiling any easy view or easy sell of his new "paintings." It was an ambiguous move: at once an expression of shame or self-defense (covering his face) and brazen self-promotion (getting in your face). Also, he didn't hang the show; he leaned his work around the room so we almost tripped over it as we came in looking for the products of the "painting machine" advertised on the poster.

Like other machines, Krebber's repeats and sometimes breaks down. The painting machine doesn't always move forward; sometimes it only turns around on itself like one of Duchamp's hypnotically static "Rotoreliefs." And by announcing and exhibiting the machine as such, rather than just the paintings it produces, Krebber relocated painting from the place where New York likes to find it (on the canvas, on the wall, in the collection) in order to make it wander from place to place (wall to floor, canvas to poster, blanket to bed sheet), and to show how this non-progressive movement is what makes the possibility of painting return—differently now—without exactly seeming to arrive. Sometimes the machine stops suddenly, like one of Krebber's dandyish brushstrokes that travels across a blank surface for a moment, and then abruptly quits. But you can't begin again unless you stop. Krebber sets impossible standards for himself. He starts against the wall or in a deep hole of aesthetic and historical debt. Known for his vampiric appropriations of other painters (Sigmar Polke's experiments with readymade surfaces, Georg Baselitz's inverted figures, etc.), Krebber makes the condition of being stuck a key operating principle. He is a "user"—primarily of everything that freezes and stops him. Following in the footsteps of so many painter-kings, any Cologne artist is always already made and positioned before even picking up a brush. There is no escape from the influence of a mentor like Markus Lüpertz or an ex-boss like Martin Kippenberger, and Krebber has famously declared his own lack of ideas, since anything good he might think of has already been thought before (his idea is not to have an idea). So he has devised two escape routes: First, don't escape. And if you do, turn yourself in. Because it's not so much by banging your head against a Polke that you're going to open up some new territory you can call your own; it's by refusing your own style in advance. Krebber has always been careful to work against himself whenever something too recognizably Krebber begins to take over. A consummate fan and disciple, his vampirism is of an entirely different nature than the appropriations and references by which most artists today position themselves and manufacture their own legible signatures. Krebber's approach underlines the fact that artists are readymades, too, and that readymades can be unmade.

As Krebber's painting machine stops and starts and displaces itself again, it exhibits its own materials as pure means, endlessly separating them from their normal ends. The canvas, the stretcher bars, the wall, the floor, the title, the exhibition invitation, the archival photograph, signature gestures of other painters, the social world that painting serves, etc., are all possible materials—ways into and out of painting. We could say that Krebber is less a painter than a strategist, and that his strategy is to repeat and to stop painting in order to go to work on the wider system that makes painting what it is today, what it was yesterday, and what it might be or stop being tomorrow. Now more than ever, we need a strategy if we want art to become possible again.

But to call Krebber a strategist is not to say that he's jockeying for a decisive, final position either for or against the medium of painting, for or against bourgeois conventions. (If he ever had a master plan, he would surely discard it immediately.) An anti-bourgeois bourgeois, as Carter Ratcliff has noted, the dandy is defined precisely by how he empties out his own position. Rather than wasting his time and energy fighting over property or his own proper place, he gladly wastes them by undermining himself. The dandy makes himself static and detached, and his endless de-centering of his own identity is the means by which he makes the world around him start to lose its grip. In the same sense that the classic proletarian strike suspends exploitative relations of production, the dandy interrupts the relations that position him as a subject: He wages a subjective or human strike. Like other strikes, this one interrupts a rhythm and opens up a gap. In this gap—in the very moment of interruption— one's own subjectivity becomes momentarily available again.

If, as he did in New York, Krebber sometimes seems to make painting go on strike, it's by no means a total work stoppage followed by total change. Krebber never stops stopping, always repeats it. His is a provisional suspension of productive norms with no other goal in mind than itself. It is a way of unlinking painting from the paint job (and, if we were to extend the analogy, resistance from official politics). It is an art of suspension and—as with repetition—a means of distancing oneself from any ideology of progress, whether bourgeois or radical. In Krebber's case, the important thing is to disconnect materials from functions, means from ends, in order to reconnect painting to its own potential, but differently now—for a moment at least. And this moment will have to be repeated.

It is probably less interesting to interpret the meaning of a ready-made, checkered bed sheet, or one depicting a moonlit, galloping horse, than to realize that this throwaway image—in its very meaninglessness—is here being reclaimed as pure means. In other words, such a gesture doesn't care to fulfill any particular end to succeed in accomplishing some ultimate significance or work. Filling the space as it does, it exhibits the "place" of painting, and returns this place to its own possibility. When Krebber hangs the readymade horse upside down, we might note that he repeats Baselitz, for example, but the important thing is that this repetition renews the possibility of Baselitz in the present moment, and thus also that of Krebber, stuck as he is. Such an "emptying appropriation" not only captures and claims the stolen gesture or image, it makes it return with a difference. Repetition, as Giorgio Agamben has said regarding both messianic history and cinematic montage, is a strategy of renewing the possibility of what was ("that which is impossible by definition, the past"), of disassociating an identity from its proper place in order to produce a transformation. Sometimes, the only way to change is by doing the same thing over and over again. Looking at a Krebber for the first time—one of those small, washy, "unfinished too soon" canvases—you get the feeling that there is maybe no Krebber behind it. There's not a whole lot to work with. For New Yorkers, Krebber is first of all something overheard, a rumor—maybe too good to be true. He's a story told by others (Germans, mostly) to each other. The story has no point and no end. It might begin with Krebber eating a beer glass at another painter's opening in order not to say something about it, or with him suddenly instructing his students never to paint again. Krebber is one of those artists they call an "artist's artist," and when you ask around, his story becomes impossible to extricate from those of the close contemporaries who are somehow or other implicated in his myth (Cosima von Bonin, Josephine Pryde, Albert Oehlen, Jutta Koether, Merlin Carpenter, Charline von Heyl, etc.). When pressed, friends and insiders begrudgingly supply half-answers ("It's a Cologne thing."), as if unwilling or unable to flesh him out in a decisive way. There are moments and contexts, certain jokes, things that are said to be "Krebberesque," the precise weight and thickness of a "legendary" opening night in someone else's memory. Krebber is like a club you can't get into, until you realize the club was built for you and you only, and maybe you are in it now, trying to describe the view to somebody back in Cologne.

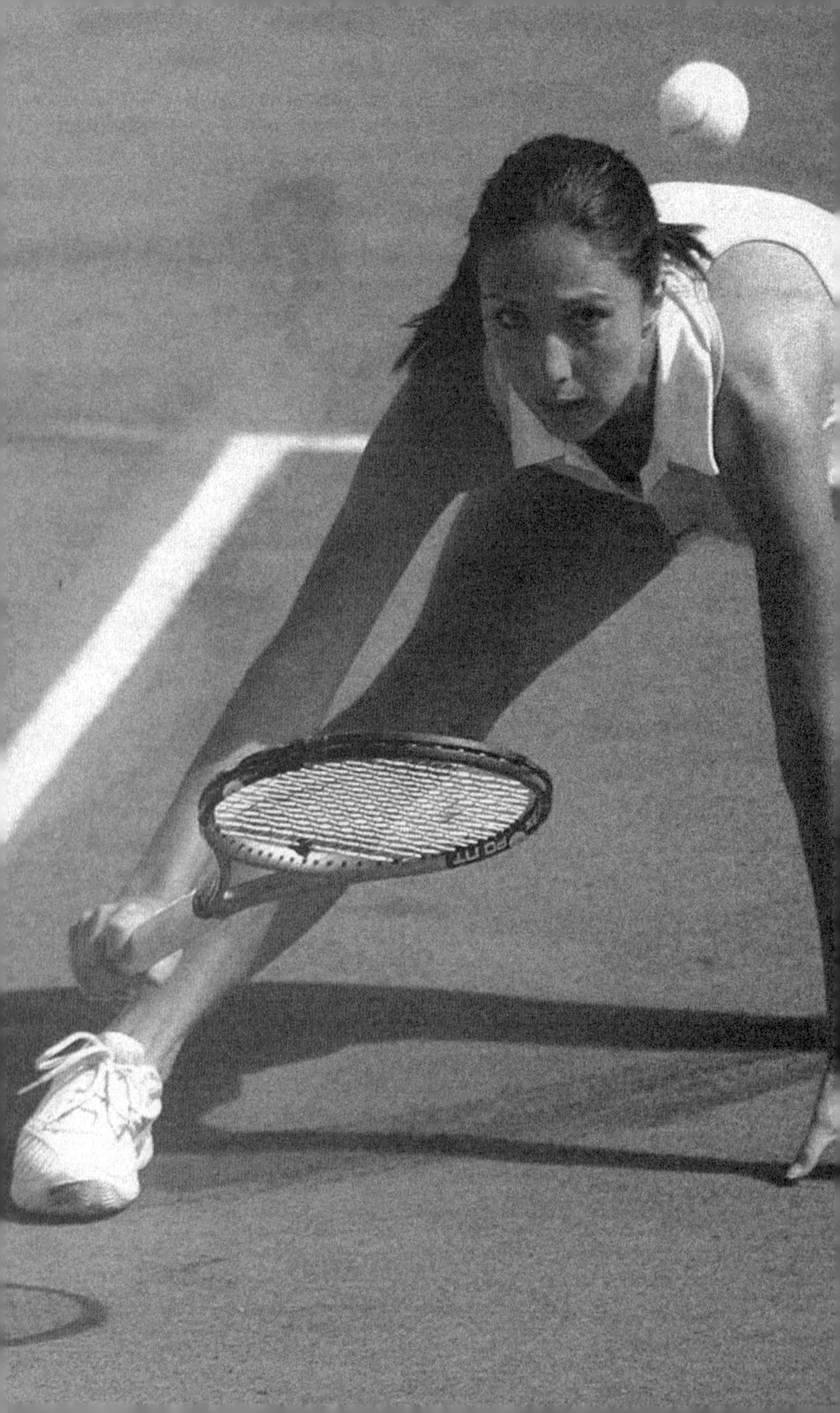

theanyspacewhatever*

Maybe we've finally given up on the "old realism of places," as Gilles Deleuze put it. In his book *Cinema 1: The Movement-Image* (1983), he used the term *éspace quelconque*—"whatever-space," or "any-space-whatever"—to describe the cinematic image of undone space that, however shattered or blurred it may be, is also a space of pure potential. It could be a wasted urban void or a shaky zoom into the luminous screen of a Macintosh. It is a postwar feeling of lost coordinates, a certain anonymous emptiness. It is a space that could be "extracted" from the familiar state of things embodied in a place like the Guggenheim Museum in New York, leaving us even more floating and detached than before in the great rotunda. It is a space both ruined and fresh.

The discourse that supports the work of the ten artists included in "theanyspacewhatever" exhibition—Angela Bulloch, Maurizio Cattelan, Liam Gillick, Dominique Gonzalez-Foerster, Douglas Gordon, Carsten Höller, Pierre Huyghe, Jorge Pardo, Philippe Parreno, and Rirkrit Tiravanija, artists who were routinely grouped together in exhibitions in Europe throughout the 1990s, but who had never before been collectively presented in an American museum—links their practices to notions of promiscuous collaboration, conviviality, Relational Aesthetics, open-endedness, and the exhibition as medium. While such claims are typically inflected with a radical if not utopian promise that sounds even less credible today than it did ten years ago, it should be said that, in their own statements, the artists themselves have been more ambivalent about the emancipatory possibilities of contemporary creative networks and exhibitions

* Originally published in *Artforum*, March 2009.

that emulate pubs, kitchens, laboratories, island holidays, or open-plan offices rather than product showrooms. Still, a long decade of effort by the artists and curators who populate this exhibition and its catalogue went into producing the feeling of a legitimate, international, hyperactive, jet-set avant-garde for these times—one that put the dream of the self-organized community back at the center of its project. It spread every-where, seeped into institutions (from which it sometimes seemed to lose any distinction), and spiraled calmly down the drain of the Guggenheim. At the bottom, Cattelan's Pinocchio floated facedown in a pool of water (*Daddy Daddy*, 2008), a Disney-fied version of a hard-core Neorealist ending to this collective story—a false ending that greets you upon entering the show.

It's usually at the very moment when an idea like "community" is on the verge of extinction that it becomes so obsessively evoked, even fetishized, in the art world. Echoing historical models such as Fluxus, but more sedately, and responding to contemporary influences such as Institutional Critique, but with a softer and more with-it attitude, the artistic strategies championed by curators such as Nicolas Bourriaud, Hans Ulrich Obrist, and Maria Lind de-emphasize the finished product in favor of discursive situations, whether these be Plexiglas "dis-cussion platforms," shared meals, semi-fictional texts, par-ticipatory "scenarios," or films based on conversations. Such scenarization and programming of social intercourse within art projects and institutions has brought frequent accusations of formalism, if not cynicism, against certain of these artists (see *October* 110 [2004]). And it's true that in the whateverworld, discourse goes hand in hand with design and décor. In the Guggenheim, for example, one encountered Gillick's floating powder-coated steel texts (information here, a continuation, etc.), which attempted to have some Broodthaersian fun with the fact that the museum is also a system of signs and commands (*theanyspacewhatever signage system*, 2008). Gordon contributed stick-on fragments of banal verbiage (nothing will ever be the same) around the rotunda, viral advertising style (*prettym ucheverywordwritten,spoken,heard,overheardfrom* 1989…, 2006/ 2008). Both of these preserved a distinctly 1990s look, with all-lowercase lettering drifted in a lot of empty white. Parreno's cartoonish, white-on-white illuminated marquee over the museum's entrance, although blank, posited spectacle—paradoxically, and in a typically "relational" move—as a site of potential communication (*Marquee, Guggenheim, NY*, 2008). Blanking out some free space in the heart of the entertainment complex can be a disruptive gesture, or it can be another way of saying that whateverspace is no longer a place to announce anything.

The show achieved a certain "badness," and a certain self-consciousness around the possibility of a flop (especially following the opening salvo of Parreno's marquee), which defused the old question of whether the work was utopian or complicit, of whether open works and promiscuous collaboration are part of the solution or part of the problem today. At the Guggenheim, the liberal-democratic call for free speech, or the relational proposal of open conversation *as art*, was answered by the glaring silence of not-great design, or replaced by free-floating words that articulated no other possibility beyond the neutrality of metropolitan spectatorship—passively distracted, anonymously addressed, mildly amused, often bored. Free because unassigned to any particular subject, these whateverwords were also devoid of any recipe for action, collective or otherwise. On the ground floor were racks dispensing free copies of the *Wrong Times*, a happily low-budget newspaper documenting the history of the Wrong Gallery (founded in 2002 by Cattelan, Massimiliano

Gioni, and Ali Subotnik) and the many collaborations and conversations that took place under its semi-fictional auspices. After the Wrong Gallery agreed to curate the Berlin Biennial in 2006, decisively dropping any pretense of autonomy from institutional power, *wrong* seemed to take on another meaning. But *bad*, *wrong*, and *empty* may also hide strategies for evading critical death traps and professional sclerosis. They became ways of undoing the Guggenheim moment and the pressures of containment here, of sidestepping achievement. Anyway, being right is a terrible way to end up, in a museum.

Besides discourse, functional seating is another trope common to many of these artists' projects, and in "theanyspacewhatever" bodies could park themselves on Gillick's handsome S-shaped benches (*Audioguide Bench, Guggenheim, NY*, 2008), on a beanbag chair in Gordon and Tiravanija's graffiti-decorated video lounge (*Cinéma Liberté/Bar Lounge*, 1996/2008), or on pillows in the carpeted area where Tiravanija's two-hour-long 2008 documentary *Chew the Fat* was playing. (Höller's bed, fitted with black silk sheets and presented within a hotel-room-like installation, presented another place to kick back, but this was available by reservation only, for paying overnight guests [*Revolving Hotel Room*, 2008].) If seating is how a socially minded artwork installs the humans who are meant to complete it— as in Tiravanija's reconstitution of his East Village apartment as a public hangout inside the Kölnischer Kunstverein in 1996— extra chairs here were stand-ins for a micro-utopian possibility that was largely banished from "theanyspacewhatever." Sitting on a beanbag in an installation in a biennial may have been a novel experience for art viewers in the 1990s, but in New York in 2009, after paying fifteen dollars at the door, one couldn't help but count the whateverminutes ticking by, wondering what had become of sociability in the city. An open seat, like a blank marquee, is a vacancy as much as an invitation, and anyway, the downward pull of the ramp was stronger. An event programmer and an urban planner lurk behind every relational artist, and these practitioners' proposals to re-appropriate common space were always elaborated in a strict and conscious relation to the fact of functionalized, policed space. It was never either/or. It was always brief glimpses of the one within the other.

At times, one had the feeling that this show had been copied and pasted, dragged and dropped, into the museum. There was a disconcerting ease, an almost dialed-in feeling, and the impression that a laptop screen was always hovering between artist and viewer. A lot of the art was screen-like, too—for example, Bulloch's illuminated starscape installed on the ceiling high above, which was less a trompe l'oeil sky than a cathedral-scale screen saver (*Firmamental Night Sky: Oculus.12*, 2008). Pardo contributed an installation of intricately laser-cut partitions along one length of the ramp, a topology of veneers that viewers had to navigate on their way down (*Sculpture Ink*, 2008). Gonzalez-Foerster used a blank white scrim to screen off a section of the rotunda, with nothing behind it except the piped-in sound of trickling water, affording the viewer a brief walk through the ambience of a New Age relaxation tape (*Promenade*, 2007). Some areas of the exhibition were left yawningly empty of art or of anything save a snippet of Gordon's vinyl dialogue. The holes that were designed into the show, giving it a loose, work-in-progress feel, were either spaces of Deleuzian pure potential or far-off echoes of Michael Asher's empty galleries, or maybe just moments of empty-handedness, and as retinal as anything that might show up on a screen.

Chew the Fat, which appeared on multiple screens, presented an extended, serial group portrait of the participating artists (joined by non-participants such as Elizabeth Peyton and Andrea Zittel). The video dares to expose certain behind-the-scenes truths about this creative milieu: the physical bodies, the way they talk, where they reside, how they treat their employees, what they eat—the lives of the artists. It is a highly demystifying maneuver, and a generous one. Some sequences are edited to reveal what is common to everyone here—for instance, a certain hunched-over attachment to titanium PowerBooks (the video could work as an ad for Apple). The artists also share the general condition of no longer emerging, and we see how it looks to inhabit a forty-something body in a polo shirt, in the comfort-able environs of one's business-hippie lifestyle, with so many projects in progress on the screen. They talk of buying real estate, sometimes even calling their homes artworks. There are brief, road-movie-like moments as artists shuttle from home to studio. Pardo appears with a big glass of red wine and even cooks a whole pig on camera. Gillick whistles along to the Clash in his sleek home office while working on the cover of an upcoming book. Gonzalez-Foerster strolls alongside a Parisian canal, com-menting that these days, she prefers to be alone. What *Chew the Fat* reveals is the fact of individuals: how they happen and how they, too, are the product of today's vanguard practices (and discourses). Here, Tiravanija risks exposing the not-always joyful anonymity that surrounds each artist, their common separation. Noticeably absent from *Chew the Fat* is Cattelan: Never appearing on camera, he is evoked by the other artists via anecdotes. He manages to exist almost purely *as* discourse, and was thus the exhibition's only escape artist.

"Theanyspacewhatever" also included programmed perfor-mances and film screenings in the Guggenheim's theater, as well as some off-site works and discussions. In the rotunda, Huyghe staged a work called *Opening* (2008), in which viewers wandered the darkened museum with strap-on headlamps, an event that took place three times over the course of the show. Huyghe is the artist who, in 1995, founded the Association of Freed Times, conjuring up Situationist calls to "never work." This gesture of appropriating free time for collective use was ambiguous insofar as it was wedded to a contradictory decision to legally register AFT with the local police. "Theanyspacewhatever" started there, on the clock and on the record, and then tried to unwork its way out again.

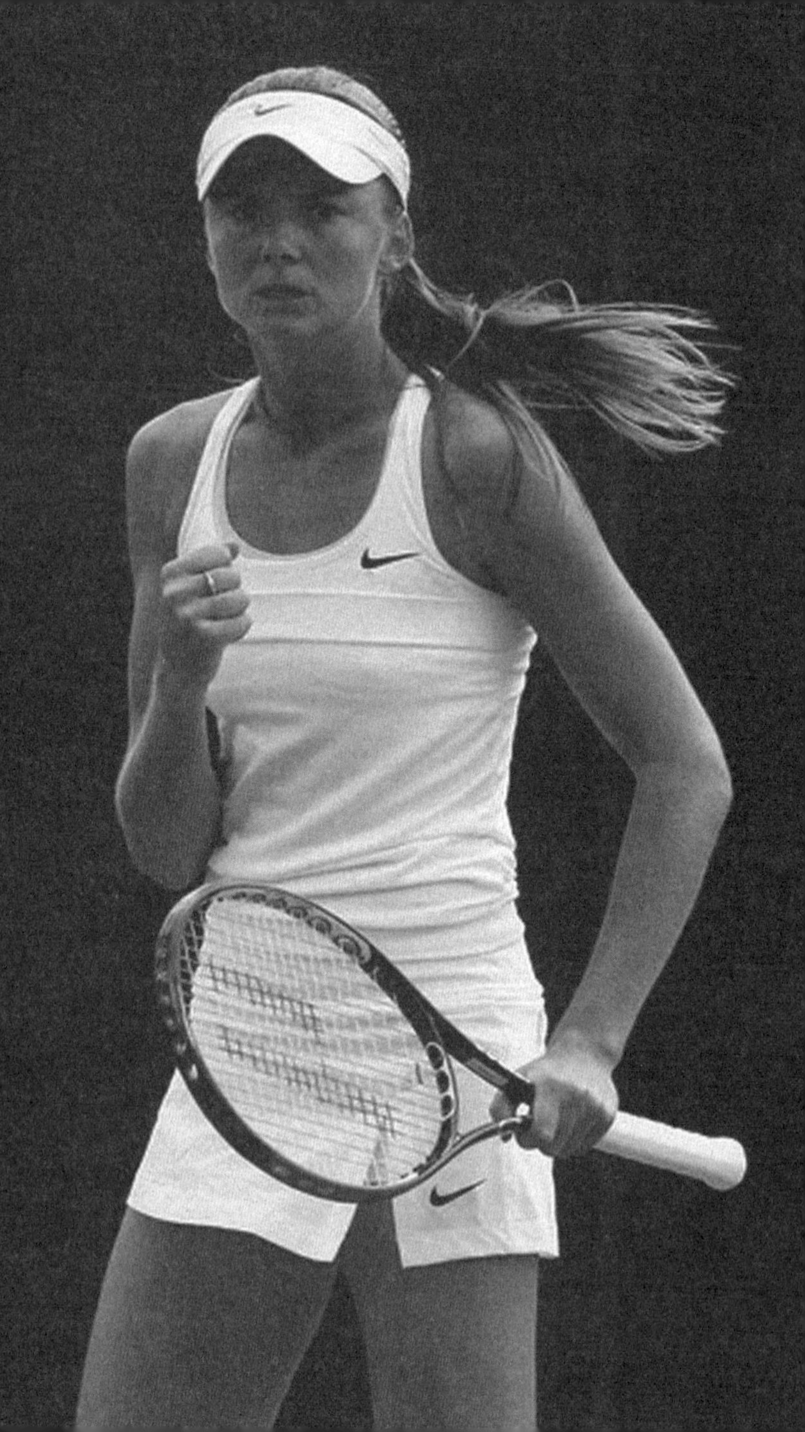

TOP 10 (2007)*

1. "Décor: A Conquest," Marcel Broodthaers, 1975/2007
Seminal, groundbreaking, and important are words typically
used to describe this two-room artwork by Belgian ex-poet
Broodthaers, which was presented for the first time in New
York this past summer at Michael Werner Gallery. Dust off the
nineteenth-century cannons and stuffed python, unpack the
twentieth-century pistols and patio furniture, and see what Mike
Kelley was talking about in 1995, when he called Broodthaers's
approach "hokey and obvious," yet admirable in its way of being
so "sincere and insincere at the same time." The work is like a
movie set propped with readymade stand-ins for Europe's modern
colonial history. Decades before "installation art" became a
household term, "Décor"—an early, more playful instance of
Institutional Critique—went quaintly and deviously to war.
The uptown display coincided with a downtown screening, organized by White Columns, of the artist's strange short films
at Anthology Film Archives.

2. *Grindhouse*
Written, produced, and directed by Robert Rodriguez and
Quentin Tarantino, this B-movie double feature is interrupted by
trailers for other fictional productions, gaps representing missing
reels, and fake print damage. The first part, Rodriguez's *Planet
Terror*, is a schlock zombie apocalypse. The second is Tarantino's
excellent hot-rod picture, *Death Proof*, a narrative that is also
split in two—like a highway, the A and B sides of a record, or
a brain. Two ensembles of actresses (including Rosario Dawson,
Vanessa Ferlito, and the stuntwoman Zoë Bell, playing herself) eat up the screen as the film veers between Rohmeresque

---

* Originally published in *Artforum*, December 2007.

conversation and bursts of bodily violence, cut to upbeat songs like "Hold Tight" by Dave Dee, Dozy, Beaky, Mick & Tich.

3. "Relax It's Only a Bad Cosima von Bonin Show"
The catalogue accompanying Merlin Carpenter's exhibition at Galerie Bleich-Rossi in Vienna is one of the most anarchically devised artists' books in print. Portraits of the artist posing with blank canvases in a hellish art-supply store, slick ads for Mercedes-Benz bicycles (which have appeared as readymades in other Carpenter shows), painters' easels and paintings of easels, and texts by Carpenter and his sister appear in separate, brochure-like sections with brutally mismatched formats, barely bound by a flimsy white thread. Designed by Non-Format, the book prefers not to come together around its author.

4. I.U.D.
Minimal, pounding, contagious noise-music made by two women—Lizzi Bougatsos (of Gang Gang Dance) and Sadie Laska—on two drum kits and two microphones. *Dead Womb*, seven inches of vinyl, was released in September on the Social Registry label, and was celebrated with shows at Brooklyn venues Studio B and Glasslands.

5. *Ode to the Man Who Kneels*
Following his *End of Reality* (2006), a play constructed around a series of monologues and brawls, Richard Maxwell's new musical is a Western set in a town called Grid, which deals out strange, stripped-down violence and "basic," even stranger language and songs. Characters are killed, but they don't stop singing. *Ode* was presented at the Performing Garage in early November with a cast including Jim Fletcher, Anna Kohler, Emily Cass McDonnell, Greg Mehrten, and Brian Mendes, and with Mike Iveson on piano and Maxwell on guitar.

6. *Freelance Stenographer*
A sort of anti-happening by Seth Price and Kelley Walker was produced on-site at the Kitchen on April 2. It began with a projected video comprising footage of a semi-fictional, New York dance-pop group named the Economist (Cory Arcangel, Emily Sundblad, and Stefan Tcherepnin) at work in the studio, video material from the Kitchen's own performance archive (a restaged Oskar Schlemmer performance), an appropriated documentary in progress about the interactive cyber-community Second Life, shots of New York skylines, and rudimentary digital effects—and was followed by a Q&A with the artists. Everything was recorded in real time by a professional stenographer whose transcription was photocopied and distributed as an instant document of its own making. The "event" was a self-recording machine instantly filed away in the no time it took to translate live into archive.

7. *Dot Dot Dot,* issue 14 ("S as in SStenographer"), summer 2007
This issue of Dot Dot Dot, a journal published by Dexter Sinister, appropriates a rejected cover design for Cabinet magazine. Inside is an interview with former Revolver books publisher Christoph Keller, who discusses dilettantism, distillation, and his current farm life while serving homemade schnapps to the editors from bottles of his own design. Other highlights deal with modern histories of book design, Richard Hamilton's *Collected Words*, and the "aesthetics of distribution."

8. Evas Arche und der Feminist
During their Sunday-night gatherings at Passerby in New York, hosts Pati Hertling, an art-restitution lawyer, and her collaborator, artist Marlous Borm, serve homemade soup and bottled beer while their artist friends eat, exhibit, drink, and perform.

For Sunday #8, which was given over to artist Kerstin Brätsch, they covered the exhibition "New York Is Dead" with sheets of black protective plastic before opening Evas's doors to a musical act by Ronnie Bass, Jeremy Eilers, and Nic Xedro; Allison Katz and Georgia Sagri (who danced with Brätsch); and DJ Antek Walczak.

9. "77 Testicular Imprints"
To make the works in his exhibition at Roth Gallery in New York, Nicolás Guagnini used oil paint and his own balls for a brush, marking and citing a series of archival documents (including an early, typewritten Dan Graham poem and personal stationery recovered from Hitler's bunker)—a brute, faux-macho gesture of signing and appropriation, but also a critical operation undermining the notions of property, inclusion, and value. The "imprints" are smart and stupid like Broodthaers's recurring, museological eagles, and as elegant in their conception—until you start to notice the pubic hairs stuck in the paint.

10. *The Artwork Caught by the Tail: Francis Picabia and Dada in Paris* (MIT Press)
George Baker's book is the first in English dealing specifically with Picabia's Dada work in Paris, and is a serious rethinking of the readymade (the other, Picabian one) based on a study of the artist's singularly multifarious practice. Once, before an audience of friends, Picabia broke open his alarm clock and used its parts as paintbrushes. He also cut a hole in a sheet of paper and called it *Jeune Fille*. Baker's book has a shiny golden cover with a reproduction of Picabia's *Natures Mortes* (1920)—a "portrait" consisting of a crucified, stuffed monkey, surrounded by the names of famous Impressionists.

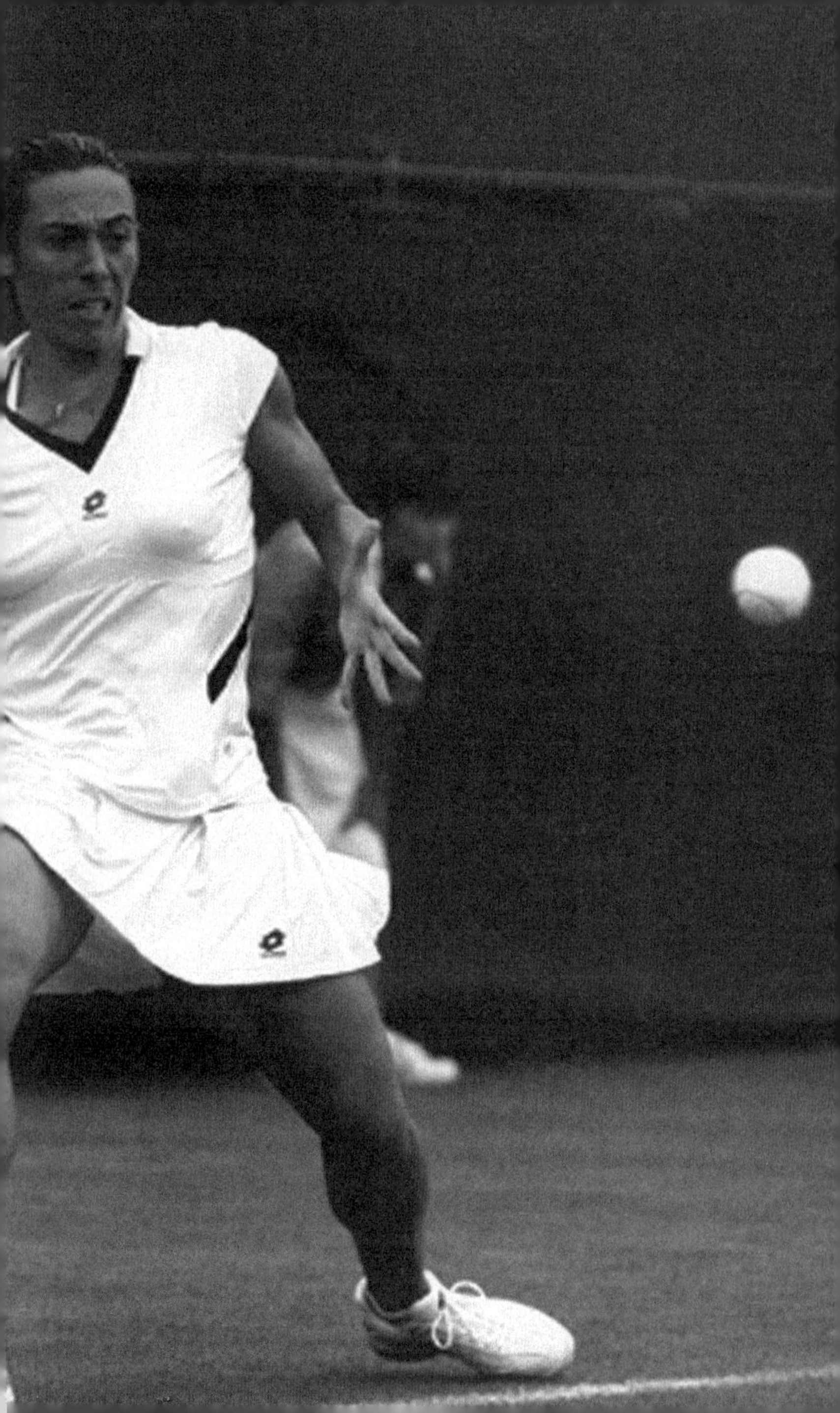

Translator's Introduction*

> The term "young" is required for advertising purposes. And the kids,
> conscious of the beefsteak they're being offered, produce nothing
> but merchandise on demand.
> —Michèle Bernstein, *Potlatch* 15

An earlier, rougher translation of Michèle Bernstein's *All The King's Horses* (*Tous les chevaux du roi*) was undertaken in 2003–04, and distributed one chapter at a time as a series of pamphlets at Reena Spaulings Fine Art, a gallery on Manhattan's Lower East Side. This serialized version of Bernstein's first novel doubled as a sort of gallery program, including in each chapter's layout minimal documentation of recent events at Reena Spaulings, as well as listings of upcoming shows and performances, some real and some fictional. The translation was done in a hasty and slapdash fashion, usually the night before an opening, with some sections of the text interrupted by JPEGs of contemporary artworks and the bodies that gathered around them at Spaulings, which at the time was known only by its street address, 371 Grand. *Tous les chevaux du roi* was still out of print in France. My source text was a photocopy of a photocopy of the original 1960, Buchet/Chastel edition.

One reason for distributing Bernstein's book in this way was to create a line in time that would cross through the various, fleeting exhibitions at the gallery, some of which were installed and de-installed in a single afternoon, and in a highly improvised manner. The gradual progression of Bernstein's chapters over the course of a year produced a narrative that ran alongside that of the gallery, which was also a sort of fiction, operated by several people under a made-up name, without a business plan

---

*   Originally published as the introduction to the author's translation of *All the King's Horses*, by Michèle Bernstein, Semiotext(e), New York and Los Angeles, 2008.

or any prior experience in dealing art. This second or supplementary narrative—Bernstein's—was intentional self-criticism, opening as it does with a boring art opening, somewhere on the Left Bank in the late 1950s. It wasn't hard to imagine the sort of work on view there: derivative, late Surrealist abstractions, a living-dead avant-garde décor, which was completely useless to the novel's young protagonists. In 2003, New York's contemporary art world—firmly installed in a renovated, bunker-like Chelsea, and experiencing a hedge fund-driven boom unseen since the 1980s, but even more extreme—seemed similarly devoid of possibilities. Art was functioning perfectly, but it was bogged down in itself and getting bored. It was clear that no new gallery could change the situation, but a fictional gallerist following in the stiletto-heeled tracks of Mary Boone, for example, performing an obviously poor imitation of an iconic New York power dealer, seemed to offer the possibility of opening up a slightly more unpredictable space of activity, or at least some breathing room for those involved. The dealer Reena Spaulings stepped right out of Bernstein's first paragraph: "The gallerist was talking about her shoes, so that an important visitor would understand she was already distancing herself from the failure she felt coming." We invented some artists too. There was a deliberate piling up of fictions in one location, in a year that also marked the release of Bernadette Corporation's collectively authored novel, *Reena Spaulings* (Semiotext(e), 2004).

The appearance of the novel *Reena Spaulings* further confused the identity and meaning of the gallery, which had meanwhile served as a meeting and writing place for the book's many authors, and which now shared its name. Partly under the influence of Bernstein, Bernadette Corporation was interested in re-appropriating an exhausted form, the novel, in order to say something insincere about New York after 9/11. A patriotic ghost of the city had been installed by citizens and police alike, the war was definitely on, and anything antagonistic to the cause was branded as terrorist. What we needed most desperately was fiction, and Bernstein's post-existentialist, anything but sincere youth novel was attractive mainly in its knowing use of popular, banal literary (and cinematic) formulas as a means of rewriting and re-inhabiting the city itself.

We had heard that Bernstein quickly disowned her own novels as minor commercial ventures, as not serious (in comparison to her husband Guy Debord's theoretical texts, for example), but this was exactly what interested us: writing under the sign of commerce, but also disowned writing. What can we make of a text that insists on both its own commercialism and its refusal of authorship? And what could we do now with the idea of a sort of post-literature, or posed literature, in a city that felt increasingly post-urban, and whose faux-bohemian art world was constantly, miraculously outlasting its own death? In addition to the Bernstein novel, other models for *Reena Spaulings* included *Gossip Girl*, a brand of sexed-up corporate literature popular among teenagers in 2002, which was also set in New York; and *Premiers matériaux pour une Théorie de la Jeune-Fille* (Editions Mille et une nuits, 2001), a "trash theoretical" tract authored by the militant collective Tiqqun, in France, which appropriated the jargon of contemporary youth and women's magazines in order to critique the increasingly biopolitical aspects of lifestyle consumption. The *jeune-fille* was the new face of control in this terrorized, cleaned-up, *Sex and the City* city, and this pretty face was our own.

Another reason for picking up *Tous les chevaux du roi* in 2003 was its ambiguous quasi-feminism, especially when read in relation to the male-dominated writings of the Situationist International. There was something awkward and problematic about Bernstein's voice, or her style of fabulation, which was difficult to reconcile with the mythic, and by now respectably academic domain of S.I. theory. Indeed, in all the many recent books on Debord and his legacy, Bernstein's fiction has been efficiently disappeared into the footnotes. What seemed unsettling and so full of potential for us, especially in the context of a semi-wild, boyish contemporary art world, was the false sincerity of the novel's Françoise Saganesque narration, which retold a season among the free-living S.I. as if it were a breezy but jaded romance for teenage girls. The names have all been changed, but it's clear that Bernstein, Debord, Asger Jorn, and others are being rewritten as flimsy parodies of themselves. There's even a drunken moment in the novel where the characters address their own fictional status: "We're all characters in a novel, haven't you noticed? You and I speak in dry little sentences. There's even something unfinished about us." What seemed useful here was the strategic return of fiction as a way of opening up another sort of distance toward what was being lived by Bernstein and the S.I., and theorized in serious books signed Debord. By rewriting the Situationist saga as a young woman's problem, as a sort of *Gossip Girl* paperback or knock-off *Bonjour Tristesse* (whose author Debord & Co. insulted in the pages of their review *Potlatch*), replete with arch social observations, flirtations, manipulations, and heartbreaks, Bernstein momentarily re-appropriates a history and an experience that are typically represented in equally posed, yet decidedly masculine and heroic modes. Her novels may indeed have been cynically commercial jobs, but it doesn't seem unlikely that they also served a therapeutic purpose for their writer, as a way of making sense of her position in relation to Debord and others at the time. Roger Vadim's super trendy movie adaptation of Choderlos de Laclos'

1782 novel, *Les Liaisons dangereuses*, starring Jeanne Moreau, had just been released in France, and by restaging the difficult, libidinal side of the Situationist experiment in that film's modishly libertine terms, Bernstein becomes both star and spectator of her own story. As a kind of performance, fiction is a means of putting oneself and one's problems at a distance, of getting rid of oneself.

Whatever Bernstein's intentions were at the time, it is possible to read her novel as both a glamorization and critique of the very milieu she was participating in, of her whole world. A *dérive* rewritten as Pop fiction is not exactly the same *dérive*. And with *All the King's Horses* and her other novel, *La Nuit*, the *détournement* of trendy literary genres is also and at the same time an ironic *détournement* of the S.I. itself by Bernstein, who, we remember, is already abandoning her role as author of these novels. We like these distancing effects, and the possibilities of dis-identification that flourish as soon as we begin to operate under the sign of fiction.

This novel may not be a great, or even a good book. All it ever wanted was to escape its young author, and maybe to make a little money. It is a hack job, and knowingly derivative, but interesting for that. Bernstein also earned money writing horoscopes for horses in the racing columns, and sometimes by reviewing contemporary fiction. There was no way a writer like that could maintain the pose of the next Françoise Sagan for long; it would be indecent (as her character Geneviève might say), and probably impossible next to Debord (or Gilles).

If, following the Lettrist International, the S.I. was the first postwar effort to politicize youth culture in Europe, it was also capable of performing the very process it despised: packaging and marketing a lifestyle product for young consumers. Around this seeming contradiction, countless present and future games can still be elaborated. Following a general disenchantment with official, party Communism, unforeseen communisms can still be found hiding—travestied and momentarily neutralized—in used-up forms such as the novel, or even right here in the mirror, in the self-controlled and controlling image of the *jeune-fille*. She is our very condition. It's only a question of how we use her.

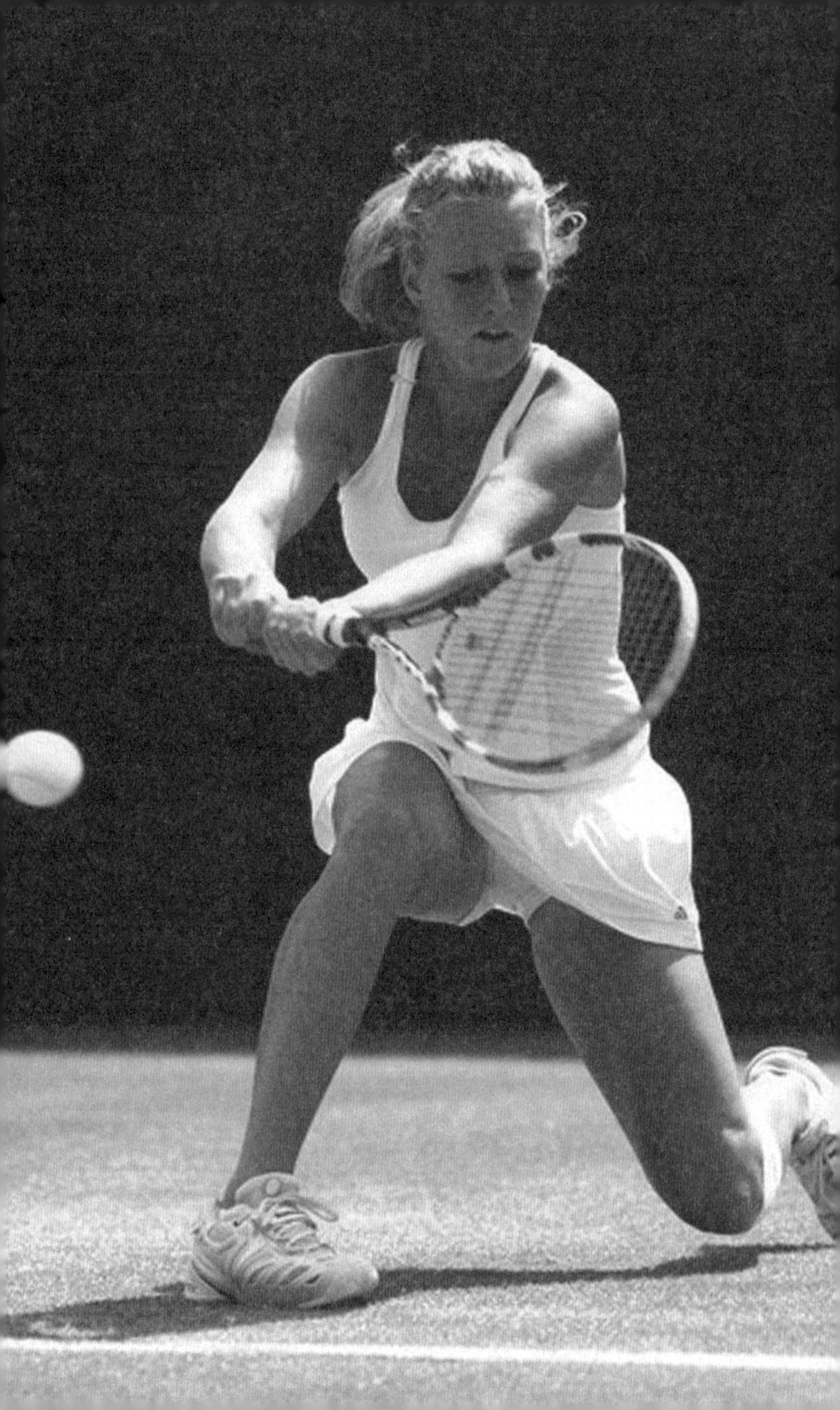

Unclaimed Bags Will Be Destroyed*

> It was not quite daylight and a neon sign indicated to me every minute
> the change of time, and naturally there was heavy traffic, and I remarked
> to myself that exactly all that I could see, except for some trees in the
> distance, was the result of thoughts, actively thinking thoughts, where
> the function played by the subject was not completely obvious. In
> any case the so-called "Dasein," as a definition of the subject, was there
> in this rather intermittent or fading subject. The best image to sum up
> the unconscious is Baltimore in the early morning.
> —Jacques Lacan

Roundtable Discussion

On our way from one party to another in Basel, a friend is saying,
"When it comes to negation, I prefer to be as subtle as possible."
This is to explain why, instead of simply blacking out his images,
he's decided to fix them in a semi-blackened state. (The fact
that we are crossing a picturesque river at sunset probably gives
the dialogue more atmosphere than it deserves.) It's true that
even the most radicalized twentieth-century cine-club audiences
could never put up with a completely dark screen, but then
reception was never the goal of such gestures. The point was not
only to interrupt a certain logic of representation, but to open
up urban time to another kind of experience: a conversation, a
problem, a collective discomfort or a fight, a feeling of presence
or whatever the spectacle was said to be robbing us of. So what
about these half-black or gray strategies that are so current in
art today? A little negation, a little affirmation, and the finger on
the fader. The work tends to set itself up as a kind of interface
between pictures and their disappearance. Like Baltimore in the
early morning, these images stage something like intermittence
or fading. The best ones produce a situation where the subject

---

* Originally published in the exhibition catalogue *Uncertain States of America*, Astrup Fearnley
  Museum of Modern Art, Oslo, 2005.

not only becomes aware of its own fading, but is able to perceive new links between this fading and the production of emancipatory possibilities, preferably extending these beyond the scope of the work, of art. In other words, an opportunity to dismantle subjectivity that also risks pushing the art a little more outside of itself, to make it fade a little too. Having said this, however, no examples come immediately to mind.

Topless
This artist is also very subtle when it comes to seduction. When he took his shirt off in the bar, he was no Arthur Cravan. He was not exactly Paris Hilton either. When Cravan undressed, it was to clear the room of everybody but his one or three friends. When Paris unveils her breasts, it's maybe to make herself contagious, or her way of distracting our attention from something else—the thing that's not in the mirror? And then there is a way of undressing that's more like changing into something a little more comfortable—another T-shirt—a little bit free but not too much. And when we tried to pin him down and fuck him, he slipped right out of our hands. We were probably a little bit drunk that night or disoriented from so much buying and selling, but when we looked up, he was gone and we all felt ridiculously seduced by this pale-skinned producer of semi-black images. There are moments when the excitement of commerce gets into bodies too, when it seems crazy to just stand there in your suit as if nothing was happening.

I Hate Myself and I Want to Die
Back in New York, publicity images of the actor Michael Pitt announce the release of Gus Van Sant's *Last Days* (2005). The seeming coup of pulling off this role with nothing more than a cheap blonde wig and a mumble says a thing or two about … how we make ourselves happen and get rid of ourselves today?

Maybe Kurt Cobain—pulling himself off with his blonde mop and monosyllabic moans and groans, in the days when all his energy had already been captured—is an image that sums up our contemporary art situation. The most dedicated fans may reject the wide-eyed, cherry-lipped, puppy dog images that Van Sant produces here, but then again, maybe it's more appropriate to do Kurt doing himself, even badly, than to really do Kurt. Anyway, the difference between Van Sant's and our Kurt is probably only that we want to fuck them for different reasons. They are strangely different Kurts, and I'm not ready to say which one is better. Van Sant's, for example, starts and ends with no energy, and that's a problem, or maybe it's just how Kurt appears in a certain masturbatory fantasy. The mystery is where the energy went, how it exploded and was then somehow put to work and turned off at the same time. And how the decision to stop producing becomes a kind of rape fantasy in his or our minds.

Bombshell

Meanwhile, on the cover of another magazine on the same rack, a very glossy image of Pamela Anderson is accompanied by a big red caption: "I think of my breasts as props!" Inside, she goes further: "I can cut glass with my nipples … a shot of tequila or espresso and they will poke through anything." Compared to Kurt, there is something disarmingly generous in Pamela's image, and in the way she circulates with it. She gives us "everything" and retains nothing. The more Pamela circulates, the more she seems to complete herself for us. You would think that the polar opposite of a dark screen is this shiny blonde screen with its screen-slicing nipples. And what is the real difference between these two blondes, the pin-up and the punk? Pamela's props are inflated, Kurt's are deflated. His pajamas maybe work like Pamela's swimsuit, except he doesn't burst out of them; he drowns. Pamela is a bombshell. Kurt is a bombed-out shell in his drowning-suit. Michael Pitt is maybe a bit of both. The answer is Michael Pitt.

Debt Relief

On the one hand, there's the big-breast market with its inflated nipples, and, on the other, more vague mumbling about the deflation of experience. In the movie, Michael Pitt is stumbling around in a satin nightie and hiking boots, stirring his instant macaroni and cheese with a prop rifle. Like our art, he is haunted by disapproving punk ghosts and seems incapable of assuming his own history in an "adult" way, whatever that could be today. And despite her apparent fullness in the present, Pamela also repeats something from the past, from the Second World War, a sweet, pin-up ease that, in her case, also suggests a violence of something ready to burst, and which resonates nicely with the all-or-nothing metaphysics of our present war on terror, for example. Cobain, who repeated punk and who is himself re-peated by Pitt, sings some kind of radical disconnection from the official time of grown-ups and markets, a regaining of something like mythic time. He was deep in debt not only to his major label, but to the major labor of the heroes that precede him. With the breast in our face and our finger on the trigger, we are starting to feel these last days could go on forever.

Rollover Minutes

If history is a record, the art of today locates itself in its scratched and skipping grooves. It's not about making or ending it; it's the hypnosis of its never-ending revolutions and the erratic skimming of a sharp or dull needle across an ever-revolving surface. This is a dark surface, an ambiguous thing, because it is both flat and deep. The stoner myth of hidden messages playing in reverse is the ironic reference of certain works today.

It's doubtful that anybody really believes in a hidden message anymore. There is the code, and then there is what you do to it. What you can do is play yourself backwards, or make yourself skip.

Sex Tape

The shiniest and best stars of today are great because of how they manage the ongoing crisis of their own image. Television is getting better and better at exacerbating this crisis, while at the same time showing us its virtuosic management in real time. Pamela, Paris, Tom, Michael, and all the others are barely sustaining the possibility of their own endless exposure, and implicating (intimating?) us in this problem or joy as we attempt to recognize them, again and again. We get the feeling that the best art now is like this too, that it brings on its own crisis and keeps happening anyway.

Mixtape

After the sex tape, nothing fills an American desert like a good mixtape. But voids are essential to the city and shouldn't always be filled. The mixtape covers the sound of breathing, of the awkward pause, of soft and hard shoes—even a smile makes a sound if the stereo is off. The other thing about mixtapes is what they do to time. Empty time is now full time. The time of a drink is haunted by the time of a prerecorded tape and even boredom has its own energetic soundtrack. Stopping the tape creates the temporal equivalent of a vacant lot, a blackout, a little ground zero. Or else we could mix tapes that have their own built-in gaps. It seems clear that, from now on, interruption can only come from outside, as a bad surprise, or will have to be somehow designed into the present by us. Can interruption be designed? This question comes up everywhere.

Neon Signs

A Chinatown storefront advertises its neon sign business with a window full of neon. Traffic and the air are heavy at 3:00 p.m., and in bright pink and green, a neon sign that says "neon signs." Is downtown New York in the middle of the day a good image of the unconscious? It's not easy to fade out here, and nothing is intermittent. Everything is doubled and tripled and even comes with a soundtrack. Two artists, unbeknownst to each other, have made blacked-out neon signs this year. You can still read the letters but their light is gone, and the black seems even blacker when it paints out a light. Neon art is nothing new of course, but how can we not keep coming back to it? And what did Benjamin say about electric street signs … it's not the sign itself that's so powerful, but its infinite reflection in the street puddles? Benjamin also wrote about the shock value of interruption in an age that is poor in experiences. Interruption is a technical strategy that opens up a gap between represented action and the action of representation. It is only by interrupting action that gestures are revealed.

No Smoking

Friends slip away from no-smoking dinner tables and meet in the street, a party as long as a cigarette. One has devised a way of smoking indoors without being noticed, cupping the illegal object in her hand and exhaling into sofa cushions and other people's hair. At a crowded nightclub, just as the security guard is about to bust her smoking, she back-hands the lit Marlboro to a friend, and when he, too, is approached by the same, increasingly irate guard, the cigarette is sneak-passed to a third, and so on. The cigarette is collectively consumed before the confused bouncer—standing right there in an obvious cloud of smoke—can catch anyone in particular in the act. In New York, desire produces itself right there in the middle of everything, with all the lights and the cameras on, and even includes the lights and cameras, the bouncers and the cancers.

Ahoy!
What else are we backhanding and sneak-passing amongst ourselves, as we hurry through these nights? Our own history. Shared techniques. The figure of the pirate sometimes appears in our midst. He cuts others and is himself cut up too. Pirates show up where things pass and circulate. They aren't simple outlaws; they often work in the gray areas of the law, and in the places where nations' borders are vague or difficult to maintain. Artists put pressure on the systems they exploit. Their images are cut from these systems; their techniques are too. Art is always put to work and escaping its job at the same time. It is double-dealing and two-faced. Thefts happen quickly, and authorship is fast behind. Our strategic play with wrappers, sleeves, file formats, and with the repackaging and rerouting of cultural information reminds us that it's a very fine line we keep crisscrossing between what we're doing with art and a more common commercial behavior, which we also partake in. Positions can be taken up anywhere along the vectors that keep all this in flux. Things get interesting when we abandon the ones we hold now.

No Smoking 2
The ban on smoke in New York is also a ban on everything that comes and goes with smoke: the very image of breath, of mystery, communication with the other side, a certain kind of time, introspection, meditative self-destruction, the intangible, etc. Smoke retreats underground, into the new backrooms and neon-lit basements of Chinatown. (Meanwhile, the city buses continue to knock us out with their exhaust fumes, as does the over-heated garbage at night when the garbage men unsettle it.

And there's a waste treatment center on the East River that continues to emit an invisible, toxic "smoke," not to mention the millions of microwaves that are invisibly smoking us.)

The Fall of Rome
We all love Pasolini tonight. He was an Italian filmmaker and poet who also wrote critical reports on urban life in his time. He loved youth, but hated youth culture and its conservatism. Pasolini hated youth culture as much as he hated the state and the language of the commodity, and while he hated the decreasing possibility of a poetic life in his time, this feeling was exactly the place where he made his poetry happen. We love Pasolini because his love/hate images are passions, and they aren't afraid to go against themselves when it feels like the most lively option. Pasolini remade the fall of Rome in the 1960s and 70s.

Party
We are talking about Pasolini at a bar in Brooklyn, where, on the same night each week, a DJ plays only "coldwave." The same twelve or twenty people always show up here, youngish men and slightly younger women. It is familiar, friendly, kind of like how we imagine Berlin. Coldwave is sparse, melancholic, early electronica, and the best bands were the ones that only made one record: late 1980s or early 1990s bisexual teenagers from remote places like Ithaca, NY, bands whose lead singers suicided soon after their first releases. The twelve or twenty regulars on this night are mostly white, mostly represented by galleries, and some are even professors. We exchange information here, sometimes saliva, but it's the coldwave that takes care of the passional element. Coldwave has romance, darkness, machines, narcissism, sentiment, youth, repetition, and creates the impression of a distant or remote world by ignoring everything

else in the world but its own taste for a vaguely feminized nothingness. In this mirror, the new themes are established, the relationships solidified, the gray strategies elaborated. Coldwave is a self-imposed constraint, as reduced in its vocabulary as a lot of the art we make today.

Packing Supplies

What is the atmosphere in New York? Can atmosphere be curated? Is music atmosphere? Is business? Before theorists discovered class relations and the structure of language, long before *Capital* and the unconscious and the centuries before aesthetics, there were ideas about atmosphere and cosmic containers, earthly and heavenly spheres, the air itself being what bound humans to each other and to their world. Today, air bubbles protect artworks so they can be shipped around the world. In his new book *Spheres,* Peter Sloterdijk uses the word "foam" to describe a present-day society of separated yet connected individualities. Bubble wrap creates a protective void around a precious object. Packing materials not only speak of containment but of the shocks and traumas that might still upset us. Think of all the artists currently working with tape. At the art fair in Miami, gallerists set up their booths in shipping containers.

Post-Kleins

A few nights later, upon entering a prominent collector's home in SoHo, guests encounter a massive black sculpture by a celebrated New York artist. The thing is a giant glossy wall supported by aluminum tubes and sandbags. A quick glance around this spacious treasure trove and you see that every work in the collection is either black, white, or transparent. These are the colors of concepts. And square are the shapes: a blacked-out screen, an empty page, frames with nothing in them, broken pains of glass, frozen film stills, grim-looking amplifiers that emit nothing but an opaque hum. The smart art of today is made by artists who have discovered the desirability of designed Minimalism. This discovery comes precisely fifteen years after Calvin Klein, and fifty years after Yves Klein; objects that are next-to-nothing are flooding the scene again. Malevich said that black was the color of anarchy. We say that anarchy is the color of design. There is the black that goes with everything and the black that's against everything. Then there is the black that wants to do both.

Rave Review

People are nervous and they should be. With this opening, the artist has suddenly outmoded them. It can happen to anybody at any moment in New York, and always does. It doesn't matter. But what is it that strikes you as being so decisive in this new blow? Not only has he repackaged your world, he did it without putting anything new into the package. This is not as easy as it looks. He outmoded you by ignoring your attachment to content, by reminding you that the format is the only message. He out-formatted you and now you are getting the message.

After-Party

Not wanting to stop here, the party moved over to a friend's apartment. The artists sat around on piles of art books in the art writer's tiny room, listening to a mixtape and gossiping about the market and other artists not present. Meanwhile, the curator who'd tagged along became increasingly upset that his artist wife wouldn't leave with him that minute. He left; she stayed. Something broke that night, if not between these two, then between them and us, or us and us. Never try to interrupt an after-party in New York. Never try to curate your wife. Never ever try to do these things in ridiculous whispers when it's already past the point of shouting. Couples like this can wreck a situation, especially one that has already so decisively abandoned any concern for what you think is proper to you and proper to me. What are your properties? Where do they belong? The after-party is one of the few places in New York where things circulate off the clock, where property is not only up for grabs, but wasted and meaningless. The panic of the after-party is at least one experience of impropriety that can sustain itself a little past bedtime. Or perhaps the real panic of the after-party is that we never stop working, and that it becomes a kind of accounting in the form of decadence. At least the curator knew when to call it a night.

Studio Visit
We hear about some artists who've been working out a new concept of the "strike," which in this case means not a total work stoppage, but the creation of a provisional space-time, where the distances and relations that normally determine us as subjects are put on hold. Unlike the Marxist general strike, this one has no goal in mind other than itself. It is a means without an end, whereby a gap is introduced between the artist and his or her own function. This gap is also a suspension of the disciplinary structures that normally ensure separation between individual producers. We are talking here about a process of de-subjectivization, following Foucault's idea that what's really revolutionary is to first of all change ourselves, Benjamin's writings on the shock-value of interruption, and Bartleby's destabilizing "I would prefer not to." To produce a gap or an interval is to create distance and strangeness, revealing another perspective on what produces us, because the artist, too, is a readymade. It can take the form of a social or technical interruption, an indifference to professional demands, a refusal of official politics, even a renewed attention to silence. This space

can only be constructed within an interruption. And in this gap, for however long it lasts, the revolutionary use-value of every-thing we've interrupted is the first thing to appear. Processes and materials, then gestures, can now be linked in other ways. How—not what—is the question, and the question of use. But it's hard to not ask what, too, and on our way out now, not to notice a drawing made with a cigarette lighter on the ceiling, some coins that fold out into knife blades, and a neon light that only turns on when you leave the room.

Group Show
By linking my production to your production, the curator also disconnects us both—whether in the name of context, theme, or simple demographics. Because we inevitably become un-available to each other in the context of an exhibition, and what-ever it is we were doing before is now doing the curator's work instead. The secret to curating a contemporary group show is that anything can go with anything, and something will always somehow connect—aesthetically, conceptually, or by mere proximity. Most of the time, we're surprised by this ourselves. In any case, there is something decidedly panoptic in the curatorial function: He is the only one in a position to view the map he locates us in, the network or idea or whatever it is we all have in common. At the end of the day, we mostly realize that we are all viewers of our own orgy. And that the secret to making contemporary art is that we aren't the ones making it, not the only ones anyway. It makes us too, so maybe it's not as useless as some people say. My video and your sculpture lost their way some time ago and it would be nice if they could meet, if they belonged somewhere, if being young, American, and in the same show were a kind of connection. A title like "Disem-bodied States of America" is maybe a way of preempting the group-show problem by announcing our non-belonging in

advance. We're not yet sure what can be elaborated within this connecting disconnection, but we feel that it somehow constitutes us, and we can only begin here. For now, this image is the best map of our disembodied states.

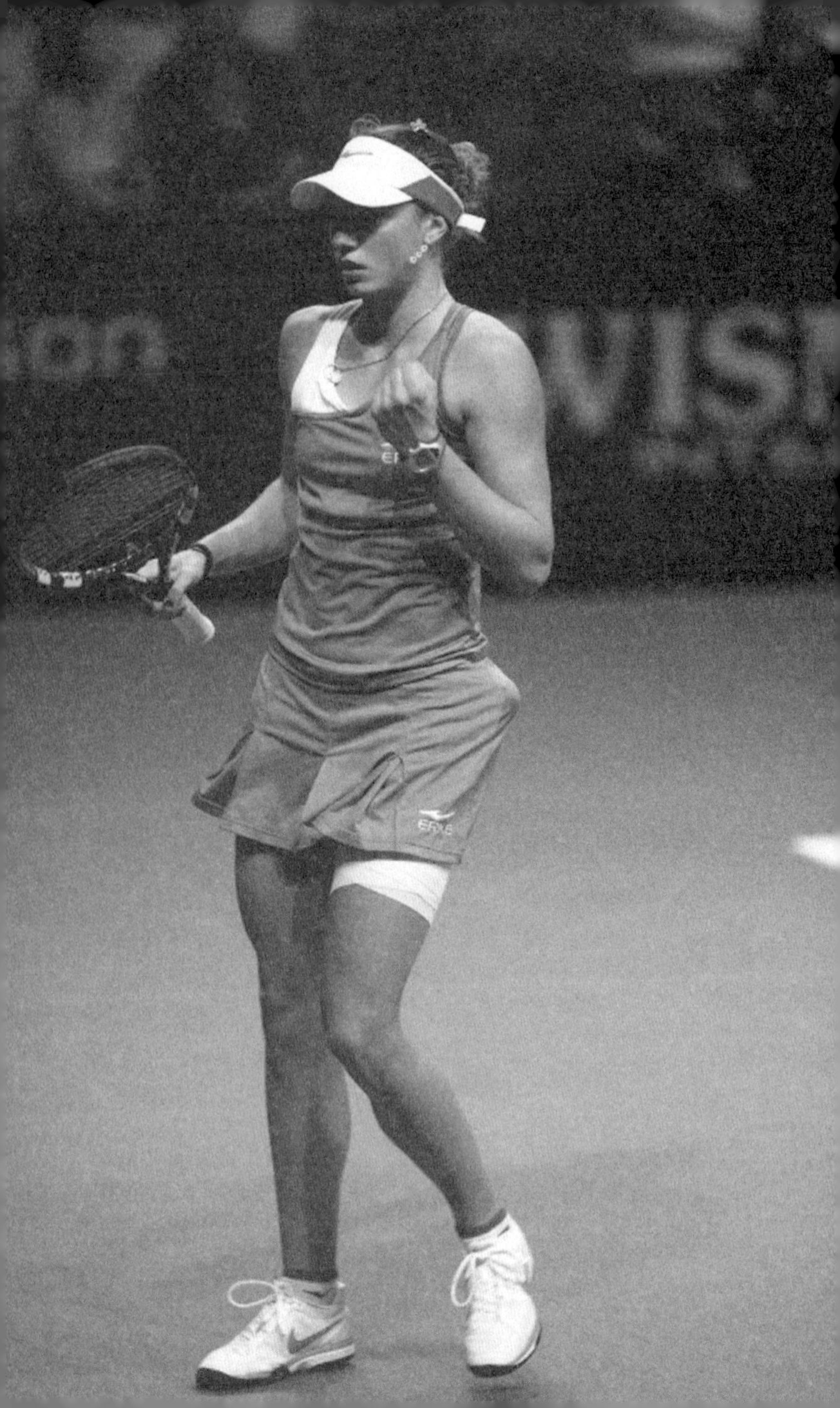

Year of the Monkey*

There was a kind of intelligence in the way 2003 blacked out midstream. Some things thrive better in darkness; some things go to sleep. But this year was halogen-lit, smooth as safety glass, and punctuated by ever-peaking terror alerts, no doubt manufactured by the Bush people in anticipation of their show of force at Madison Square Garden. The year may go down as the most *managed* in the history of New York, the year that so many potential and imaginary explosions were defused or diverted, the year that the wartime climate served as a consistent and dependable stabilizing device. It's tempting to consider all the ways that 2004 almost happened, or could have happened but didn't. But whether it did or not, the year had a certain managerial logic, a logic that applied to daily life as well as to cultural production, guiding the movement of money, people, and art into and out of New York.

There were some brief moments in the streets on the occasion of the Republican National Convention. There was Critical Mass, a roving party of five thousand bicycles circling Manhattan on the first evening of the event. During two minutes of mayhem on the steps of the New York Public Library, a battalion of riot police manhandled some over-lively kids, and ensnared many less-lively ones in orange plastic netting. And as the sun came up on the last morning of the RNC, all of the city's major fountains flowed bloodred (until the cleaning crews quickly corrected the anomaly). Later, Andre 3000 appeared downtown to support the more than one thousand illegally detained, bureaucratically "lost" protestors. But nothing was broken during the RNC; nothing really got out of hand or exploded.

---

* Originally published in *Artforum*, December 2004.

As if the 1980s might be possible all over again, money and art once again decided to quit fooling around and shack up in 2004: Their many children suddenly filled Chelsea from end to end. These well-educated artists proved to be experts at manipulating today's second and third appearances of 1960s, 70s, and 80s countercultures, but could do nothing either to disrupt an insanely policed Republicanizing of their own city or to resist or refuse their own instrumentalization by an art market increasingly fine-tuned to the momentary whims of young collectors and curators. It seems that nowadays we will appropriate everything but our own time and place, and appropriation will always feel a little too cool and vague if it doesn't take that extra, possibly criminal, step toward misappropriation, or a theft that *actually* takes something. In 2004, insider-outsider, faux-rebel art appeared as the rising sign of the ambitious post-MFA artist-monkey. Every pretty picture and scrappy drawing hanging on a gallery wall seemed to stand for a defused desire, a wallpapered-over possibility, a patch in the sails of the happy ship that carried us smoothly into another cold, bright winter.

So as the election loomed closer, a remarkable amount of pictures were shown and a lot were sold. Some will say that it's going too far to claim that this apparently contagious phenomenon was the result of so many galleries catering to the Judith Rothschild Foundation's desire to invest one million dollars in young drawings as part of a proposed gift to the MoMA. They will say it's going too far to claim that, in 2004, the New York art world was dominated by private collectors and their easily predictable spending habits. That this is why so many galleries presented show after show of loveable little works you could slip into your briefcase. That these same galleries are increasingly connected to a sturdy yet flexible feeding tube: the Columbia

University MFA Program. That art students are now trained, above all, to manipulate this tube from their end too. That museums offered no viable antidote to this epidemic. That this year, young artists even helped create the décor for the Whitney Museum's gala ball for young collectors. That everyone (except every single artist I know) seemed to agree that Assume Vivid Astro Focus was the hottest thing since Wendy Airhole (because they dared to create retro-poppy, theme park-like environments rather than small, handmade things?). That things have suddenly become so amazingly transparent as far as art and money go, as well as in terms of a generalized libidinal investment in the smooth functioning of the high-speed, art-school-collector connection. We all see it, and the fact that it's so easy to see is precisely what makes for a stable market, a steady production, a safe and manageable art.

An autopsy of a year requires sharp tools. But while writing this in October (with the second presidential debate droning in the background), 2004 reveals its particular and extreme amnesia. All the things missed or forgotten in New York, all the shows we knew didn't matter but went to anyway. We forgot drawing. We forgot "goth." We forgot our Biennial. We tried to remember Minimalism. After three years without it, we almost forgot the absence of MoMA in Manhattan (will we still recognize her when she unveils her extreme makeover in November?). But 2004 also produced its own particular life forms, and the following words are addressed to these other New Yorks, the ones you can actually live in. Because a few things do stick.

I remember the Downtown for Democracy Liberty Fair on 22nd Street in mid-September. Although the word "democracy" has recently taken on a distinctly empty and pornographic flavor, and although voting—or voting Kerry—is now the be-all and end-all of political engagement for most New Yorkers, the street fair was remarkable for the momentary shock of a festive afternoon it unleashed on a normally battened-down Chelsea block. A spontaneous, collectively produced feeling exposed the ordinarily anti-festive, low-intensity character of this zone—an open window, a stopped clock, a sudden, joyful critique of the normal situation. Contributions to this rare Carnivalesque atmosphere included Rachel Harrison's pay-to-enter/pay-to-exit "jail," samba lessons by Andrea Fraser, a kissing booth starring Emily Spears-Meers, boxing with Cecily Brown, some disorderly conduct with trash bags and whipped cream, and an open bar in broad daylight. And for many of those involved, the feeling hasn't faded.

Speaking of the changing terrain of 22nd Street, 2004 was the year that Colin de Land's American Fine Arts, Inc. finally closed its doors. The most adventurous art gallery of the 1990s, AFA pioneered a critical-collaborative enterprise that kept its doors and its agenda wide open to alternative practices. It offered a humorously dysfunctional model of what a New York gallery could or should be—a willfully difficult model that now no longer exists in Chelsea. And in characteristic fashion, AFA went out with a string of excellent shows. There was Andrea Fraser's *Official Welcome* (2001–2003), an Oscar-worthy thank-you speech (in conjunction with an exhibition across the street at Friedrich Petzel Gallery that documented her literal consummation of a deal with a collector). There was "Get Real Estate," Gareth James's exhibition of conceptual origami. There was Patterson Beckwith's transformation of the gallery into a free schoolhouse, with a month-long program of events and artist collaborations. There was Lutz Bacher's excellent and mordant "Jokes." And finally, "Election," a group exhibition organized by James Meyer. As if in hysterical reaction to the loss of AFA, eighteen new Chelsea galleries mushroomed overnight this fall. We can only hope these young dealers and their artists will put as much energy into redefining something that resembles a local New York art as they will into churning out product for NADA-Scope-Liste-Frieze. This was, after all, the year that art forgot New York, which, every month, shipped another part of itself to Miami, Basel, London, or a Utopia Station near you.

In 2004, we witnessed the unexpected return-with-a-vengeance of Alex Bag at Elizabeth Dee Gallery. Many have felt her influence, but few can match her comic genius when it comes to exposing the insidious links between contemporary lifestyle culture, the global economy, and our latest wars. Another unexpected return was David Wojnarowicz, who haunted Roth Horowitz gallery in October with his freshly unearthed "Rimbaud in New York" series, shot in 1978 and 79. Whoever ventured up to 70th Street to encounter these images couldn't help but feel the frisson of a now extinct life form that once stalked the East Village: obsessed, poetic, committed, addicted, out of control, a community of exiles, a long-gone bohemia, not that long ago. And more untimely still: Dieter Roth, Lee Lozano, and Lee Bontecou.

There were some noteworthy visits from Europe. German painters Albert Oehlen and Michael Krebber both presented New York shows in 2004, and demonstrated, each in his own way, that if the old painting as endgame still has a few matches left to play, it's because fresh art can be made by assuming this paradoxical living death in a robust way, and by using it as a point from which to question all other forms and media whose vitality are so taken for granted today. This is very close to what Londoners Nick Relph and Oliver Payne proposed regarding urban life in their new faux-experimental film *Gentlemen* (2003), which was one of the first shows at Gavin Brown's new space on Greenwich Street. How can we inhabit a dying city in a lively way? What poetic revolutions might be lying dormant in a post-post-revolutionary, totally streamlined metropolis (the first shot is of an out-of-focus urinal in Starbucks)?

I also remember Gary Indiana's slapped-together, freestyle cabaret nights at Passerby, and at the same venue, Stephan Dillemuth's video-performance *People of Light in the Slush of the Sun*. The latter, based on the artist's research project about how the Third Reich absorbed previously-thriving lifestyle cultures into its own machine, was in fact an explicit and hilarious critique of the present. That same night, Dillemuth reappeared on the Lower East Side at Reena Spaulings Fine Art (a gallery admittedly close to my heart), where he presented an hour-long exhibition consisting of sculpted spaghetti, photographs of anuses, and a single flashing light bulb.

I remember music: a No-Neck Blues Band/White Magic concert on the steps of P.S. 1, and the very first live show of Rita Ackermann's Hungarian New Wave band, Disfunctionixs, at Tonic. Also, the mysterious rise of Animal Collective and Gang Gang Dance, the persistent, meandering trajectory of Black Dice, and the discovery of local metal band Early Man, whose impromptu concert at the Hole goes down as one of the most deliriously fun nights of the year. Each of them—whether by noise, collage, *détournement,* chance, contagious rhythms, guitars or no guitars, abstracted song structures, or theatrics— added another facet to what might be called a downtown sound, which isn't really a sound so much as a collective com- mitment to keeping our music local, but just out of reach, so we're kept guessing and wanting more. I also remember food:

Agathe Snow's guerilla catering concept, "Feed the Troops," reinvented eating in 2004 with its Dadaesque culinary interventions at various parties, picnics, and art openings. And thanks to the young women of *LTTR*—the radical feminist and transgender journal, whose three-week performance and lecture series at Art In General and Reena Spaulings Fine Art unleashed a dense cannonball of otherness into the heart of the same—I remember that I am not a man, no longer a bio-boy, but, as of this year, a "non-trans-man."

It seems appropriate to conclude this faulty memoir of a still-unfinished year with two big shows this month that deserve mention, only because they serve as warnings: The Jet Blue-sponsored group show in Terminal 5 at JFK airport, which was closed down by the Port Authority police on its opening night, and the Guggenheim's Rirkrit Tiravanija event (bankrolled by American Express at the former Ace Gallery), which met a similar fate during a Dead Meadow concert. That art can be arrested today for a little vomit, broken glass, or noise is bad enough. Worse is that the artists and musicians involved felt the need to apply their talents to such cynical, crassly promoted, high-security, bogus utopias in order to do their thing, *and* were shut down anyway. So I'll leave the year in mid-stride with the example of these two forgettable un-happenings, and all my votes for a less stabilized and compromised 2005. Next year we'll all blow up.

John Kelsey is a writer, artist, and gallerist based in New York City. He is a permanent member of the artist collective Bernadette Corporation (since 1999) and co-founder of the gallery Reena Spaulings Fine Art (since 2004). His texts on contemporary art have appeared frequently in *Artforum*, where he is a contributing editor. Other texts included in this selection have been published in *Texte zur Kunst*, *Parkett*, and various artists' catalogues.

John Kelsey

Rich Texts: Selected Writing for Art

Editors: Daniel Birnbaum and Isabelle Graw, Institut für Kunstkritik,

Hochschule für Bildende Künste, Städelschule, Frankfurt am Main

Publisher: Sternberg Press

© 2010 John Kelsey, the editors, Sternberg Press

All rights reserved, including the right of reproduction in whole or in part in any form.

First published 2010, first reprint 2012, second reprint 2014.

Managing editor: Matthew Evans

Proofreading: Melinda Braathen

Design: Miriam Rech, Markus Weisbeck, Surface, Berlin/Frankfurt am Main

All texts republished here with the permission of the author and with the help of the

publishers, magazines, institutions, or artists noted at the beginning of each text.

Printing and binding: BUD Potsdam

Cover: Munken Print White 1.5 Vol., 300 g/m^2

Paper: Alster Werkdruck gelblichweiß, 1.75 Vol., 90 g/m^2

Typeface: Arno Pro, Akzidenz-Grotesk BQ

ISBN 978-1-934105-23-8

Sternberg Press

Caroline Schneider

Karl-Marx-Allee 78

D-10243 Berlin

www.sternberg-press.com